Urban Geography

Urban Geography

L.N. Verma

RAWAT PUBLICATIONS
Jaipur • New Delhi • Bangalore • Guwahati • Kolkata

ISBN 978-81-316-0041-2 (Hardback)
ISBN 978-81-316-0042-9 (Paperback)

Reprinted, 2020

Published by
Prem Rawat for *Rawat Publications*
Satyam Apts., Sector 3, Jawahar Nagar, Jaipur 302 004 (India)
Phone: 0141 265 1748 / 7006 Fax: 0141 265 1748
E-mail: info@rawatbooks.com
Website: www.rawatbooks.com

Delhi Office
4858/24, Ansari Road, Daryaganj, New Delhi 110 002
Phone: 011-23263290

Also at *Bangalore, Guwahati* and *Kolkata*

Typeset by Rawat Computers, Jaipur
Printed and bound in India

Contents

Preface

This book primarily is a work attempting to summarize an area of the branch of Human Geography related to its urban sector. It is heavily based on the research done by other scholars of our country as well as from other parts of the world. It is intended to provide a vision about urban phenomena in an outline for students preparing for colleges and universities' examinations. It should not be treated as full length treatise on urbanology. It is hoped that the book will provide understanding both of the streamlines developed in India and also in the developed world sector.

Urban life has become a common way of living among small towns and villages and people have a lure looking towards metropolises and capital cities for pastimes and also for seeking newer jobs – technical, managerial, educational, commercial, etc. This has brought a change in the attitudes of majority of population in the country. They seem to be eager to have a taste of various urban patterns and levels of urban activities. The contents of the present book might fulfil their hopes to have a glimpse about the urban order and system going in and around India.

Most of the chapters included in the book are based on my lectures delivered to the students of the university where I taught the subject for more than two decades. Many of the ideas expressed in the book have been built up by experience in teaching and by contacts with fellow teachers and scholars conducting research in the field of urban geography.

I cannot forego the valuable academic guidance that I received from my respected Late Prof. A.N. Bhattacharya during the course of my own research in urban settlements. I would like to acknowledge with deep sense of respect and sincerity the masterly comments and suggestions I had been receiving from time to time in the Department of the University as his colleague. I am also indebted to my own students for having interaction with them on various topics discussed in the book.

The book contains some of the maps taken out of the geographic literature of foreign and inland authors to explain the concepts. I acknowledge with gratitude their usage and the due references for the same have been made at the appropriate places in the book.

I thank heartily my family members for their assistance they have been providing me during the course of my writing work.

In the end, I feel a deep sense of gratitude towards the staff of the Rawat Publications for their cooperation and help provided to me. The final editing of the manuscript was done efficiently, and I sincerely thank the editor whole heartily for the labour entailed by him.

March 2006
Udaipur

L.N. Verma (Retd.)
Head & Reader
Department of Geography
M.L. Sukhadia University
Udaipur

List of Figures

1

Introduction

The Urban Environment

City and Environment

World's population touched a billion mark by the 19th century, and, more so it was 3 billion in 1968. At present it is estimated that the global population might have crossed the limit of six billion. Out of this tremendous increase in numbers, cities contain nearly 50 per cent people, and as per the United Nations Report (1969) the urban world would definitely cross this limit of half and half.

The phenomenal increase by the 19th and also during the 20th century is generally said to be associated with migration factor. But now it is coupled with the widely spreading phenomenon of industrialization, and cities got boom of factory labourers from neighbouring countryside. This has given rise to lame settlements known as 'shanty' in almost all metropolises, and people unwontedly squatted in and around heaps of garbage to make 'slums' of unhygienic unhealthy environment. Three-fourths of the population in metropolitan cities are huddled uncomfortably and living inhumanly where their density per square kilometre surpasses nearly seventy-five thousand figure. In the late 20th century what was happening in

Kolkata may make the fact clear about the pressures and values arising from the process of urbanization and industrialization.[1] "The congestion of buildings within the city becomes heaviest at the banks of the Hooghly River, particularly at each end of the Howrah bridge. The wharf-roofs and the factories stretch like a broad, dirty ribbon for miles up and downstream from the heart of the metropolis.... According to an official estimate – two-thirds of the people live in 'kutcha' buildings. More than 57 per cent of the multi-member families have one room to live in. For more than half of the families cramped into one room quarters there is only 30 square feet or less per family member." One study showed that the indigent in the 'bustees' share a single water tap among 25.6 to 30.1 persons and a single latrine among 21.1 to 23.

Objectives of Urban Studies

To summarize, the study of cities should invariably be associated with environment comprising the very life of the people living there and also the involved activities performed by them. Two main themes of study of towns include their distribution 'in area' and the town itself 'as area'. But the orientation of urban studies must not escape the overall environment formed by the town fabric. There are certain aspects which actually are enveloped by environment and these should form the major objectives of urban geography. As outlined by Harold M. Mayer[2], these are:

(i) a real association of activities within urban places;
(ii) economic base of cities;
(iii) the areas which cities serve in one way or another;
(iv) patterns of distribution of cities; and
(v) morphology of cities – planned or unplanned.

Dickinson[3] too has stated that the objective of urban studies is:

(a) to determine the characteristics of site and situation of urban settlement;
(b) the historical development of a town; and
(c) its limits which it has currently attained.

Harold E. Murphy[4] while analyzing the scope of urban geography has aptly stressed on 'spatial aspects of urban development' as one of the major objectives of urban studies. This includes all areas that are sufficiently city-like in housing density and land use characteristics. Murphy has pointed out that urban geographer is concerned with cities as entities – their locations, characters, growth, relations to the countryside and to each other. He has further stressed about the interior patterns of the city – land use, social and cultural patterns, patterns of circulation and patterns of the natural environment – all as they exist in interrelation and interaction in the urban area.

The changing character and the role of the city in consequence of growth of urbanization are of prime significance as objectives of the urban studies. Recent growth of urbanization in the developing countries has given rise to a giant urban area where the great majority of people depend on urban jobs and urban services. This radical change has brought about the change in urban environment, the impact of which, in terms of measurements like commuter zones, service areas and the exchange of goods and information, expands to involve each part of the city area in a complex series of interactions with other parts. The objective is not only to study attitudes to the city which are common within the prevailing culture, but also and at the same time, the new trends and fashions manifest themselves. Urban geographic phenomena are not static, but changing over time – being dynamic.

Into the process of change, of course, the slow crystallization of urban geography into a clearly structured systematic study, came the 'quantitative revolution'. Harold Carter[5] has stated that "out of theory came building of models to be tested in the real world. That testing involved statistical analyses of data, hence the quantitative revolution". In the light of this development Johnston[6] effectively summarized the objectives of urban studies as:

(a) quantitative approach to description;
(b) behavioural approach, and
(c) radical or structuralist approach stressing the constraints that society as a whole impose on the behaviour of individuals.

Urban Environment in India

During the first half of the 20th century, city environment in India was simple and manageable wherein one could go about one's normal activities with the least amount of strains and stress. By the end of the century, urban life and city's physical environment became unadjustable because of growth of urban population, unlimited demands and ambitions of urban dwellers, congestion and crowd in residential buildings, transport hazards and unsafe movement within the city. Above all, unhygienic conditions, poor drainage, heaps of garbage, pollution of air, water, food and erosion of social values have made the city life in India intolerable and miserable.

The result is that conditions in Kolkata, Mumbai, Chennai, Hyderabad, Ahmedabad and Kanpur (to mention only a few cases) are indescribable and intolerable. Even in this age of technical boom, thousands are without any home or shelter and have to live in open spaces or sleep on pavements in most of the metropolitan cities of India, Lewis Mumford[7] has opined that industrial pollution has vitiated beyond imagination the civilization and culture of the Orient. The pleasure of being a city dweller has now disappeared because of deteriorated urban conditions and unhealthy environment. There has now been developed a wide gulf between the standard of life of upper and lower classes of people living in cities, unequal distribution of wealth and its confinement into the hands of a few. Materialism has overshadowed urban amenities and eroded service institutions of cities, ultimately to create ecological unstability of urban base.

Concept of Urban Environment

City environment is the composite effect of city terrain, drainage including water bodies, modes of transport and movement within the city as well as from-and-to the city. Population of the residential areas, density of buildings, industries and commercial areas, alignment of roads and streets, workplaces and institutions of economy, health and education, and also cultural, all what is that form urban infrastructure give rise to the concept of urban environment.

Duality of Urban Environment

Positive Organs of City Environment

Urban environment has a dual-facet role to play. Various institutions providing services to the residents of a city are positive organs of urban functions. These institutions, and also centres of production provide some of the essential services, concerning health, education, marketing in consumers' products as well as facilities for residence, light, water and movement from one place to another within the city. Safety of one's life by seeking help of administrative institutions, police stations, courts of justice and law too form part of instruments of healthy, smooth and comfortable city life.

Negative Organs of City Environment

Use and misuse of organs of environment affect directly on the day-to-day working and life of urban dwellers. With the increase of urban population working capacity of positive organs become weak, inefficient and even polluted, thus resulting into discomfort to their users. Recently, due to tremendous increase in city population, both due to immigration and industrialization, city environment has become polluted to the extent that the very life of city dwellers is at stake and unsafe. Air, water and land have gone out of the track and their misuse has been threatening existence of city people.

Problems of Today's City Life

The day-to-day growing population of urban centres in India has also compoundly increased urban problems. These problems are concentrating day by day, particularly in metropolitan regions, thus posing a major challenge to national progress. The present infrastructure of services and community facilities have become outmoded because of the ever-increasing population density including density of residential buildings. In Indian metropolises more than 25 per cent of the working population is living below the poverty line and is too poor to obtain its own shelter of any sort. More than half of the people suffer from poor, unsafe and unhygienic housing. Thousands of people in Kolkata and Mumbai, and in Delhi live in 'jhuggi-jhonparis' or slums with mud-heaps overcrowded dwellings which lack the barest essentials of sanitation. The dwellings are old and dilapidated with ill-drained narrow lanes where neither sun's rays reach nor fresh air is available. Such environment is unfit for human habitation.[8] In these areas life tends to the breakdown of social structure. Cities indicate high rate of cases of thefts, criminal breach of trust, cheating, kidnapping and abduction including molestation of women. People in capital cities have developed negative attitude towards public property and flout provisions of laws by anti-national activities like strikes, processions, demonstrations, and several times, these agitation lead to violence.

Attacks are done on transport system and buses, railways suffer large-scale destruction. City life in India has reached a deplorable state of affairs. Under the vicious urban environment people lead a life of tension and mental torture.

Strategy for Creating Healthy Urban Environment

Now, time has come to step up plans for urban development in India. In this context some of the suggestions which were approved in the Habitat Conference of Vancouver[9] may be considered for creating healthy urban environment in our country:

(i) Former Prime Minister, Indira Gandhi vehemently expressed her concern about growing urbanization in India and she favoured its immediate control so that towns may reshape their individuality. This is possible only when decentralization of institutions is adopted in the true sense of the term. Medium-sized towns and also country-towns should now be given priority and preference for locating some of these administrative institutions. Eemployment-based production centres as well as technical institutions may be started in rural areas in order to check migration of people from countryside.

(ii) Channels of villages and vice versa may help to link private and public enterprises. This too would help in releasing undue pressure from metropolitan areas to their surrounding small urban centres lying within the sphere of economic influence of metropolises

(iii) Nearness and accessibility of urban institutions and their economic viability to the consumers might make our towns more serviceable.

(iv) Pedestrians within the towns must feel safe, and parking places of vehicles getting adequate space would relieve the towns of unnecessary troubles. Footpaths, zebra crossings, parking spots, traffic lights on crossroads are some of the essentials to provide safety to people.

(v) Regulations and laws enforced by city corporations, urban improvement trust and urban planning department must not be impractical and these should be utilizable by builders and engineers.

(vi) Cities in India have expanded into the adjoining rural areas in a haphazard and unplanned manner. City people too have started moving to the countryside. This reverse process has adversely affected agricultural lands because of its usurpation by industrial and residential use. These newly occupied areas are mostly devoid of basic urban amenities of drainage, sewerage, piped water supply, electricity, roads, etc. This can be managed by workable urban development schemes to provide healthy urban expansion.

(vii) Multi-storied complexes are coming up in a number of lakh-towns, and overcrowding metropolitan cities. This development in cities of our country have negatively affected community life. A closed urban life of multi-storeyed complexes in which residents drawn from different regions and different states of India have greatly marred our ethos and values, and there is a greater degree of hybridization of culture which is neither Indian nor Western. Vertical expansion[10] of a city should be weighed properly against social distance, security, hygiene, health and culture.

Notes

1. Bose, N.K., "Calcutta: A Premature Metropolis", in Kingsley Davis, *Cities: Scientific American*, W.H. Freeman & Co., San Francisco, 1973.
2. Mayer, H.M., "Geography and Urbanism", article in *Readings in Urban Geography*, Allahabad, 1967.
3. Dickinson, R.E., "The Scope and Status of Urban Geography", in *Land Economics*, 1948, pp. 221-38.

4. Murphy, Harold E., *The American City: An Urban Geography*, McGraw Hill, New York, 1966, p. 2.
5. Carter, Harold, *The Study of Urban Geography*, London, 1995, pp. 5-6.
6. Johnston, R.J., *Urban Geography: City Structures*, Progress in Human Geography, pp. 118-29.
7. Mumford, L., *The Culture of Cities*, Seeker & Warburg, 1938.
8. Hoselitz, B.F., "Cities of India and their Problems: A Review Article", in *Annals of the Assoc of American Geographers*, 1959, Vol. 49, pp. 223-31.
9. United Nations Habitat Conference, Vancouver, May, 1976.
10. Rao, V.L.S.Prakasa, *Urbanization in India: Spatial Dimension*, Concept, New Delhi, 1983.

2

Urban Geography

Meaning, Scope and Concepts

Nature and Scope of Urban Geography

Urban geography is the study of urban places with reference to their geographical environment. Broadly speaking, the subject matter includes origin of towns, their growth and development, their functions in and around their surroundings.

The subject of urban geography has gradually taken a special place among the various branches of geography in the period after the Second World War in various foreign and Indian universities and colleges. With the increase of population globally, towns and cities have become magnets of economic, social and political processes. The changes brought about by these processes have become instructive as well as interesting too in case of the single phenomenon, i.e., city in a spatial context. Under these circumstances, the study of towns and cities have formed an essential part of the branch of Human Geography.

Meaning of an Urban Place

It is one of the most essential and immediate problems to decide 'what is urban?' How does it differ from its counterpart, i.e., rural? In everyday life we are aware that difference between rural and urban depends upon their nature of work – the former being engaged in agricultural operations and the latter in non-agricultural activities. But it is a difficult task to transform the above stated meaning between the two different nature of settlements into precise and scholarly terms. This is because of the fact that 'an urban place' has been defined differently by different scholars and agencies. Even the *United Nations Demographic Year Book* (UN, 1990) has given a wide range of examples covering the various countries defining demographically. UNO defines a permanent settlement with a minimum population of 20,000 as an urban place. But several countries have their own minimum such as Botswana (5,000), Ethiopia (2,000), Argentina (2,000), Israel (2,000), Czechoslovakia (5,000), Iceland (200), Norway (200), Portugal (10,000), Japan (50,000), Australia (1,000), India (5,000), etc.

But, the *UN Demographic Year Book* concludes: "There is no point in the continuum from large agglomerations to small clusters or scattered dwellings where urbanity disappears and rurality begins; the division between urban and rural populations is necessarily arbitrary."

A review of the problems of rural and urban centres as revealed by the Census Reports of various countries identifies a few bases for reckoning a place as urban. These are:

(1) a place designated by administrative status;
(2) a minimum population;
(3) a minimum population density;
(4) a concept of contiguity to include or exclude under suburban area or loosely scattered settlement;
(5) a proportion engaged in non-agricultural occupations; and
(6) a functional character.

In case of our country (India), the census of 1981 has identified the following places as urban:

(1) centres having Municipality, City Board, Cantonment Board/Notified Town Area;
(2) a minimum population of 5,000;
(3) 75 per cent males engaged in non-agricultural activities;
(4) a minimum population density of 400 persons per square km or 1,000 persons per square mile; and
(5) centres defined by urban amenities prescribed by the Director, Provincial Census.

Two important facts must be borne in mind before accepting the meaning of urban and rural. One is the fact that it is rather impossible now to identify a dividing line between the rural and urban – the two being merged to create a sort of diffusion and present a landscape which is neither purely agricultural nor engaged wholly in tertiary activities. Industrialization has brought into being a large number of settlements which are not certainly villages but are nucleated settlements of agricultural population. Another problem is about the concept of what is urban, which is not static and is subject to change with time as well as with space. The proportion of population engaged in agricultural activities is the most effective measure. But capitalization of agriculture in modern times and rural depopulation by commuting urban workers have made the criterion of proportion irrelevant, Thus, to conclude the discussion one reaches to the point that with the changing nature of both rurality and urbanity, there has developed the functional overlap between the two. Therefore, the distinction between what is urban and what is rural has lost its meaning in reality.

Attributes of a Town

What are the attributes or characteristics qualifying a town? Several qualities of a city or town may be summarized as:

Table 2.1
Urban Attributes

Genetic	*Structural*	*Functional*	*Evolutional*	*Relationship*	*Townscape*
Origin	Morphological	Residential	Growth as organism	Surrounding area	Environment
Site-considerations	layout – Extent	Economic	Age-decay	Umland	image
Location – situation	Demographic	Cultural/Social	Rejuvenation	Intra and inter relations	Future
	urbanization process	classification	Redevelopment		planning
		Typological			
		land use			

(a) Town is a kind of settlement having a social organization of much greater scope than a simple rural establishment.

(b) It does not represent a mere greater number of people agglomerated in a vast area. But it represents a stage of civilization quite different from a locality expressing rural way of life.

(c) Cities and towns have their historical origin. Blache has pointed out that cities characteristically possess mythical halo surrounding their genesis (ritual, eponymous hero, etc.).[1]

(d) Towns and cities are creatures of commerce, and politics accompanying the earliest developments such as: Babylon, Athens, London, Paris, Delhi, etc.

Emrys Jones has also expressed various attributes of towns and cities which also resemble whatever has already been discussed above:

> ...a town is a physical agglomeration of streets and houses, a centre of commerce and administration, a kind of society, even a cultural frame of mind of urbanite or a way of life.[2]

Attributes forming the scope and contents of urban geography have been summarized in Table 2.1. The details of these and their explanations follow in the ongoing chapters in their respective place.

Scope of Urban Studies and Definitions

Urban geography studies urban centres in the context of geographical factors. The factors operate spatially to explain processes – economic, socio-cultural and also political. But the subject of urban geography has its limited scope in the sense that it deals with these processes in relation to only one phenomenon, i.e., town or city.

Some of the general principles on which a town is based form the subject-matter. Commonly, it includes in the very beginning, consideration about the origin of an urban place. The genesis about a town is invariably related to its history. Who is behind its origin? What is that which makes a town to take its root where it is, and why it is there? Town site or the ground on which it is sited has some specific and geographic attributes. These need explanation to bring forth personality of a town.

Another point which has been emphasized by D. Stamp to cover the scope of urban geography, is the study of the actual town itself, i.e., town as an entity. He further has added that influence of the town on its surrounding area too forms a significant aspect of the study.[3] This means that 'townscape' and also hinterland including 'umland' are vital issues for studying urban geography.

One of the pioneer scholars in urban studies in India, R.L. Singh has stressed on three broad categories under the scope, viz., (a) the physical structure of the city, (b) the stage of its historical development, and (c) the process influencing the structure.[4]

Dickinson defines urban geography as the study of a city commanding the surrounding region. He describes the city as a king among the surrounding towns. His trait for cities of all ages has been institutional supremacy for their surrounding territory.[5] Their existence depends upon the resources of the surrounding areas, and also, by virtue of their interaction through their physical, social and economic infrastructure. Their interdependence with their surrounding regions is the spatial reality.

Raymond E. Murphy points out the dual role of urban geographer, i.e., (i) to analyze cities as entities in terms of locations, characters, growth, and relations to the surrounding countryside, as well as, (ii) to discuss patterns of the city's interior – land use, social and cultural patterns, patterns of circulation, and above all, natural patterns of environment – all as they exist in interrelation and interaction in the urban area.[6]

Harold Carter opined that since the geographer is concerned with the analysis of the variable character of the earth's surface, and thus, "the populations and the buildings agglomerated together to make up towns, constitute the special interest of the urban geographer".[7] Since considerable population of the world live in towns, and the problems of the urban environment are paramount, the study of urban geography is important and its relevance to applied geography needs no further stress.

Towns and cities have their wide impact on human life and activities. Overall growth rate of city population has been faster during the last two-three decades. It is only after Second World War that the study of urban geography got due recognition in the universities in India and abroad. Prior to that period, it was taught as a theme within human geography where its scope was restricted to the description of site-situation of towns including their description as a part of settlements.

Since the publication of the major work of Doxiadis,[8] urban geography has made much headway in and outside India. Brian J.L. Berry also encouraged the urban studies by introducing urban systems as consequences of economic development.[9] In the present circumstances the scope of urban studies has reached far-flung areas and is not restricted to its site-situation structural approach. The ICSSR Report of the Fourth Survey of Research in Geography[10], covering the period 1976-82 in India has pointed out various themes of urban phenomena bringing into light the scope of the subject. These include trends and patterns of urbanization; rural-urban migration; urban systems and hierarchical orders; morphology; economic base; land use; functional housing classification; slums and squatter settlements; rural-urban fringe, surrounding areas of influence, umland and interaction between a city and surrounding settlements; urban environment; pollution; poverty; crime and quality of life; urban services and amenities;

urban politics and administration; tourism; urban planning and problems including urban metropolises.

N. Baransky, the founder of Soviet economic geography, has pointed out that study of cities has a wide scope in the sense that it has now become the subject matter of historians, geographers, statisticians, economists and sociologists. Similarly, planners and plan designers are interacted in cities, each in their own way, as well as architects, financial specialists and representatives of a number of special fields. He further advocates that the studies of cities may vary in terms of their territorial scope and can be studied in a global context, in the context of a country, or in the context of an individual region. One may carry out comparative studies of cities belonging to a particular category. Finally, one may engage in a geographical study of a particular city constituting the subject of a monograph. Baransky stresses that from an economic-geographic point of view a city together with its network of roads constitutes the skeleton on which everything else hangs that defines the relevant territory, and endows it with a specific configuration.[11] About planning, Baransky has opined that cities may be viewed as applied urban microgeography.

Bases and Concepts

Cooley,[12] in his treatise on transportation, made it clear – "why is a town there, where it is?" He has pointed out the geographical qualities which govern the site of a town is 'binary'. On the one hand, it is bountiful with respect to its resources and facilities of production, while on the other, it is equipped with transportational facilities.

Site-Situation Concept

Taylor's[13] various classes and types of cities are the product of their natural site like hills; cuestas; mountain-corridors; passes; plateaux; eroded domes; ports, including fiords, rias, river-estuaries, and roadsteads; rivers, falls, meanders, terraces, deltas, fans, valleys, islands; lakes, etc. All of these are 'controlled' primarily by the topography of sites.

Dickinson's point of view about a city is that of natural beginning. But with the passage of time, town's natural setting is changed by its utilization of the available resources and its adaptability with the locality and the surrounding region. Its growth and expansion sometimes diffuses natural site to the extent to make it beyond recognition. In this context there was little scope for the development of a true urban geography. The aim was restricted and hardly it was possible to explain a complex economic function and social system. Crowe[14], writing on methodology, pointed out that treatment of towns as "indicative of the inability of geographers to penetrate beyond the superficial". He further stressed that the application of the 'site and situation' formula was meaningless "where site had nothing but historical interest as situation was viewed in terms of routes and not currents of movement". Such state of affairs rejected the stereotyped concept of 'site and situation'.

Concept of Ecology

Plant ecology came into being to influence geographical phenomena during the two World Wars. Robert Park[15] opined that because of increase in population and city region there came a change in the ecological processes of a city. Urban ecology influenced the relationship with the surrounding areas of a city and had its sway over the people and their environment. Park, in 1925 published a book *The City* in which he introduced the typical process of the expansion of the city. The process of expansion was best illustrated by Burgess[16] for number of American cities in general and of Chicago in particular. He made it clear that during the course of time city – land use tended to display a zonal organization concentrically arrayed about the city centre. Encircling the downtown area there is normally an area of transition which is being invaded by business and light manufacture, a third area is inhabited by the workers in industries who have escaped from the area of deterioration but who desire to live within easy access of their work. Beyond this zone is the areas of high-class residences, and further out beyond the city limits, is the commuters' zone – suburban areas or satellite cities.

The concept of Burgess, of course, initiated the specialized spatial patterns where residential zones of varied ecology made their headway characterized by successive areas with different land uses. Nevertheless it is a model in the proper sense, but it was criticized on the ground that by the late 20th century it was anachronistic and limited to large Western industrial cities. It is true that urban ecological and social patterns are determined by geographical, economic, industrial and transportational factors but these do not have their evenly spread impact everywhere and in all times on socio-economic life of cities.[17]

Behaviouralism and Urban Centres

Berry's contention about city and its growth is related to its consumer's behaviour[18] who are the befitting choice makers for using land. It depends upon three variables, viz.,

(1) value of residential unit – buying cost or rent?
(2) quality of residence, and
(3) relationship with place of work and neighbourhood?

Family income is an important component for the choice of site in the city, and this depends upon the ability of behaviour to interact with space by its users. But as a general tendency, it is evident that people of almost the same income group agglomerate make their choice for an even space. In the context of India, social relationship and behaviour are the products of caste-ridden values and culture. These have given rise to 'mohallas' of the same communities. The city, of course, has its geographical base, but nonetheless important is behaviour of its citizens and their socio-cultural background. It is because of this behaviouralism of the residents that cities have been able to infuse in them their own smell.

Concept of Radicalism

An important aspect of the urban world is the concept of 'total change' brought into play by development of metropolises. This has changed totally the consumers' ideas. These ranged from the relative deprivation of immobile residents of small-country towns who are isolated from standard urban services which are concentrated at only big cities. The people of inner city are better placed than the residents of the peripheral sectors. These sorts of people have to depend on the private institutions. The situation becomes worse when these institutions exploit the common masses, and finally, control the city. These radical reactions also affect urban planning and capitalist city overpowers the rights of the masses. Radical urban concept "stresses the constraints that society as a whole, and particularly certain groups within it, impose on the behaviour of individuals".[19] Radicals believe in the replacement root and branch of the operation of 'laissez faire' market forces and the inequities generated by them. They offer alternative system of 'socialist city' – the city of planning controls and central directions ensure egalitarianism as well as plenty for all.[20]

But recent events have revealed that the radicals' proposals are no more than an Utopian dream. These bring about economic conditions even worse than those of market forces. The rigid totalitarian control are far from reality. They are responsible for breeding massive bureaucracies.

Concluding the discussion, urban geography is more of an amalgam of different approaches. It is nearer perhaps to a multidisciplinary analysis of its object rather than a systematic geographical study. The town cannot be viewed as an object of study as a geologist would appraise a piece of rock. The urban environment has a vast domain of world's people spending their lives with a central theme of humanism. The prime objective is the fact that people of varied nature within a city aspire for the good life with a degree to which it may be met spatially.

Notes

1. la Blache, P. Vidal de, *Principles of Human Geography*, (ed.) E.D. Martonne and Trans. from the French by M.T. Brigham, Constable, London, 1926, p. 471.
2. Jones, Emrys, *Towns and Cities*.
3. Stamp, L. Dudley, "Some Aspects of Urban Geography", in *Applied Geography*, Pelican, London, 1964.
4. Singh, R.L., *'Banaras': A Study in Urban Geography*, Nand Kishore Brothers, Banaras, 1955.
5. Dickinson, R.E., *City Region and Regionalism*, London, 1947.
6. Murphy, R.E., *The American City: An Urban Geography*, McGraw Hill, 1966.
7. Carter, H., *The Study of Urban Geography*, Arnold, London, 4th Ed., 1955.
8. Doxiadis, C.A., *'Ekistics': An Introduction to the Science of Human Settlements*, OUP, New York, 1968.
9. Berry, B.J.L., *Urban Systems and Economic Development*, Eugene, USA, 1962.
10. Gosal, G.S. (ed.), *IV Survey of Research in Geography*, ICSSR, New Delhi, 1999.
11. Baransky, N., *Selected Works in Geography*, Progress Pub., Moscow, 1981.
12. Cooley, C.H., *The Theory of Transportation*, 1894.
13. Taylor, Griffith, *Urban Geography*, Methuen, London, N.Y., 1949.
14. Crowe, P.R., "On Progress in Geography", *Scottish Geog. Mag.*, Vol. 54, 18, 1938.
15. Park, R.E. and Burgess, E.W., *The City*, University of Chicago Press, 1925.
16. Ibid., *The Growth of the City*, Chap. 2.
17. Nelson, H.J., "The Form and Structure of Cities: Urban Growth Patterns", *Journal of Geography*, Chicago, USA, Vol. 58.

18. Berry, B.J.L., *Geographic Perspectives on Urban Systems*, USA, 1970.
19. Johnston, R.J., "Urban Geography: City Structure", in *Progress in Human Geography*, pp. 118-29.
20. Carter, H., op. cit., p.7.

3

Conceptual Explanations of Urban Places

Concept of a Town

What is a town? What is that which constitutes a place which can be called 'urban'? How is a 'town' different from its counterpart: 'village'? These are some of the fundamental queries, which should be clearly understood before probing into their regional relationships. A town may be a small country-town, and it may be a giant metropolise or megalopolis. Concept of a town is not uniform and same everywhere. It is differently followed in different environment, and it is but essential to know the difference in the context of space, time, culture and the stage of economy of a country.

Town and village are two opposite concepts, but it is difficult to draw a sharp line of distinction between these two. On what grounds, and with how much addition a village becomes a country-town, this too is not based on an universal rule to decide. It is only a matter of regional understanding and people's mental preparedness to define it as a large village or a country-town. The scale between them differs from country to country and the differences between town and country "become very difficult to transpose into precise and scholarly terms".[1] Even then, there is something acceptable to reach to a point of agreement. In the *United Nations Demographic Year Book*, 1988 some of the samples are recorded defining the urban population covering the wide range of examples from all the continents:[2]

(1) *Botswana*: Places having 5,000 or more people with 75 per cent non-agricultural.

(2) *Egypt*: Governorates as well as district capitals.

(3) *Ethiopia*: Localities of 2,000 or more inhabitants.

(4) *Argentina*: Populated centres of 2,000 or more inhabitants.

(5) *Peru*: Populated centres with 100 or more dwellings.

(6) *Canada*: 1981. Places of 1,000 or more inhabitants having a density of 400 or more per km^2.

(7) *USA*: Places of 2,500 or more inhabitants and urbanized areas.

(8) *India*: Places having 5,000 or more inhabitants (municipal administrative) with at least 75 per cent adult male employed in non-agricultural activities.

(9) *Israel*: Places more than 2,000 inhabitants (Except those settlements where at least one-third of households participating in the labour force earn their living from agriculture.).

(10) *Japan*: Cities having 50,000 or more inhabitants with 60 per cent engaged in urban types of business, manufacturing or trade.

(11) *Czechoslovakia*: Towns usually of 5,000 or more inhabitants with density of more than 100 persons per hectare of built-up area.

(12) *France*: Communes containing an agglomeration of more than 2,000 inhabitants.

(13) *Iceland*: Localities of 200 or more inhabitants.

(14) *Netherlands*: Municipalities with a population of 2,000 or more.

(15) *Norway*: Localities of 200 or more inhabitants.

(16) *Portugal*: Agglomerations of 10,000 or more inhabitants.

(17) *Australia*: Population cluster of 1,000 or more inhabitants.

(18) *The former USSR*: The cities and urban-type localities officially designated by each of the constituent republics.

(19) *Gambia*: Banjul only.

Town and Vidal de la Blache

The above definitions show that the division between urban and rural populations is necessarily arbitrary (UN, 1955). It is impossible to identify satisfactorily a dividing line, which is conceptually meaningful between an isolated farm and metropolitan area. In this context, the statement of the Human Geographer P. Vidal de la Blache[3] is very near to reality. According to him "there is a difference of 'kind' rather than of 'degree'. It is not a mere question of number or of area". A city, as observed by Blache, represents a social organization; it is the seat of administration, institutions of various functions and a symbol of culture. It expresses a stage of civilization.

Built-up areas of cities have single and multi-storied houses where sufficient density of population is living and people are busy in activities other than agriculture like buying and selling goods, manufacturing products for the use of local population, as well as for the people living outside the country, and are also busy in cultural, recreational and all sorts of social activities. Cities are served by various sorts of channels of movement of people – roads, streets, footpaths, etc., along which stands houses and buildings. But some of these qualities are present in a village too. For examples, modern villages have quite a good number of 'pucca' houses and some of them are double or multi-storied also. Similarly, villages have now developed a market place where buying and selling and all kinds of businesses take place and there are also developed institutions – health-centre, community and culture centres, administrative offices, etc. In villages quite a good amount of population is found engaging in secondary and tertiary occupations. Again, therefore, it becomes difficult to draw a sharp line distinguishing between an urban or rural centre.

Criteria Distinguishing a Town and Village

A single criterion based either on population or structure of settlement or activities of people might not explain sufficiently and satisfactorily the distinction between rural and urban centres; the issue should be decided therefore on the basis of a set of some variables or components.

Components Distinguishing Rural and Urban

These may include: (1) demography, (2) economy, (3) society and culture, (4) morphological structure, and (5) functions of a place constituting an urban environment.

Demography

What should be the demographic cut-off point distinguishing a town from a rural centre? The population of a town on a global scale differs very much. In India too a town may be having as low as 5,000 persons or it may start from 20,000. The census in India decided a minimum population of 5,000 for an urban place. Besides the number, the density of population in a town is generally high from that of a village. In India, the density of a rural centre per square kilometre on an average is found around 500. The Census[4] along with certain other conditions, fixed the density of at least 400 persons per km^2 for an urban place.

Economic Activities

Settlement's economic activities fall under two major groups: agriculture or non-agricultural. The working population in a village invariably is found engaging in agriculture, while in towns people perform activities mostly of non-agricultural nature. Therefore, one may conveniently decide whether a place is rural or urban. Here again, the same problem has to be faced to decide of how much of the population be fixed as 'agricultural' for the settlement to be called village. The cut-off point may be any number of percentages above 50, because in a village too, same people earn their living by secondary or even tertiary activities. Quite a good number of villagers are engaged in skilled-works and are carpenters, blacksmiths and goldsmiths, teachers, washermen, etc. Some are employed in cottage or household industries, producing household articles. In view of this, the Census has fixed that for a town at least 75 per cent of male working population is required as non-agricultural.

Social Organization and Culture

Villages and towns are far away from each other from the point of view of social life and culture. In villages social distances are closely knitted, and people know each other very intimately. Villages participate in each other's social functions irrespective of caste, creed or religion. They share frequently and without any constraint, in one's joy or sorrow. They also provide economic assistance to each other without going for any legal process. In contrast, the town's social set-up is full of complexities where social distances among people are far and wide. They meet each other only occasionally, and only for their self-motives. In cities and in metropolitan areas even next-door neighbours do not know each other. They have no time and mind to share one's joy and sorrow.

Culturally speaking, rural centres are tied with their localities. Truly speaking villages are the product of their soil as against towns, which are alien to the ground on which they stand. Rural culture is simple and without complexities and is based on traditions of the area. Towns and cities have a social organization of much greater scope, and represent a stage quite complex and also diffused as compared to villages. Cities are negligent of human feelings; they are cold, a harsh enterprise devoid of the amenities for living; they harbour a larger number of divergent groups than any rural area. They seem to make group relations more contentious, or at least more unstable and problematic, than rural communities do.[5]

Morphology, Form or Structure

Villages and towns differ in their physical structure; the latter are being occupied by 'pucca' built-up areas having multi-storied residences, while the former display 'kuchcha' dwelling distributed haphazardly along unpaved lanes and blind alleys.

Morphologically, urban places have a distinct core area, which is occupied by residences built up with bricks, cement, mortar and often have more than one or two storeys. The core is flanked by a busy market where pedestrians and various forms of vehicular traffic make their way through a crowd. In contrast, the core of a village is relatively open, silent, peaceful and occupied by shops, which are few in number and are scattered. The dwellings too are piled haphazardly and built with local material - mud, thatch, tiles, pieces of bricks and stones including waste articles. The very physical appearance may be used as a criterion distinguishing a village from town.

Function as a Criterion

The criteria based on various functions performed by a town identifying it from a village are widely accepted. A village is dominated by a population engaged in primary functions like agriculture, quarrying and mining, and in producing articles of daily use like baskets, mats, etc. Some of the village people are engaged in producing pots, pitchers and bricks too; others are service performers like barbers, sweepers, carpenters, tailors, weavers and also shopkeepers.

Functions in a town are generally of secondary and tertiary sectors. People in a town are salaried and wage earners working in various types of institution. Many of them are businessmen and some are industrialists. Quite a good number of people are labourers and live in between the middle and central zone of a city. Because of the nature of tertiary type of functions in a town, a substantial proportion of the population consists of people coming from outside regions who are different in culture from the local people.

Concepts of Urban Places: A Typological Frame

Both the terms 'urban' and 'cities' are used to convey almost the same meaning. In the geographic literature of the Western and American world, urban areas are city-like, but not actually cities. These areas having population of 2,000-2,500 and are in commercial use and livelihoods not dependent directly upon the land. Cities are incorporated places based chiefly upon size and functions. But the size rule may vary; its functions are a better measure.

Census and Urban Places

The Census Organization in India has defined the concept of urban places. But, the difficulty is that the criteria have changed from time to time. The 1981 census defined it as:

(1) a place with municipality, corporation, cantonment or notified town area; or

(2) a place having minimum population of 5,000 plus, at least 75 per cent of the male working population non-agricultural, and plus, density of at least 400 persons per square kilometre.

Urban places by census are vague because some of the marginal cases may be deleted or added at the discretion of the Director of Census. The state-level officers exercise their discretion in an arbitrary manner.

The Geographical City

Geographical city is a place with contiguous built-up area. It is limitless and in case of larger towns built-up area spills over the administrative boundary with a few vacant or even agricultural plots. But in case of the smaller towns, the built-up area is generally smaller than the administrative areas. This has given rise to the concept of 'over-bound city' or 'under-bound city'. In the over-bound case, the administrative city is larger than the geographic city; while in case of the under-bound, the geographic city is the larger. There may be a case when the geographic and administrative cities both have the same limits. But in practical situation it never takes place.

The spilled and the contiguously built-up area in and around the administrative city have been also termed the real city, the brick and mortar city, the physical city and the geographic city. In the real sense, "the geographic city refers to the built-up area extending in all directions until significantly interrupted by farms, forest or other non-urban land or by water bodies".[6] Delhi, in India now has experienced its tremendous growth and sprawled in all directions to include Ghaziabad and Loni in Uttar Pradesh, Faridabad, Gurgaon and Bahadurgarh in Haryana and Narela urban communities of Delhi on other side of the Yamuna River.

The process of growth of a city and its rate keep the geographical city ever changing, and its limits, cannot be determined without intensive fieldwork or aerial photographs taken from a plane flying at 10,000 feet elevation. The edge of the geographic city is not sharp and one of transition. Thus, it is almost impracticable to reach to its exact definition.

Nevertheless, the concept of geographic city is significant for the studies of urban land use and planning.

The Administrative City

The American terminology defines an administrative city as legal or corporate city having its boundary lines fixed by law and is governed as a unit either by a major and board of alderman or a city manager and a city council. Administrative boundaries of urban places in India are clearly defined on the ground as well as on maps. Such maps are available at the state level with the Urban Improvement Trust (UIT) or with municipalities, cantonments, and also with township committees.

Some of the administrative cities have their limits of boundaries extended far beyond the limits. The idea of town-group was also severely criticized in the IGU Congress (1968) in Delhi on the grounds that it is impractical for preparing city plans for its being disjointed set of settlements. It bears hardly a sense of cohesion as one unit. The concept finally was replaced by the concept of urban agglomeration.

Urban Agglomeration

Urban agglomeration (UA) is a contiguous urban area including other municipal towns, Census towns, revenue villages and outgrowths in the form of colonies or residential or commercial complexes. In 1981 census there were 293 urban agglomerations. Some of them had a core city of one lakh or more population, while on the other extreme the smallest UA in 1981 had a population of less than 5,000 and had only two small townships within. Dalhousie in Himachal Pradesh was a UA of only 4,178 population with a municipal committee area plus Cantonment Board area. In contrast to this was Kolkata UA of 9.16 million people having as many as 107 contiguous units. This means that there was no minimum fixed population of the core of UA. Besides it, no definition of an urban area can be fixed for its limits likely to be expanded in future. The UA is a concept very similar to the concept of geographical area. It is of the geographical cities. These are known as 'over-bounded city'. Greater Mumbai is an over-bounded city, which includes large and as yet unbuilt-up areas for future growth. On the other hand, the city of Kolkata is an example of 'under-bounded city' where the urban area extended far beyond the limits of the legal city.

The administrative boundaries of urban areas keep on changing with the time. The adjoining villages when legally are annexed to a city, its boundaries are altered. It makes often difficult to compare the decennial Census data regarding the population of individual cities.

Town-Groups

In the census of 1961 in India, a new definition of urban areas was coined. When a group of towns adjoined one another to form a single urban locality, the cluster is known as 'town-group'. Certain clusters or groups are not simply a matter of adjoinment of one or two places, but these represent agglomerations where satellite towns and cities, industrial towns or close by neighbourhoods may be surrounded by rural countryside. The population of town-groups is generally more than one lakh. The number of town-groups (in 1961 census) was 132 out of total number of 2,700 urban settlements; the concept of town-groups was abandoned in 1971 because of its being diffused in definition. The number of satellite towns of a town-group varies from time to time and its inability to qualify the minimum size too makes it a defunct concept useful in the sense that it accurately reflects the limits of an urban place. UA is formed of an outgrowth having a special status. The outgrowth is neither a town, nor a revenue village. Its special status is in the forms such as railway colony, university campus and townships built by public sector undertakings.

Standard Urban Area

The concept of Standard Urban Area (SUA) was introduced in 1971 to reinforce the concept of urban agglomeration. It is different in nature from UA by the fact that it covers the built-up city as well as a rural countryside likely to be urbanized in the future. In the census, the SUA is defined as a core town having a minimum population of 50,000 plus rural contiguous areas having a close mutual socio-economic links with the core. The rural contiguous areas should project an urbanized trend likely to be urbanized in the coming two or three decades.[7]

The possibility of SUA seems viable only when a core town crosses the limit of one lakh population and shows a trend for rapid growth to usurp rural areas. The concept of SUA is the lively subject of research and planning process for those who are keen in studying rural-urban fringe within the urban area. The SUA provides a reliable base for drafting a city master plan. However, the delimitation of SUA takes into consideration several variables like: (i) density of rural and urban population, (ii) the growth rate, (iii) percentage of non-agricultural workers to the total population of core town and contiguous rural units, (iv) rate of increase in literacy among males and females, and (v) land use including built-up areas. These may help in deciding objectively the cut-off point for inclusion a exclusion of the fringe rural areas in SUA.

Metropolitan Area

The process of urbanization got a fillip after the Second World War. It is because of the industrial growth as well as because of economic competition that urban growth was considerable, and specially million-cities appeared nearly in all parts of the world. In India, a dozen of million-towns existed in 1981, and at present there are 23 million-towns in our country. Around the million-cities, SUA began to merge and usurp the standard urban areas of bigger towns. These in the course of time gave birth to a new urban phenomenon known as 'metropolitan'.[8] The core of the metropolitan area was million-city. Around Delhi, the SUA of number of towns like Ghaziabad, Faridabad, Gurgaon, Bahadurgarh, Narela, etc., form a contiguous geographical area. Such an area is termed now as metropolitan area. The core of Delhi has linkages of economic, political, social and cultural nature within the metropolitan area. Its association within the metropolitan area is due to increase in industries and also because of diversification of Delhi's economic base. Mumbai and Kolkata are other metropolitan areas, larger in extent than even Delhi.

Conclusion

As projected by the United Nations[9], "there is no point in the continuum from large agglomerations to small clusters or scattered dwellings where urbanity disappears and rurality begins; the division between rural and urban populations is necessarily arbitrary". It is actually a difficult task to draw a line, which divides conceptually the continuum between metropolitan area and the countryside. Continued metropolitan growth and spill-over beyond administrative boundaries is actually not a new trend. It is continuation of the one, long established.

The standard way for the identification of urban areas may differ from country to country. Therefore, it is advisable to draw up a series of rules for drawing lines among various categories of urban places. It constitutes the basic problem and needs empirical studies to decide criteria for each of the countries.

Notes

1. Carter, Harold, *The Study of Urban Geography*, Arnold, 1995, p. 10.

2. *UN Demographic Year Book 1988*, UN, 1990.
3. la Blache, P. Vidal de, *Principles of Human Geography*, Trans., M.T. Bingham, Constable, London, 1926, p. 471.
4. *Census of India, 1981*, Tables A-3 and A-4.
5. Davis, K., *Readings from Scientific American*, in Introduction, Section V, p. 264.
6. Murphy, Raymond E., *The American City: An Urban Geography*, McGraw Hill, N.Y., 1966, p.13.
7. *Census of India, 1971*, Monograph No.1.
8. Murphy, R.E., op. cit., p.15 (Ideally, the metropolitan area consists of a recognized, substantial population nucleus and the adjacent areas of countryside and scattered urban development that have a community of interests with the nucleus).
9. *United Nations Demographic Year Book*, 1952, U.N., New York.

4

Origin and Growth of Towns

A Historical Resume

Ancient-Early Beginning

The origin of towns came into being as early as 6000-5000 B.C.[1] But these were mostly based on Neolithic agrarian culture. Later on with the inventions of plough, wheel-cart, boat, metallic implements, etc., and also system of watering fields ushered development and valleys of Nile, Tigris, Eupharates, and Indus started surplus food-grains production. Consequently, there evolved a social organization in which certain strata comprising religious, administrative, trading and artisans' communities could appropriate for themselves part of the produce grown by the cultivators. Such groups settled in towns to perform non-agricultural activities. In the river valleys, thus began a culture of certain groups who were having skill for writing, accountancy as well as knowledge of solar calendar and bureaucracy. There in the real sense town-cult began around 3000 B.C.

After this up to nearly 2,000 years, the ancient urban process ceased. Early cities went into eclipse.

River Valley Urbanization

Towns of river valley civilization were small affairs – Babylon being walled only in 3.2 square miles area, while Ur with its canals, harbours, and temples occupied some 220 acres. Similarly, Erech's walls encompassed an area of just two square miles.[2]

Urban culture of the Indus-valley according to Wheeler flourished during 2500-1500 B.C. with its prime centre Mohenjo-daro, where presence of copper and bronze affected the way of life. Mohenjo-daro and Harappa were two metro cities of the Indus Empire. Both seem to have conformed with certain distinctive and evolved principles of urban planning.[3]

Egypt had earlier beginning and was the crossroad of ancient world civilization. The Nile valley as well as the copper belt of Sinai peninsula gave impetus to the contemporary urban revolution. The valley became the centre of art, architecture, philosophy, religion and science. Hieronkonpolis, Thebes, Giza, Aphroditopolis, Memphis, Karnak were some of the known cities.

Mesopotamia forms the Doab of Tigris and Euphrates rivers where a fertile belt, also known as 'Fertile Crescent' gave rise to empires known as Sumerian, Babylonian, Asoyrian and Childian. Mumford described the Doab as 'magnetic container' where water from all directions inflow to enrich it. Urban centres like Ur, Erich, Lagash, Susa, Babylon, Kish, Agade, Assure, Niroveh, Nippur, Khurasabad came into being to give rise to commerce, industry, irrigation and civic-administration.

New World

The first urban revolution touched even the New World where it spread in the Central America, Mexico and Peru where Mayan civilization had its sway in about 1000 B.C. It was based on the cultivation of maize with Mexico as the capital city. Towards southward in and around Andes, the mountainous country of Incas grew. The replicas of their strongholds, palaces, and temples provide enough evidences of the empire. Yucatan peninsula was the centre of Mayan civilization where Mayapen, Uxmal, Chichen were the principle new towns that grew to ease the pressure on cultivated land.

Bases for Ancient Urban Growth

The origin of ancient towns in the river valleys and everywhere including China and Central America has common attributes as under:

(a) Their bases exclusively had agrarian cult with intensive farming, irrigation for surplus food production so that favourable conditions could be generated for non-agricultural activities like trade, commerce, and also, art and culture.

(b) Under the conditions of surplus food production there developed opportunities for mutual economic affairs and also means of transport for contacts around urban centres.

(c) Ancient urban development is not a matter of chance and accident. It is actually the product of community living. Of course, the centres of community life were not well organized, but, they had their origin based on social positive-understanding and cooperation.

(d) Establishment of trade and growth of centres for organization and administration of exchange, storage and redistribution of goods were some of the attributes giving impetus to the then urban scene.

(e) Above all, it should be understood that ancient urban growth was not purely an economic phenomenon, but must have been pre-eminently a social process.

(f) Religious activity was an important force of change. The rise of temples played a significant role in the change.

(g) Ancient towns characteristically were symbols of civilizations known as their 'cradles'.

Towards Mediterranean Coast and South-East Asia

The first urban revolution made its headway from the cradles of river valleys to the sea coasts of Mediterranean Sea and in the A.D. reached as far as south-east Asian countries and islands.

Greek Towns

Between 3000-1000 B.C., the eastern Mediterranean became the theatre of urban growth. On the Greek mainland on Asia Minor, towns flourished. They were of course small, having high agricultural population percentage. Knossos, Troy and Mycenae were important trade centres dealing in high-value goods. Several islands were nurseries for sailors and there were artisan population around Aegean Sea having skilled craftsmen.

To the Greeks town life was a manner of living in a political community. Several Greek city-states were developed during 800-700 B.C. According to Aristotle, the city (or 'polis') must have a population which is self-sufficient for the purpose of living the good life after the manner of a political community.[4] But Thucydides expressed that even in the 5th century B.C., the majority of Athenians lived in the country. Only a few cities were having a population which was convenient for a self-sufficient life.[5] Actually Greek towns were parasites and dependent on the surrounding rural population. The Greek city-states had three attributes in their origin:

(1) They were 'capitals', for example, Athens.
(2) They were 'federal capitals', for example Megalopolis.
(3) There were cities which developed as instruments of colonization, such as Ephesus and Miletus, and in the new colonies of Sicily and Italy, such as Selinus and Naples.[6]

Some of the salient qualities of the Greek towns may be summarized as:

(1) They had their origin as political communities.

(2) Each city was independent politically having autonomy and a source of municipal administration.[7]

(3) Ancient Greek cities were symbols of rural-urban symbiosis. Cities had olive gardens and were surrounded by stone or wooden walls.

(4) City-states in Greece were responsible for changing the kinship into citizenship. This consequently gave rise to brotherhood, cooperation and community life. Tribal organizations now had been changed into patriotic state-administered units under an elected leader's control of the state.

(5) Wealthy group of people in the city-state had extraordinary privileges and the right to collect taxes in wartimes and in the event of emergency. But later on the relations between the rich and poor or serfs with their masters became strained. Gradually, this became one of the major causes of the downfall of the Greek city-states.

By 500 B.C., urban life shifted to the Ganges of India and to the south-east Asian coasts and islands. Urban growth in Hellenistic and Roman Empire was due to improved communications and weapons.

Roman Towns

Roman towns and cities were not only the means of good life and trade – they were a mini-world in themselves and were actually like the state having all essential functions like administration, culture, religion and trade. Roman cities had a network of roads and were effectively integrated into the foolproof system to defend the Empire. The alluvial Po Basin had as many as eighty garrison towns, while the peninsular Italy had a network of some 350 towns in the Augustan period.[8] The Iberian peninsula had also urban centres where Roman life and culture made its sway. Tarragona, Sagunto, Merida and Coimbra were some of the monumental examples. The

Romans, to stabilize their empire, developed a system of urban hierarchy ranging from a 'castrum' (the simple military camp), through the small market centres around a local 'forum' on the highway, to the great regional capitals or 'civitates'.[9] Rome, Turin, Nimes, Lyons, Treres and Autun were capitals of varying size but having a close network by the roads.

Towns in the Gangetic Plain

Around 1000 B.C. in the Gangetic plains Aryans settlements spread from Kurukshetra to Patliputra and use of iron opened up new horizons by replacing copper tools. Several capitals of the various kingdoms came into being and important among those were Hastinapur, Indraprastha, Ahichhatra (Northern Panchala), Mathura, Ayodhya, Kashi and Kosambi.[10] During 1500-500 B.C., there appeared 'janapads' and according to Atareya and Taitareya Upnishads, the Aryan country Aryavarta was divided into eight janapads or tribal territories.

The cities of the post-Vedic period were few and far between. Their emergence is to be attributed to economic forces. The Aryans were essentially Iron Age people, the use of which set the stage for urbanization.

Early South Indian Towns

In general, South India shows a continuity in urban development from the 5th century B.C. because of the absence of foreign invasions. The classical literature *'Sangam'* in Tamil language provides ample evidence of an independent urban civilization in the South. The major Tamil cities were Madurai, Vanji, Urayur, Puhar and Korkai. Magasthenes's account of travels mentions about the southern cities of Madurai and Kanchipuram in the Mauryan court. Kautilya's *Arthasastra* too refers about the trade between the Mauryas and the cities of

Madurai and Kanchipuram in the 3rd century B.C. The southern cities had trade contacts with the Arabs, and later on with Greeks and Romans too, around 1000 B.C.

South-East Asian Towns

Urban development in South-East Asia remained a slow process as compared to the Western world. It has because of the fact that there was diffusion of political and religious organizations. The tribal cells adopted political organization based on Brahmanic and Buddhist beliefs. But later on, around 2nd century A.D. economic base gained strength. Traders from the West as well as from India made their headway for various islands. By the end of the 2nd century three prominent areas came into being where urban centres appeared, viz.:

(a) Lower Mekong and its delta under kingdoms of Funan;

(b) The 'Champa' Empire in the neighbourhood of modern 'Hue'; and

(c) The empire of Langkasuka on the Kra Isthmus having its ties with the opposite side of the Malaya Peninsula.

These areas were economically rich because of their favourable geographical position on the trade route between China and India. Vyadhpura grew as the capital of the Funan Empire and was an important centre of foreign merchants. Nakorn Pat'om was another important coastal port of Dwaravati in the valley of the Chao Phraya in Thailand. Srivijaya State in Sumatra was a trade based Empire on the river Palembang. Akor-thom was the capital of Khmer Empire and Pagan was a flourishing centre in the Upper Burma region.

The South-East Asian trade centres were representing a civilization of wealthy priests and artisans who were specialists in non-food production. Diversification of economic activity was the rule of the trade centres which were capitals also. In other words, they represented an 'universe'[11] with all sorts of material facilities and were properly guarded by the Place,

Temple, Wall and Ditch. Cities' habitations were having an hierarchical pattern ranging from administrative and wealthy trading communities and priestly citizens attached to the palace to a common artisans and foreign traders. Backward classes were having their quarters outside the city wall.

Attributes of Towns in the Middle Ages

On the continent of Europe, during the Dark Ages, it was only in Italy that any semblance of urban life was visible. In the 9th and 10th centuries, the urban revival was centred around the church and defence needs. There were some 286 bishopric towns and 32 defence settlements survived in Italy and France respectively. In Scotland also 'royal burghs' were there to provide military control over the region. In Britain military garrisons as well as trading towns developed. In many parts of Europe including Flemish and Saxon coasts, and in Central and Eastern Europe and some in Russia, there were nuclei around which 'military burgs' and trade centres could develop.[12] Defence was an important base in the 12th century in the creation of towns. But the local rivalries of lands attached to these 'castella' or garrison-centres, account for the spread of many 'bastides'. Bastides were towns to which autonomy was granted by 'Charters'. These charters of demands by peasantry were introduced in France, Germany, England, Ireland and Scotland during the 14th century. Hundreds of bastides originated around church and fortress to assure a guarantee of protection to an agricultural population including increased production. The charter made the peasantry free of the clutches of landlords. Farming population was granted land ownership and also the minimum-tax facility on cultivated lands. They were also freed of the bonded labour and 'serfdom'. In France between Guyenne and Languedoc out of 50 towns at least 20 were bastides. These bastides besides being market towns were also centres of Christianity.

Between 1500-1800 A.D., the bases of town's origin were both simultaneously with defence and trade considerations. Military needs later on became redundant to give place to the process of economic competition. Between 1450 and 1710 on the Continent, the tributary areas of the royal burghs became punctuated with the market towns. Throughout the Middle Ages town-country relations were close enough to sustain trade.

Medieval towns had a typical plan known as 'baroque planning' in the 17th and 18th centuries. Madrid, Munich, Vienna, Budapest, Warsaw, St. Petersburg and Copenhagen, and many others in Scotland, England, and France represented the spirit of this age in their formal layout, public squares, ornamental gardens and the uniformity of design. Mumford has stated, "town plans changed from medieval diversity to baroque uniformity, from medieval localism to baroque centralism and from the absolutism of God and the Catholic Church to the absolutism of the temporal sovereign and the National State".[13] Baroque towns were having stylish late Renaissance architecture.

On the Continent, great cities could grow in regions where agricultural productivity was high and where trade routes met, such as the Po Basin, the Netherlands and Belgium and the loess belt of Central Germany. During the 17th century, urban consolidation was a phenomenon of great commercial activities which multiplied the gains of capital cities at the expense of smaller towns. For example, growth of Paris in France was a matter of the decline of Nancy, Besancon and Toulouse. Nationalism played an important role in the growth of the capital cities. Nationalism itself was being strengthened by the communicational integration of nation states plus foreign trade and manufacturing. Retailers and handicraftmen abandoned country towns and resort to London because not only the court but also that the provision of things most fit for it might easily be fetched from thence.[14] London at the close of 17th century was having one-quarter of the total urban population of England.

In India too, conditions responsible for urban growth were not very different from that of Europe. Al-Beruni (1017 A.D.) and Ibn-Batuta (1333 A.D.) came to India and wrote about the geography of the country. Ibn-Batuta spoke eloquently about the grandeur of Delhi and considered it one of the greatest cities in the world. He mentioned its four nuclei as main Delhi, Siri, Tughlakabad and 'Jahanpanah'. It had its trade relations with the Arab countries in the West and China. Abul Fazal, during the time of Akbar (1556-1605) mentioned in his two works *Ain-e-Akbari* and *Akbarnama* that the Empire was divided into 105 'sirkars' each having number of townships. In 1594 A.D. there were 2,837 small trading centres distributed in Agra, Oudh, Allahabad, Bihar, Bengal, Malwa, Khandesh, Berar, Gujarat, Ajmer, Delhi, Lahore and Multan. Sirkar's (district) headquarters were fertile in grain and also rich in the handicrafts and small-scale industries like white cloth, silk, cloth of gold, silver and indigo. Lahore was a wealthy trading centre as pointed out by Manuchi in 1756 A.D., dealing in tents, carpets, saddles, swords, boots and shoes. Like their European centres of trade and capitals, medieval towns in India too dominated the urban scene; while non-capital towns were only commercial and small-scale and handicrafts industrial nodes. The towns were distributed fairly on fertile soil including facilities both of land and water routes, and they were producing variety of local products contributing to the prosperity of urban scene.

Moorland[15] has described some of the urban characteristics during the time of Akbar: "There were no metalled roads in the surrounding areas, though the main routes of land-travel were closely defined. In some cases, the 'sarais' in which travellers and merchants could pass the night, were enclosed by walls for safety and flanked by the avenues of tree."

Almost up to the 14th century in India, the urban development after the reigns of Chandra Gupta and Harshavardhan became sick because of the diffusion of the Central power. It was only under the Muslim rulers that urban life in the areas such as Sutlej-Yamuna Divide, Yamuna-Ghaggar area and Yamuna-Ganga Doab, was governed by handicrafts, trade, art and architecture and agro-industries. Some of the towns like Multan, Lahore, Bhatinda, Rewari, Ranathambhore, Nagarkot, Jaisalmer, Ujjain, Kalinjar, Mathura, Meerut, Kannauj, Kasi, etc., were having good business and activities. In the South, the town life was confined to sea coasts and near the ports and harbours. Dwarika, Somnath, Kanchipuram, Puri, Tamralpta, Dwarasamudra, Tinevelli, Tanjore, Calicut, Rajamundri were having trade with the outside world and were prosperous business centres. Most of the urban centres were sensitive areas being historically significant nodes of chieftains.

Salient Characteristics of Medieval Indian Towns

(1) Medieval period in India was a transitional time and it was not possible under the unstable political conditions for the planned and systematic urban growth. Only fortress towns under the patronage of chieftains and petty rulers could grow.

(2) Towns along the main routes of travel, and by the river-side had trade in foodgrains, cloth, swords, carpets, perfumes and several other handicraft articles.[16]

(3) Small urban centres was the 'rule', and only capitals were having busy life. Jaunpur was the capital city under the rule of Firozshah.[17]

(4) It was only under the rule of Akbar that the disturbed urban life was reconstituted and redeveloped.[18] All centres – 'dasturs' (districts) as well as 'parganas' (tehsils) beside

capitals in nature were also 'garrison towns' where armies were invariably stationed for protection.

(5) Medieval towns, whether in India or anywhere else, were walled, encircled by an outside moat. The town resembled "an island when its gates were locked at sundown".[19]

(6) Medieval town site was usually governed by physically significant terrain; it was either on a hill flanked on the other side by a water body, or it was guarded by a ring of mounds.

(7) Medieval town used to have its first nucleus often as a fortress of walled property of a landlord, its internal roads being controlled to connect the market place lying directly before the gate of the castle or place of worship. Nucleus of the town was "the stage on which were enacted the daily drama of buying and selling, religious pageant, tournament and procession".[20]

(8) Urban centres of the medieval times were surrounded by agricultural land, and farmers and labourers commonly were having their dwellings near or outside the town limit. The areas within the walls of a town near its bound were occupied by artisan castes engaged in handicrafts. Wealthy merchants were having their mansions around the market place in the central area, while the administrative officials and high-ranked army personnels' residences were around the palace or castle, church, abbey and the place of worship. The entire structure of a town was divided into socially hierarchical classes controlled by the chieftain or bishop.[21]

Geographical Bases of Origin and Growth of Modern Towns

Modern towns have their roots in the Industrial Revolution which began on the Continent of Europe at the end of the 18th century. In 1800, the population of Europe was about 175 million, of which 1.6 per cent lived in 20 cities of over one lakh population. The phenomenal increase due to industrial impact was felt during the 19th century and number of cities in Europe between 1800 and 1890 with one lakh inhabitants increased from 20 to 120 cities.[22] The great increase was a change from the economic spatial relations between towns from trade to manufacturing industries, related to the introduction of steam power and its utilization in the factories. The colonial activities of the European nations exploited the countries of the Third World by the useful raw materials brought to Europe in their factories for manufacturing products of daily use. However, the impact, of course a bit late, too influenced towns of the countries outside the continent. But the positive and maximum advantage of the Industrial Revolution turned the cities of Europe into big urban nodes. McGee expressed aptly that the majority of the Third World countries have inherited their modern economic structure from an era of colonialism.[23]

In Europe, three important factors are responsible in the general growth of towns, and the disproportionate expansion of the giant cities. These are:

(1) the spread of railway plexus across Europe,
(2) the development of the coalfields, and
(3) the continued increase of the capital cities.[24]

In the mid-19th century eight cities of over one lakh population were located on the coalfields and 16 were ports in western Europe. But the handicaps of costly inland transport and the slow movement on canals and natural waterways were removed by the railways. The combination of the new form of transport plus the added factor of point production made possible by the steam engine, caused the disproportionate growth of industrial centres. In England also the development of railway gave impetus to the industrial conurbations of the woollen and cotton towns.

Growth of modern towns made it possible to increase the number of service centres where increased population engaged in tertiary activities was taking shape because of the decreased artisans engaged in handicrafts.

One other factor came into prominence in the case of Great Britain where due to excessive industrial growth and pollution people sought to relieve their pains by migrating from the smoky 'Black country' to the sea-side. The spread of railways too played the role and several sea-resorts came into being. Smailes observed the phenomenon of the growing holiday resorts and expressed:

> A concomitant of the intense industrialization of Great Britain, an island country with stretches of sea-side now within easy reach of all major concentrations of population, has been the development of resorts on a scale unmatched in any other country. As a class of towns, resorts are here both more numerous and more highly specialized in function.[25]

Growth of seaside towns spread all along the coast of the Mediterranean sea in Spain, France, Italy, Yugoslavia, etc. Urban expansion in Europe due to holiday and health resorts was tremendous during 1801-51, being 254 per cent, followed by the manufacturing towns with 224 per cent, mining and metallurgical towns 217, seaports 195, London 146 and the country towns 122 per cent.[26]

By the mid-20th century, in Europe, there were some 300 cities with over one lakh inhabitants. This represents the greatest urban growth in the world because the total number of such cities was 700; Asia had 215 and the Americas 155 cities.

Development of 'conurbation'* is another spectacular phenomenon of urban growth in Europe. In Britain, by the end of the 19th century, out of 40 towns with over one lakh population, 27 were on coalfields to form conurbation. The census of 1951 in England shows six conurbations having 41 per

---

* The term 'conurbation' was coined by Patrick Geddes representing an urban unit or rather the contiguous administrative districts that make up the urban unit (Geddes, P., *Cities in Evolution*, London, 1915).

cent of the total urban population. In the north-western part of Germany the Ruhr Coal region had some forty coal-towns welded into conurbation spreading from Duselberg to Hern and between Dusseldorf to Hagen.

Throughout Europe in the 20th century there has been a common factor of the supremacy of a national capital or commercial city in each country. As aptly observed by Houston, "the national feeling was a tremendous force or a general tidal advance when compared to all other population movements which were merely ripples".[27]

In India, urban modernism truly began with the advent of the British rule. In 1872, India's first census of population was carried out. This showed that in 1872 there were only 16 cities of one lakh population and all of them were trading centres situated either on sea coasts or on river banks. Kolkata was a premier city grown due to its trading activities through its rich mineral-bearing hinterland. At that time England had evolved as a major industrial node of the world as a result of the industrial revolution and India became its main market for British goods. Moreover, the economic policies of the European colonial powers proved detrimental and the raw-materials from India fed the factories of Europe. It resulted into both decline as well as growth of some of the Indian urban centres. Kolkata, Chennai, Mumbai, Patna, Surat, Varanasi and Delhi showed a growth of nearly 10 per cent in their population when compared to 1800 A.D. Kolkata was having eight lakh population in 1872. On the contrary to this fact, old ancient and medieval towns like Agra, Lucknow, Srinagar, Ahmedabad, Gaya, Baroda, Indore and Tanjore lost their former importance due to negative approach to the colonial powers towards the traditional industries, especially handicrafts and cotton textiles of India. Earlier, trade centres which were largely on the Ganga river lost their importance. Mirzapur may be cited as an example which became a 'sick-town' in the beginning of the 20th century.

Another factor is the network of railways which contributed to the urban growth in India. Inland towns, and even cities of large size which were on the railways, developed. The railways had their profound impact since 1931 and the census of 1941 showed that there were 49 one lakh cities, and in all, around 2,500 towns were on railway lines.

The 19th century also witnessed in India the emergence of a new class of towns in the hill areas, particularly for the British to enjoy a cool temperate climate to get relief from the agonies of the summer heat. By 1870, there were over 80 hill stations in India to cater the needs of four clientele areas, viz., (a) Simla-Mussoorie-Nainital near Delhi, (b) Darjeeling-Shillong near Kolkata, (c) Mahabaleshwar near Mumbai, and (d) the Nilgiri-Kodaikanal in Tamilnadu.

The major railway heads, hill stations and centres of manufacturing peculiarly had the British ethos. Modern development in towns of India indicate a striking contrast between their indigenous sector and the other Anglicised part.[28] It is because of the modification of the urban landscape of the existing capital towns with the introduction of civil lines, cantonments, railway colony, establishment of townships, and also with the addition of amenities like clubs, administrative and educational and hospital campuses as well as the central commercial areas flanked by the massive buildings of Roman styles.

In the post-independence period, urban growth in India has entered a new phase. Cities having one lakh and even more population, grew rapidly. Some new cities also came into being because of the partition of the country. The displaced people began to settle in and around Delhi, and there was a phenomenal rise in the population of towns in northern India. This was followed by industrial development which was responsible for three to four-fold increase in the urban population. Rise in commerce, trade and communication, and also new administrative set-up gave rise to urban development.

In India, bases of origin or urban centres were not different from that of the western world. Towns primarily originated and developed in the areas which were fertile agriculturally. Most of the towns have village origin, and small towns have a substantial part of their work-force engaged in agriculture. Market towns also appeared in and around agriculturally fertile areas to collect and dispose food-grains.

Religion also played an important force for the origin of towns. Varanasi, Allahabad, Haridwar, Rameshwaram, etc., have come into being predominantly because of religious sanctity at the point of their site.

Another significant base of origin in India has been political. Princely states had their capital cities originated, grew and even deserted with the beginning, rise and fall of kingdoms during the course of history. Patliputra, Vijayanagar, Aurangabad, Bijapur, Golconda, etc., are some of the examples representing their political origin. After independence also, the new state capitals like Chandigarh, Gandhinagar, Bhubaneshwar, Dispur, etc., came into origin because of the political need.

Concluding the trend of origin and growth of urban centres around the world, this may be conveniently established that the underlying reasons are multifarious ranging from economic to cultural, social and political. The economic forces either generated by the ancient river valleys or by Greek's voyages around the Mediterranean played significant role. Roman political organization and the Aryan states in the Gangetic plain or later on the colonial activities of the European powers too made their marks in the origin and development of towns. Industrial Revolution during the 19th century coupled with production and vast labour forces generated the creation of entirely new urban agglomeration in great contrast to the earlier urban development. Urban gravitation is being encouraged by the development of modern transportation and communication.

In the entire world, the capital cities, especially in Europe and India, as well as, strong point towns of state rulers and emperors have given a fillip for origin of urban centres. Enayat Ahmad[29] has summarized in the case of India, the village origin, religious origin as well as industrial, commercial, transport and whim of rulers as factors of urban origin and growth.

Notes

1. Davis, K. and Hertz, H., *The Pattern of World Urbanization*, New York.
2. Childe, V.G., "The Urban Revolution", in Possehl, (ed.), *Ancient Cities of the Industries*, Vikas, New Delhi.
3. Wheeler, *Civilization of the Indus Valley*.
4. Aristotle, *Politics*, ii, 5.2.
5. The Miletan town-planner, 'Hippodamus' pointed out that 10,000 was the right number to have in a city population for the good life of city-state.
6. On Greek cities authoritative work in English is, Wycherley, R.E., *How the Greeks Built Cities*, London, 1949.
7. Munro, W.B., *Municipal Government and Administration*, Macmillan, 1923, Ch. 1.
8. Frotheringham, A.L., *Roman Cities in Northern Italy and Dalmatian*, London, 1910, p. 98.
9. Houston, J.M., *A Social Geography of Europe*, G. Duckworth, London, 1953, p. 142.
10. Wheeler, *Civilization of the Indus Valley*.
11. McGee, T.G., *The Southeast Asian City*, G. Bell & Sons, London, 1967.
12. Houston, J.M., op. cit., p. 143.
13. Mumford, L., *The Culture of Cities*, London, 1938, p. 77.
14. Stow, J., *A Survey of London*, London, 1598, W.J. Thomas, (ed.), 1876, p. 265.
15. Mooreland, W.H., *India at the Death of Akbar*, 1920.
16. Ahmad, E., "Settlement in the United Provinces", unpublished Ph.D. thesis, London University, 1948.

17. District Gazetteer, Jaunpur, 1908, p. 152 and p. 238.
18. Mooreland, W.H., op. cit., p. 167.
19. Mumford, L., *Culture of Cities*, Sacker and Warburg, London, 1945.
20. Dickinson, R.E., *The West European City*, London, 1962, p. 316.
21. Ibid., p. 324.
22. Meuriot, P., "Des Agglomerations Urbaines dans l'Europe", Paris, 1897, pp. 30-31. Quoted from Houston, J.M., op. cit., p. 152.
23. McGee, T.G., op. cit., pp. 17-18.
24. Houston, J.M., op. cit., p. 152.
25. Smailes, A.E., *Geography of Towns*, London, 1953.
26. Weber, A.F., *The Growth of Cities*, London, 1899, p. 57.
27. Houston, J.M., op. cit., p. 157.
28. Bharadwaj, R.K., *Urban Development in India*, National, Delhi, 1974, pp. 59-60.
29. Ahmad, Enayat, *Geographical Essays in India*, Kusum Prakashan, Patna, 1954.

5

Location, Site and Situation

Urban geographers have always been interested in seeking the answer to the question as to why a town is located where it is. Speaking concisely, location of a particular point on a map can be explained "in terms of latitude and longitude, or distance and direction from other established points".[1] Further, location of a place may also be explained to bring forth the interconnections between a town on its economic and social plane, and the productive activities in its peripheral region. Another important fact about the location of a town is to know about the interplay of physical characteristic of its immediate ground such as river bank, confluence, terrace or abandoned river bed, mountain gaps, piedmont and a plain, or the presence of lakes or the sea. Nonetheless important is a fact that town's place is the product of culture of the people of the region.

The concept of town's site represents both a history and a geography.[2] Historical fact of a town is expressed materially in its created landscape and sequence occupance of the space in time. The geographical fact is no less important than the historical, because it reveals the human environment with the economic activities. It includes the identification of site and location factors in relation to the growth of town.

Traditional Concept of Location

Traditionally, location means a position of a point on a map of the earth's surface in relation to equator. It is expressed as its angular distance from the equator known as 'latitude'; and 'longitude' is another angular distance of a given point measured in degrees east or west of the Greenwich meridian. As stated earlier, location of a particular point is explained in terms of latitude and longitude. But this is not suffice and capable to answer the question fully, "where is it?" If a town's position is only explained in terms of location then it would be more than a mere information not sufficing to serve the geographer's purpose who generally seeks all sorts of spatial relationship.

Modern Concept of Location

The site and situation of a point (rural or urban) actually present a milieu - a base, which is more reliable to answer geographically the question "where is human settlement?" In a strict sense of the word, 'site' means the actual ground where a town or village stands. The word 'situation' carries a wider plane and it includes the place of a settlement within its surrounding environs. It was Ratzel who could recognize first the distinction between the site and the situation of a town.[3] In a study of Berlin he noted that the city had a site negative to its active expansion, but that its situation on the North German Plain was an important factor in its growth.[4] In case of London, Paris and Istanbul, site and situation are both favourable resulting in their long famous history. Population growth and the function of towns are the product of their situation; whereas site determines urban morphology.

Town's development is not a matter of chance. It is the process in which are juxtaposed potentialities of the original site, and also functional viability – trading, commercial, administrative and cultural services. Both may well be understood in relation to its regional resources and its national interests.

Positive and Negative Aspect of the Site and Situation

The site and situation both possess positive and negative aspects. These may be properly understood when studied in relation to the expansion or growth of a town. A favourable site of a town has all possibilities of its fullest expansion horizontally in all directions. Generally, it possesses inestimable advantages of almost all types – natural drainage, protection or security, easy accessibility to the hub of the town from its different corners. In this respect we may look into the case of Paris (Figure 5.1) which is interesting both geographically as well as historically. Its site is just below the confluence of the Marne with the Seine, at a point where a river crossing was fixed by a north-south route running north through a hill gap, that Paris has grown. Its site is advantageously created by 118 miles of the underground 'Metropolitian' which pierce under the Seine in five tunnels.[5] Thus, Paris is today the result of creative forces rooted in the 19th century. It is for such qualities of the site of Paris endowed to it by the created landscape that it is now called "Paris is what Paris has made". Another interesting case from our own country India is of Varanasi (formerly Banaras). It is sited on a high ridge of 'kankar' (lime concretion) forming the northern bank of the Ganga quite above normal flood level. The character of its site has made the position of the city so stable and enviable that it is amongst the few cities of the world which shows little shifting of its site. The Ganga was, at the same time, not only a protection from hostile invasion but it also provided an easy highway. The city owes its importance to the site by various advantages. These not only attracted the early settlement to this spot, but they also continued to exert their influence in the nature of the city's growth during different phases.[6]

Figure 5.1
Map Showing Site and Growth of Paris

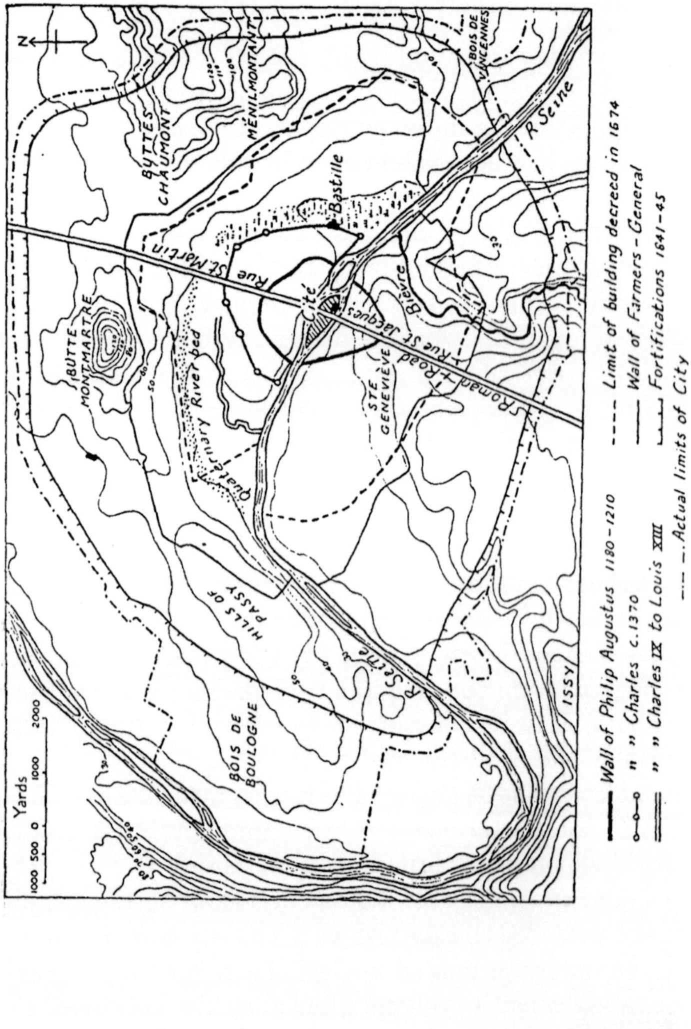

Figure 5.2
Site of Jodhpur

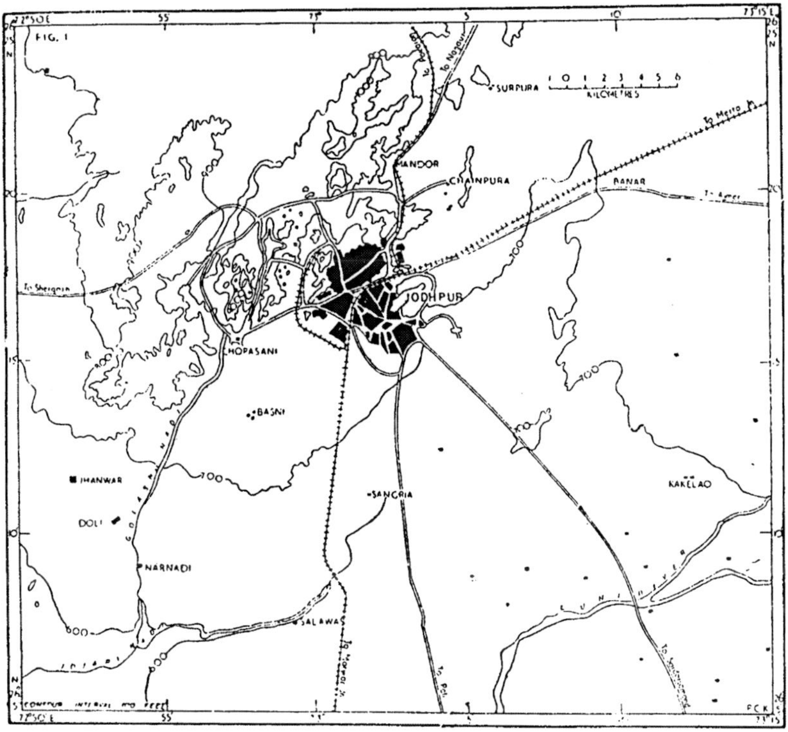

The site of Jodhpur (Figure 5.2) reflects both positive and negative aspects. By traditional standards, Jodhpur has an excellent natural defensive site at the north-eastern extremity of a small, detached, steep and flat topped ridge of sandstone. The medieval city lies on an irregular surface, in the form of 'horse-shoe', sloping upwards towards the base of the rock surmounted by the fort. The northern side, being wholly occupied by a desolate and rugged rock, is too inhospitable to attract any settlement while the extensive rolling plain of the south has offered opportunities for town-spread.[7]

But the cities which possess site and situation both favourable or positive, as are London, Paris and Istanbul, become famous universally and historically for they are in the position to command local, regional, national as well as international advantages.

As already pointed out earlier, negative town sites have limited opportunities for horizontal expansion due to the presence of either a ford of the river, a tank, a steep ridge or hill, sea coast or any island or any other such natural obstruction hindering town growth in one or the other directions. Such sites of towns back the advantages of all-round accessibility, and their plans too become amorphous. Towns having negative sites being squeezed physically, their expansion of the built-up areas may be found forcibly vertical rather than horizontal. Greater Mumbai and New York[8] can be cited as best examples where buildings have been going up-and-up to house their ever increasing population wave.

Often with the development of a town, its site no longer remains positive and does not fulfil the conditions which it originally offered. Canberra and Brasilia initially originated on favourable sites, but later on, their growth could not retain the site-advantages. This contradiction has presented extremely serious problems. But, technical progress, fortunately has come to the rescue and kept pace with urban growth.[9] For Rouen, which was favourably established on the concave bank of the river-loop remains no longer advantageous. But the technical skill used to make its expansion possible on to the convex bank of the river. In case of Hamburg the two banks of the Elbe are joined by a tunnel. City of Caracas continued its expansion by clearing the hills and filled-in valleys. Large number of bridges, tunnels and ferries over the Hudson and the East River have had to be provided as the agglomeration has grown. Delhi towards east of the river Yamuna and Panjim (Goa) too have overcome the disadvantages on the old site by using technical skill for providing new outlets. The new towns of the pre-Soviet Union bear witness to the supremacy of technical methods.

Significance and Purpose

The study into site-situation consideration in geography has an important role to play. Site is the actual space occupied by a town. It may be undulating terrain or level ground. It may or may not be flanked by water bodies. It may be coastal land or a loop of a river. Whatever the physiography of the site, it governs the morphology of a town and plays its role in growth. Its role may be positive or negative. Site of a town and its natural setting determine the drainage and transportational channels in their own way.

Situation of a town has different role to play. It reveals town's connectivity with its surrounding areas – regional, national or even international. It is important to know the situation of a given country or even a single settlement to transportation linkages, markets, and major industrial, trade, administrative, and cultural centres. Dickinson distinguishes between the concept of a site and of a situation. "The situation embraces the general conditions, both physical and human, throughout a wide area around the town that affect its origin, development, and character. The site embraces the precise physical features of the ground on which the town began and over which it has spread."[10] This distinction itself reveals the significance of site and situation.

Location has a very different significance. Traditionally location of a town is often understood to mean: so many degrees of eastern or western longitude, and, so many degrees of northern or southern latitude. The locational concept is useful for identifying a specific point of a settlement in a map or on a globe. It is of much use for beginners of geography for understanding town's position globally. In the wider perspective its significance includes the relation of a given point to some regions, countries or continents of the world. It means that the concept of location is also related to territorial sector of geographical significance. For example, it can be conveniently stated that Stalingrad is on the right bank of the river Volga.

Enayat Ahmad following the same notion about location, has classified towns into riverside, interflurial, confluence, zone of contact, break-o-bulk, hill, frontier, fall-line, seaboard and bridge-head locations.[11]

Function and Geographical Situation

Town's situation is invariably related to its particular function. It is found generally situated at the place best suited for the exercise of that function. For example, an estuary part is situated at the highest point reached by the tide to take advantage of the sea downstream and at the same time the lowest easy crossing point of the river. Panjim (Goa) is an ideal example on the river Zuari estuary.

In economic geography, the situation must be defined in relation to conditions that are created by man's activities in the course of the historical process.[12] When an economic geographer approaches the study of a city, the first question that arises in his mind is "why a city emerged and developed precisely at a given point and not elsewhere?" This may be best analyzed by an example of Leningrad. It is situated, on the one hand, at the point where the Atlantic Ocean reaches farthest into the territory of the Russian Plains; on the other, there are internal waterways passing through that point – by linking the rivers of the lake basin with the Volga through canals. Further, the Volga provides a route to Moscow, as well as, to the Urals. Leningrad is thus a point that may benefit from the low cost rates of water transportation in receiving diversity of raw materials from vast internal regions through the Volga, the canals, river and maritime routes.[13]

Classification of Town Sites

Site of each town is peculiar in its own way, and it is not easy to recognize its particular type because "a particular town may claim as a representative of different site-categories".[14] Each town site is, in a sense, unique and possesses only relative values.

But, on the other hand, topographical features of the nucleus, the original function, initial development, needs of defence, communication, etc., of a town may comprise the standard relative values of judge and classify urban centres. A tentative scheme is being attempted to identify site-categories as follows:

Town Sites

Sea coast and Bridgehead	*River Valley*	*Lake/Depression*	*Hill Sites*	*Sites on flat terrain*
	(a) Long Valley (b) River Meander (c) River-loop (d) River-spur (e) River-island (f) River-confluence of 'doab'	(a) Nest Site (b) Re-entrant (c) Trough		(a) On level terrain (b) On high-level terraces or plateaus

The above scheme of classification of town site is very general in nature and it should not be regarded as a series of pigeon holes into which every town can be neatly placed. The categories mentioned in the scheme are not mutually exclusive. Site on flat terrain is the common category visible everywhere on level topography (Figure 5.3). A sea coast site may occur both on a plain as well as on a hill. Therefore, the present analysis may only be taken as suitable for some representative towns and cities in India. Only stray examples are given to represent the characteristics. These neither cover the entire country, nor do they represent a well-marked and complete region.

Sea-front cities have the access to a view of the sea, and in some of the cases these are flanked by beaches which are the sources of recreation and attract tourists and local population

Figure 5.3
Level-Site Markets

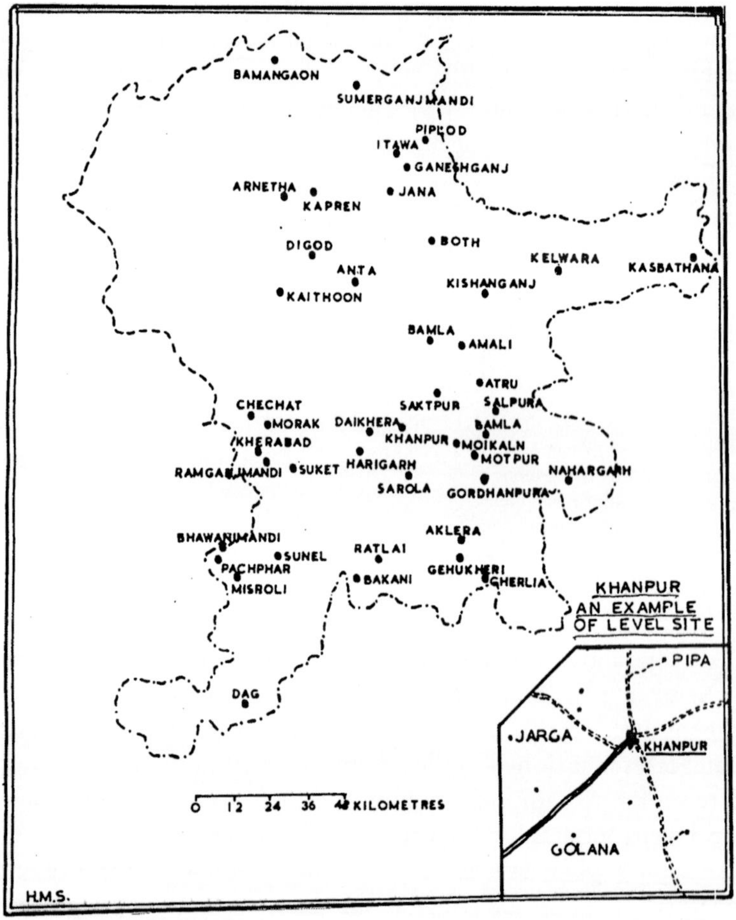

Source: Geography of Transport and Market Centres by H.M. Saxena.

Figure 5.4

Some Examples of River-Site Markets

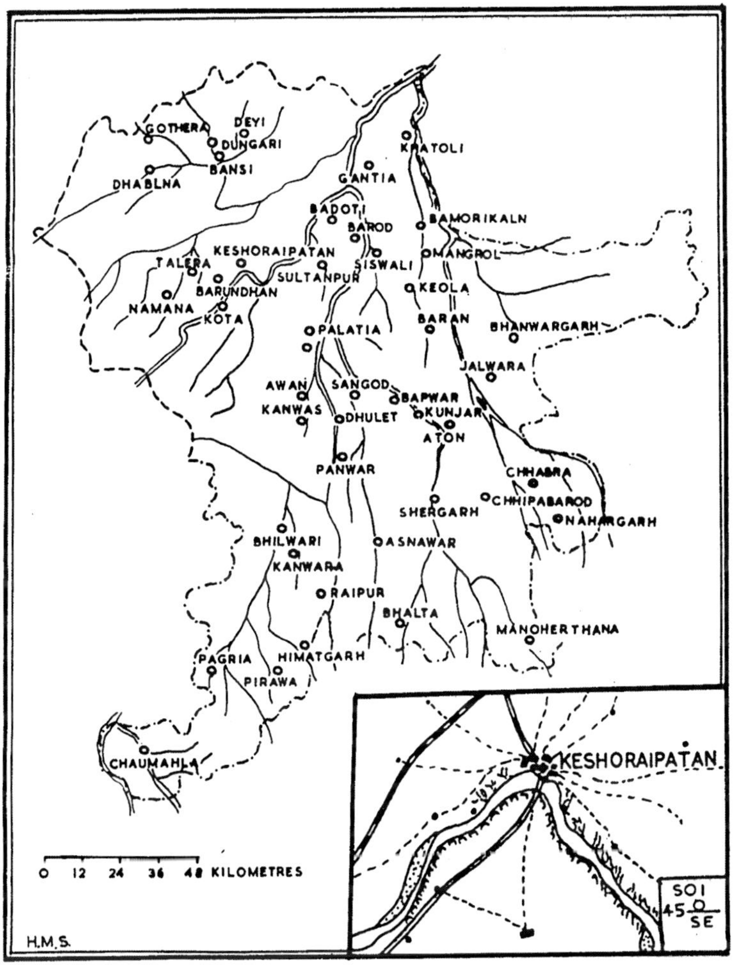

Examples in Map from Hadoti Region (Rajasthan) – (Courtesy: H.M. Saxena).

also. Chennai, Trivandrum, Calicut, Panjim have beautiful beach sections. Vishakhapatnam and Mangalore have rocky shorelines.

River-front sites (see Figure 5.4) are numerous in India. This type of site is favoured by towns seeking proximity to the route, river crossing points, ford, ferry or bridge. Most of them are on raised land above the flood-limit along the river plain. Mathura, Varanasi and Prayag are sited on the banks of Yamuna or the Ganga. Madurai, in South is on the river Vaigai, Nasik on the Godavari, Tanjore on the Kaveri and Nagarjunakonda on the Krishna are typical towns on the river-front.

On the uneven rugged terrain streams and rivers develop valleys where typical sites are favoured by towns seeking proximity to the route, river crossing points, ford, ferry or bridge. Sone and Jons river valleys of the central, eastern and south-eastern parts of Vindhya region have quite a good number of settlements representing valley route site (Jhukhehi in Satna district), valley floor site (Churhat in Sidhi district), Step-site (Anarpur in Shahdol district), transverse-valley site (Venkatnagar in Shahdol district), and valley-exit-site (Maihar in Satna district).[15]

Besides the above, river-meander site of Unnao in Datia district of Madhya Pradesh is an excellent example where the town on the river Pahuj is at the point of converging roads from north-west, north-east and south directions. Annuppur in Shahdol district occupies a site on a spur rising 500 metres above the sea-level. Orchha in the Bundelkhand historic region is a classic example of the river-island site where the town is sited on the edge of the Betwa river in a hollow with a fort on an island defended by a wall, river water and marshes from all sides.[16]

Depression or tank as a town site are most commonly found on the Bundelkhand Gneiss plateau where natural and semi-artificial tanks are formed by dykes constricting the streams frequently. Tikamgarh and Jatara are typical urban

Figure 5.5
Foothill, Trough and Gap-Site Markets

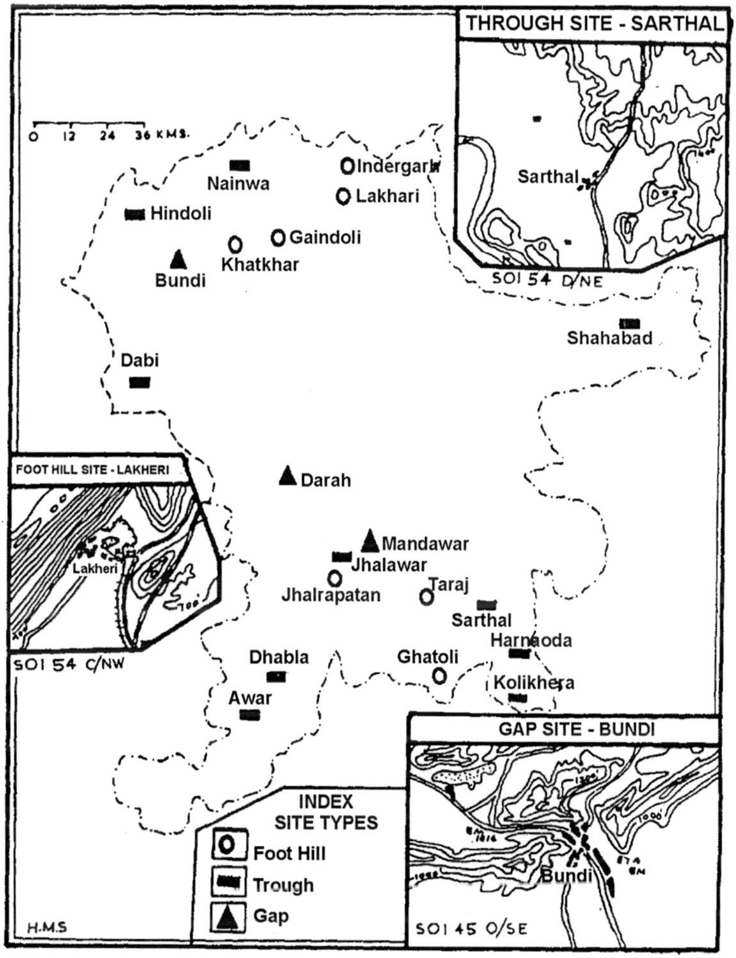

Hill sites examples from Hadoti region are shown in the Map (Courtesy: H.M. Saxena).

settlements where site consist of tanks built by the Chandella rulers.[17]

Hill sites (see Figure 5.5) refer to the presence of prominent hills within the developed area of the city. The Golden Rock Temple in Tiruchirappalli, the temple on Palni hill and Sri Venkateswara temple at Tirupati are all examples of hill sites.[18] In India hill site usually is supposed to be the most common abode of 'deva'. Uttaranchal presents excellent hill sites for the famous pilgrimage centres of Kedarnath, Badrinath, Gangotri and Yamunotri. Hills and the associated forts with their ramparts are typical sites in Madhya Pradesh and Maharashtra. Aravalli hills from Gujarat to Delhi are studded with numerous settlements which have been princely states during medieval times. Alwar, Ajmer, Jaipur, Udaipur, Salumbar, and Deogarh are some of the examples whose sites represent gaps within the hills of the Aravalli system.[19] Walled towns within the hills everywhere represent generally "a tendency to converge, even to concentrate, at the angle of slopes, at the intersection of different gradients".[20] Thus, the actual ground occupied by hill towns represents either hill top or hill slope or foothill. Udaipur is flanked by a fort and palace on top of the ridge extending from south to north, whereas the habitation occupies the slope of the ridge from west to east, and finally the post-independence built-up area is now occupying the eastern-southeastern site within the outer ring of the hills; the eastern hill being only 783 metres as compared to its western counterpart having the height of 939 metres.[21]

Conclusion

Consideration into site-situation is significant aspect in urban geography. It reveals the purpose and also the function for which town or city is there where it stands. Its site is actually the space best suited for the exercise of its particular function.

All the three basic concepts of location, situation and site differ from each other, but their impact is simultaneous in determining the growth of urban centres of various orders.

Care must be taken to distinguish the situation of a town from its site. Beaujeu Garnier distinguishes between these by stating their function: "the situation commands; men use it as best they can for their own ends, and the site is the result of this arrangement".[22] Site, according to Blache, determines the dwellings, and sites of cities have a tendency to multiply and to crowd into certain areas.[23] Site governs morphology of a city and also produces a typical plan by virtue of its various forces – natural and cultural.

Location of a city makes us known with its position on a globe geomentically, while its situation reveals the relationship of the centre with the surrounding areas regionally and also beyond the national limits. But the concept of an urban site includes the inherent qualities of a space actually occupied by the settlement. Each town site is, in a sense, unique. It involves relative values. Its values are responsible for the town's initial growth, its functions, its needs of defence and communication with other centres. As an urban geographer, the site must be studied three-dimensionally, i.e., its topographical features governing towns's growth; the influence of topography on the plan of the town; and the created landscape modifying the original site by urban spread. Site is the core of the complex features of a city's anatomy and physiology.

Notes

1. Smailes, A.E., *The Geography of Towns*, London, 1958, p. 41.
2. Houston, J.M., *A Social Geography of Europe*, London, 1953, p. 159.
3. Ibid., p. 137.
4. Aurousseau, M., "Recent Contributions to Urban Geography", *G.R.* XIV, 1924, pp. 444-55.

5. Crone, G.R., "The Site and Development of Paris", *G.J.*, XCVIII, 1941, pp. 33-47.
6. Singh, R.L., *Banaras: A Study in Urban Geography*, Nand Kishore and Bros., Banaras, India, 1955, p. 14.
7. Kumbhat, P.C., "Urban Morphology and Planning of Jodhpur", in *Essays in Applied Geography*, in memory of the Late Prof. S.M. Ali, University of Saugar, Sagar, 1976, p. 192.
8. Huntington, E., "The Water Barriers of New York", *Geog. Rev.*, 1916.
9. Beaujeu-Garnier, J. and G. Chabot, *Urban Geography*, Longmans, 1967, p. 210.
10. Dickinson, R.E., *The West European City*, London, 1951, p. 5.
11. Ahmad, E., *Geographical Essays on India*, Kusum Prakashan, Patna, 1954.
12. Baransky, N., *Selected Works in Geography*, Progress Publishers, Moscow, 1981, p. 110.
13. Ibid., pp. 121-122.
14. Smailes, A.E., op. cit., pp. 44-49.
15. Verma, L.N., *Environment and Human Habitation*, Himanshu Pub., Udaipur, 1991, pp. 152-153.
16. Ibid., p. 153.
17. Ibid., pp. 153-154.
18. Ramchandran, R., *Urbanization and Urban Systems in India*, Oxford, New Delhi, 1999, p. 159.
19. Verma, L.N., "Some Forms of Town Sites in the Aravallis", *Indian Geogl. Journal*, Madras, Vol. 41, 1966, pp. 52-63.
20. la Blache, P. Vidal de, *Principles of Human Geography*, Trans. Bingham, London, 1921, p. 283.
21. Verma, L.N. "Walled Town and Trends in its Post-Independence Built-up Area", Proc., Autumn School in Geography, Aligarh Muslim University, Aligarh, 1966.
22. Garnier B. and Chabot, G., op. cit., p. 113.
23. la Blache, P. Vidal de, op. cit., p. 277.

6

World Urbanization

Urbanization is a process indicating growth of urban centres in number as well as in the population occupying these centres. The phenomenon of urbanization is present everywhere in the world, but it is conspicuously found in the western world where urban population proportion is about 75 per cent. Regionally speaking, nearly 68 per cent of urban population resided in more developed regions comprising Europe, North America, Japan, Australia and New Zealand in 1970. It increased to 75 per cent in 1994 and is estimated to jump over 80 per cent by 2010.

Looking at the phenomenon in terms of number of urban centres by size, the problem becomes more intense. As evident from the statistics of the United Nations, the world population living in agglomerations of the size 20,000 and more increased from 132 per cent in 1800-1850 to 193 per cent in 1850-1900, and further 240 per cent in 1900-1950; the corresponding increases in cities with one lakh population or more were 76 per cent, 222 per cent and 254 per cent respectively. If these figures are compared with world's total urban population (1 billion in 1970, 2.5 billion in 1994, and nearly 4 billion in 2010), it becomes obviously clear that urban growth of lakh population cities would be tremendous.

Concept of Urbanization

Urbanization simply does not mean increase in number of urban people and increase in number of urban centres either of lakh-towns or million-towns. The concept of urbanization specifically means a process involving an increase in the proportion of the population that is urban in relation to the increase of the total population as in relation to the proportion of non-urban population of a region.

This means, that "rate of urbanization" differs from the "growth rate of urban population". The rate of urbanization is the percentage increase over a given period in proportion to the total population living in urban communities. Here, urban communities, again a complex notion, differs from country to country. The UN defines as 'urban' any settlement with at least 2,000 residents; however, some countries use threshold populations of 5,000, 10,000 or 20,000.[1]

The rate of urbanization is different from the "growth rate of urban population" which refers to the percentage-increase of the urban population without necessarily relating it to the total population.[2]

Whatever is stated above, can be summed up by referring to the calculation of the degree of urbanization over a period in a region. It may be $\alpha = \frac{U}{T} \times 100$, where α means degree of urbanization which is proportion of urban population to the total population in terms of per cent.

Significance of Urbanization

Urbanization and a probe into its relevant knowledge is essential by virtue of its four-fold reasons. First, the fact of urbanization has been now felt pervasively over the entire world. It has now become a global phenomenon because sizeable proportion of the population now lives in cities. Second, it is a fact that urbanism has its impact on our social life to the extent that people's attitudes towards values have altogether changed. Even the surrounding rural milieu is being changed by urban appendages. Third, is the fact that cities have become centres of power and are capable enough to determine economy, polity and social relationships. The last point of significance characterising a number of problems which are the outcome of the continuum process of urbanization like housing, transportation, employment, appearance of 'bustees' or 'jhuggi-jhonpadis' or shanty quarters, insecurity, social distance, etc., in the city life. These problems are mostly unsolved, and a sort of uncertain and bleak future has grabbed materialistic city environs.

Historical Perspective

The first cities appeared sometime between 6000 and 5000 B.C., but in the true sense of the term, cities came into existence by 3000 B.C. Their number grew and the degree of urbanization gained some pace between 600 B.C. to 400 A.D. It was only with the Romans that large cities had sufficient potentialities to support the population of several hundred thousand. Rome and Constantinople had fruitful hinterland rich in cultivation.[3] The Dark Ages (400-1000 A.D.) witnessed the collapse of urban wave in Europe with the decline of commerce and the establishment of hereditary social system. It was only after 1200 A.D. with the regaining of energy by trade, urban centres once again became significant. Florence, Venice, Antwerp, London, Frankfurt, Nuremberg began to revive on the basis of improvements in agriculture, trade and transport, and, above all, the rise in productive activity.

A true urban revolution took place in the 19th century with the appearance of factories run by machinery and fossil fuel. England was the foremost in the race of urbanization. In 1801 only 10 per cent of its population lived in cities of 100,000 or more, by 1901 this increased by threefold. Its 58 per cent population was living in cities of 20,000 or more in the beginning of the 20th century. Further, by 1951, the figures of the percentages reached 38.4 and 69.3 respectively of the two above stated levels. Since then, urbanization has gone rapidly ahead in northwestern Europe.

It is also evident that earth's total population has grown extremely at a rapid rate since 1800, reaching 2.4 billion by 1950. But the share of urban population was far ahead. In 1800 there were about 15.6 million people living in cities of 100,000 or more. By 1950 it was 313.7 million, or more than 20 times the earlier figure. (Table 6.1). In 1950, there were close to 900 cities of 100,000 or more people.

Table 6.1

Showing Percentage of World's Population Living in Cities, by Regions (1950) (K. Davis)

	In cities of 20,000 plus	*In cities of 100,000 plus*
World	21	13
Oceania	47	41
North America (Canada and USA)	42	29
Europe (except USSR)	35	21
USSR	31	18
South America	26	18
Middle America and Caribbean	21	12
Asia (except USSR)	13	8
Africa	9	5

If the same rate of urbanization continues, then more than half of the world's people will be living in cities of 100,000 or more in the year 2050.

Dominance of Urbanization

The most significant fact of urbanization is the recency of its dominance. At the beginning of the 19th century nearly 3 per cent of the world's population lived in towns of over 5000 inhabitants. At present the percentage figure is above 40. Between 1950 and 1970 the world's urban population rose from 28.2 per cent to 38.6 per cent. But the increasing trend went on unceasingly and by 2000 A.D. the figure reached 50. The number of cities having over 1 million population too indicated the similar trend. In 1921 there were 24 cities of over 1 million population which rose to 41 in 1941 and 113 in 1961. By 1988 their number reached 240 (*UN Demographic Year Book*, 1990). It is actually a swing from developed to developing countries rather than simply the southern shift.[4]

Changing Urban Milieu and Urbanization

As stated before, the shift of the trend in urbanization is from developed to developing countries; the fact is also being supported by the changing regional distribution of urban population. Asia is steadily increasing its share of the world's urban population by hosting as many as 11 mega cities (over 10 million population of each) viz., Tokyo, Mumbai, Kolkata, Shanghai, Dhaka, Karachi, Delhi, Jakarta, Osaka, Manila and Beijing. It is estimated that by 2020 the urban population in Asia and Pacific Region would be 1.97 billion or 46 per cent of its total of 4.3 billion. This means that three-quarters of the world's urban dwellers will live in cities and towns of Africa, Asia and Latin America (Figure 6.1).

Figure 6.1
Third World Urban Development

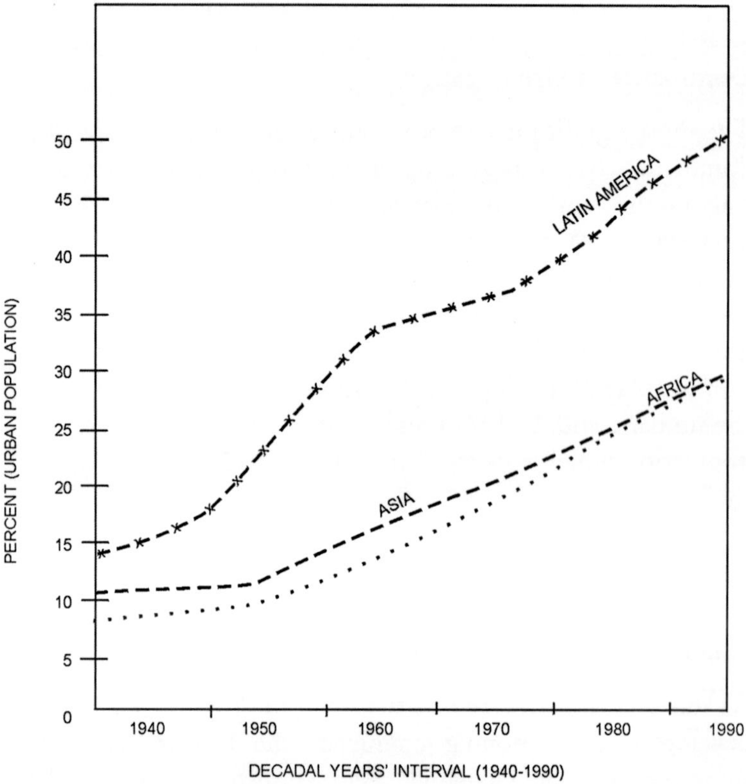

Source: World Development Report – 1983.

When cities begin to experience the pressure of population beyond their capacities and urban dwellers' life become uncomfortable, there is the situation which is termed as 'over-urbanization'. From the mid-20th century the populations in big cities have been increasing by leaps and bounds. The classic example of such a situation is found along the north-eastern seaboard of the United States, where there is a

Figure 6.2

Megalopolis, North-Eastern Seaboard: USA

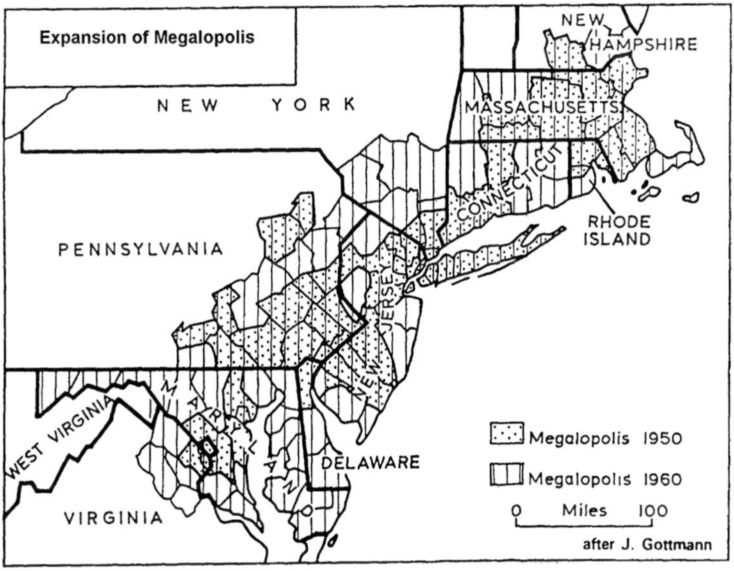

continuous stretch of urban and suburban land use, with a main northeast-southwest axis stretching about 600 miles and a population in 1960 of 37 millions. Here, a chain of metropolitan centres, often great ports, have grown. The entire seaboard is being "encouraged by the impact of the motor car on urban travel and by the dynamic nature of the economies of these cities which are based on diverse maritime, commercial and industrial functions".[5] The seaboard area has been termed 'megalopolis' by Jean Gottmann (Figure 6.2).

The phenomenon of spread of large cities has been now shifted to the tropical lands during the last three decades, particularly since the end of the Second World War. Mumbai, Kolkata, Mexico City and Sao Paulo had reached a population of more than one million. Now, there are at least 15 largest urban agglomerations, ranked by population size in 2000 (Table 6.2).

Table 6.2

15 Largest Agglomerations (by size) in 2000 A.D.

Rank	*Agglomeration*	*Population (in millions)*
1	Tokyo	26.4
2	Mexico City	18.1
3	Mumbai	18.1
4	Sao Paulo	17.8
5	New York	16.6
6	Lagos	13.4
7	Los Angeles	13.1
8	Kolkata	12.9
9	Shanghai	12.9
10	Buenos Aires	12.6
11	Dhaka	12.3
12	Karachi	11.8
13	Delhi	11.7
14	Jakarta	11.0
15	Osaka	11.0

Source: UN (2000) World Urbanization Prospects (1999 Revision).

The table indicates that urban growth is now taking place at a much faster rate in the tropical lands than in Western Europe of North America. The growth of very large cities in the tropics, of course, is due to political awakening. But even today many of these countries still depend on the export of raw materials and the import of manufactured goods. Hence, many of these million-cities are ports. But, in case of India, the history of urbanization reveals a number of processes at work, the important being the emergence of new social order through a process of change, rise and fall of cities as a result of changes in the political, the growth of cities by virtue of new productive processes, and the physical spread of cities as a result of the inflow of migrants in search of newer and profitable employments.

The changing urban phenomenon on regional pattern is another interesting point to make. There has been noticed a net-immigration in developed countries. The developed world receives hordes of people of various ethnic origin mainly from Asia, Latin America and Africa. Consequently, the racial and cultural milieu of Europe and North America is being loosened and is becoming heterogeneous gradually. During the last decade, the world witnessed flows of refugees in Euro-Asia due to the break-up of the USSR, and also the dismemberment of the former Yugoslavia. In Sub-Saharan Africa where genocide in Rwanda (1994), and civil war in the African Horn, Angola and the Western Africa, refugees were forced to move internally as well as externally. At the start of the new millennium, there were 22 million refugees and internally displaced persons in the world, especially the majority in Asia, Africa and Europe.

Table 6.3
Million-Cities (1870-1991)

Year	*Numbers*
1870	2
1900	20
1939	57
1951	95
1964	140
1979	213
1991	300

Urbanization has turned the cities into crowded places everywhere. The result is being felt in the form of overwhelming densities because of the urban explosion. In the mid-20th century in India nearly all cities having million-population or more became crowded with nearly 1,000 persons per hectare or even more. Mumbai has the density of 3,000 persons per hectare in 1991. The same is the case in the central areas of cities everywhere in the Third World countries. Ibadan and Singapore has 2,000 and 2,500 persons respectively in an area per hectare. The central areas are much more congested, the figures being 55,000 for New York, 52,000 for Montreal and 49,000 for Moscow per hectare (1991). Kolkata had as many as 69,000 persons per sq. kilometre in its central area.

Levels of Urbanization[6]

Level of urbanization indicates the proportion of total population residing in urban places. The world population between 1800 and 1950 living in urban agglomerations of 20,000 or more persons increased from 132 per cent (1800-1850) to 193 per cent (1850-1900) and 240 per cent in 1900-1950. The corresponding figures with 100,000 or more persons for urban settlements were 76 per cent, 222 per cent and 254 per cent respectively. It is estimated that the world's population which was 1 billion in 1970 and 2.5 billion in 1994, would be approximately 5 billion by 2025. The proportions of urban population for the respective years are 37 per cent, 45 per cent and 61 per cent.

The level of urbanization on the regional plane differs in case of the developed and developing world. It suggests that about 68 per cent of urban population resided in the developed regions comprising Europe, North America, Japan, Australia and New Zealand in 1970. This was further noted as 75 per cent in 1994 and projected to 84 per cent in 2025. This is clear that the level of world's urbanization at the turn of the millennium was 50 per cent urban, and by the quarter century in the new millennium (2025) urbanization is projected at the level of nearly two-thirds of the total population. It is also estimated that in the Asia and Pacific Region the proportion of the total population residing in urban places will be 1.97 billion (46%) of the total of 4.3 billion by 2020 A.D.

In such a precarious and tense situation in the urban world due to pressure of over-urbanization, people would be experiencing shortage of food from land and be looking for food from oceans and forests. Concluding his essay on 'Urbanization in the World', Kingsley Davis remarked that "urbanization in the sense of emptying the countryside and concentrating huge numbers in little space will reverse itself – not, however, in the direction of returning people to the farm but rather in that of spreading them more evenly over the land for purposes of residence and industrial work. 'Rurality' would have disappeared, leaving only a new kind of urban existence".[7] A situation comes about, therefore, where not only is population growing but the bonds which held that population to countryside are wakened.

World's Major and Minor Urban Areas

Urban areas contributing their share in the process of urbanization may be broadly divided into two categories, (i) highly urbanized, and (ii) low-urbanized areas.

The above division generally corresponds to the well-known division of the world into developed and developing world. The developed world includes the countries where proportion of urban population to the total exceeds 50 per cent. The level of urbanization exceeding fifty includes: (a) Australia and New Zealand (84-85%); (b) Japan (77%), North American countries (72-75%), South American countries, Latin America and Europe (nearly 70%), Central America and former USSR (65%).[8] This group largely is included in the developed world. The rest of the world's countries which are both of developed and developing categories are unmistakenly mixed such as Singapore,

Hong Kong, Kuwait, Shanghai, etc. These too have urban proportion of above 50, but do not form part of the developed world being part of Asia. However, for convenience it is more valid to have three categories based on cut-off point of percentages. The countries having proportion of more than 50 per cent urban may form part of first order urbanized region. The second order includes countries having proportion of urban population ranging between 25-50 per cent, and the last, third order includes areas of urban proportion to the total less than 25 per cent.

The first order urban region includes areas of north-western Europe, North-eastern USA, Canada, Australia and Japan. In this section, the cities have reached almost to the point of saturation. Belgium, Sweden, Germany and some of the other parts of the Western Europe have more than 80 per cent of the total population as urban. Here, large urban centres because of their dynamic economies and their existing immigrant populations, attract more than their share of new immigrants, who come from both short and long distances. In these areas, motor car and the lorry have encouraged urban inflow including manufacturing industry. North-eastern seaboard of the USA where a chain of metropolitan centres, often great ports, have grown together, encouraged by the impact of the motor car on urban travel, and also by dynamic nature of the economies based on diverse maritime, commercial and industrial functions.

The second order of urban region is that of medium-level urbanization, where areas having a proportion between 25-50 per cent urban to the total population are included. These are countries which are commonly included in the developing world sector. Although the proportion of urban to total does not rise beyond 50 per cent, but the individual cities having population of million or more persons show spectacular increase. In this category are included some of the cities of Brazil, China, India, Argentina, South-East Asia, etc. Cities such as Kolkata, Mumbai, Delhi, Manila, Singapore, Mexico City, Karachi, Jakarta, Buenos Aires, Shanghai, Rio de Janeiro, etc., are big metropolises, and individually they represent first order urbanization. But, as a part of region, they are included in second order group of urbanization. In much of Asia, the rate of urban population growth during the 20th century has far exceeded that of Europe. But, at the same time, the level of urbanization is still much lower than in the Western world. The fact about expansion of cities in the group of second order urbanization is immigration from rural areas This is partly related to the 'push factor' administered by the economic state of the countryside rather than the attraction of the town. The migrants are often unskilled, uneducated and casual workers. For them migration may not be beneficial.

The last, third order region of urbanization includes areas where proportion of urban population to the total varies between 10-25 per cent. Asia, Africa, Siberia and South-America have many cities where industrialization, transport and communication and also technical development show the low ebb in growth. McGee has termed the nature of urbanization in these countries as 'pseudo-urbanization'. The failure to reform agricultural structures in these countries has resulted into rural poverty. Rwanda, Burundi, Malawi, Uganda and Upper Volta in Africa have many towns which are even today based on farm-cum-forest-based economy. The urban proportion in the cities is too low to sustain their growth.[9]

Urbanization in India

Urbanization is the process resulting into increase in the proportion of urban population to the total population in an area. In India, the urban population during pre-independence time was 13.9 per cent (1941) which rose to 17.3 per cent (1951) after the independence. The rise in urban population during the decades kept growing and by 1991 it reached 40 per cent.

Table 6.4

Percentage Increase of Urban Population During the Decades from 1941 to 1991

Decades	*1941-51*	*1951-61*	*1961-71*	*1971-81*	*1981-91*
Percentage increase of urban population	41.4	37.0	38.2	35.4	40.4

Source: Census of India, 1991, Series 1-2.

The above table indicates that during the five decades between 1941 and 1991, the growth rate of urban population was between 3.4 and 3.8 per cent every year, the average increase being about 38.5 per cent. Before the independence of the country nearly 15 per cent people were living in towns, and now their share has become more than double. The reasons in increase of the urban proportion of the total population may be very many, but mainly the Indian urbanization is the result of movement of rural population to urban areas.

Growth of urban areas in India, particularly of the lakh-cities, and also, million-cities, is related unquestionably with the shift of a significant proportion of the population of urban areas from the surrounding countryside. It may be partly a function of natural increase, but the migration factor is dominant one. Migration actually is a change from one place to another. Speaking from geographical point of view, it is of spatial character. The movement of people from one place to another which affects the process of urbanization may be of three types: (i) from rural villages to towns, (ii) from smaller towns to cities or capitals, and (iii) from surrounding urban fringe or peripheral villages.

Again, this fact needs emphasis that in India people often take a risk to migrate from rural to nearby large urban centres. In 1961-71 itself about 24 million people migrated from rural to urban areas. Every year, speaking on an average, about 4 million rural people migrate to the cities of Mumbai, Delhi and Kolkata. McGee has described this type of migration in the Third World countries as 'pseudo-urbanization'.[10] It is not the consequence of industrialization or other allied causes but is the product of failure to reform the agricultural structures of the majority of the Third World countries, which, consequently resulted into rural poverty. Large number of families living under the poverty line are incessantly moving to metropolises in search of employment. But they are mostly unskilled workers, uneducated, aimless about profession and are mostly incompetent for specific jobs. For them, the search for employment proves ultimately a daydream. In metropolises many of them become an undesirable part of the population. The pseudo-urbanization is a large and growing problem in Africa and Asia including India. The reality is that, because of the sick urban phenomenon in million-cities of India unemployment has risen, earnings have gone down, and working conditions have been endangered. However, for millions of workless migrants in India, social and economic hardships continue.

The trend and direction of urbanization in India can be visualized by a look into Table 6.5:

Table 6.5

Trend and Direction of Urbanization: India (1901-1991)

Census Year	*Total Population (in lakh)*	*Urban Population (in lakh)*	*Urbanization Rate (per cent)*	*Decadal Increase (per cent)*
1901	2384.0	259	10.8	—
1911	2520.9	254	10.3	0.35
1921	2513.3	281	11.2	8.22
1931	2789.8	335	12.0	19.14
1941	3186.6	441	13.9	31.97
1951	3610.9	624	17.9	41.38
1961	4392.3	789	18.0	26.41
1971	5481.6	1091	19.9	38.28
1981	6833.3	1597	23.2	46.02
1991	8443.2	2171	25.7	36.19

Source: Census of India: Series 1, Papers 2 (1991) Provisional Population Totals – Registrar General, New Delhi – 1991.

Figure 6.3
Percentage of Urbanization in India by Regions

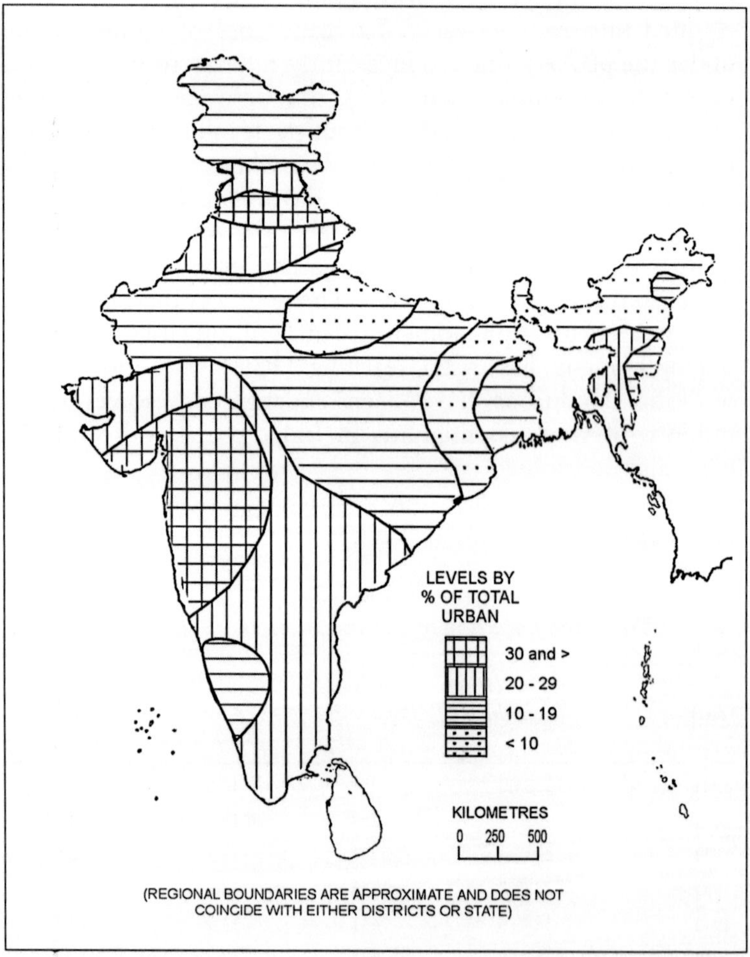

In 1991, the level of urbanization was 25.72 per cent, whereas in 1981 it was 23.34. Annual growth rate was only 0.24 per cent which is very slow. Maharashtra had 39 per cent level which is the highest against the lowest in Assam (11%), the reasons being pace of industrialization, transport links and trade. Orissa and Bihar had also low pace and were urbanized below the average of 25.7 (see Figure 6.3). This indicates that India is still not in a satisfactory position in terms of urbanization in the world and its 70 per cent population is living in villages. The world's average of urbanization level was 45 per cent against India's 25 per cent. If we compare India's position with Australia and New Zealand where nearly 85 per cent level has been reached, there remains no doubt about India's backwardness in the world of urbanization.

However, the pattern of urbanization in India varies very much, the highest being of Delhi (90%) to the lowest of Dadra and Nagar Haveli (8.5%), both union territories. In other union territories the figures vary between 25-65 per cent. In case of various states Mizoram, Goa, Maharashtra, Gujarat, Karnataka and Tamilnadu vary between 30 to 45 per cent, largely because of their economic status which represent above normal conditions. West Bengal, Uttar Pradesh, Rajasthan, Punjab, Madhya Pradesh, Himachal Pradesh vary between 20-30 per cent and may be of medium level of urbanization areas. The rest of the areas which show below the average level are of low urban order. These include Arunachal, Assam, Bihar, Orissa, Sikkim, Tripura, etc., where transport links are weak and the development of industries too is slow.

Causes of Urbanization

What are the reasons for the overwhelming trend of urbanization throughout the world? This question is an important aspect of geographical urban pattern to explain its growth trend. Generally, urban phenomenon is supposed to be the consequence of economic growth. But there have been found many bases in a city which are responsible for urbanization and are held attached for its growth. The bases for urbanization vary from time to time. In recent times, industrialization and economic development are found predominantly responsible for urbanization. But, the historical context of the problem reveals that social, cultural and political forces too have their profound impact in the process of urban growth.

Figure 6.4

World Urban Growth (1800-1950) by the Impact of Industrial Revolution

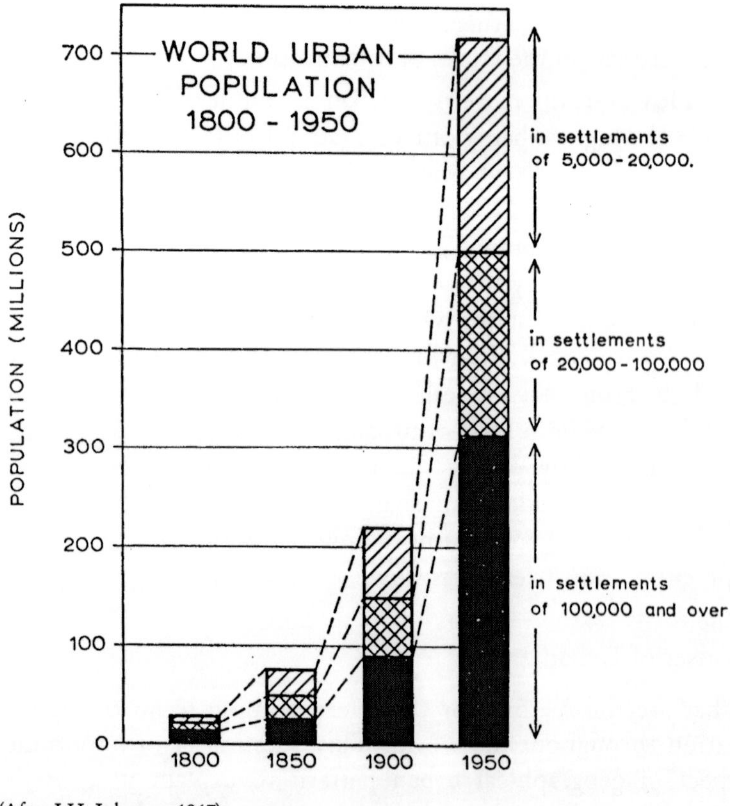

(After J.H. Johnson, 1967)

Industrial Revolution

In Europe cities grew occasionally with the impact of Renaissance, and which were associated with economic development tied with Industrial Revolution and advancing technology. The result was a profound alteration in the size of cities, in the proportion of people who lived in them, and in the rate at which urbanization was taking place (see Figure 6.4). New industrial towns came up from the larger units of production.

Economic Development

Economic growth and urbanization are intimately associated. Economic development can be measured by Gross National Product (GNP) per capita. Figure 6.5 explains urbanization in relation to economic development. The countries like Sri Lanka, India, Haiti, China, Gambia, Kenya, Nepal, Ethiopia had an urban percentage below 30 and their GNP per capita was less than US $1,000, whereas Egypt, Chile, Brazil, Cuba, Iraq, Iran, Portugal show a better economic status between US $2,000-4,000, and their share of urban proportion varies between 40 and 80 per cent. Of course, these countries do not form part largely of the developed world but their urban share is due to their resources which have been largely utilized by the countries of the developed world. The countries like Netherlands, UAE, France, Canada, Trinidad, Austria, had 50 to 80 per cent urban share and their GNP too is US $12,000 to US $15,000. The highest level of urban share of 75 to above 90 per cent includes the countries like Iceland, Denmark, Japan, USA, Norway and Switzerland with their per capita GNP ranging between US $15,000-20,000.

Large Agglomerations and Urbanization

Large agglomerations are sources of providing pace to urbanization. Once a large city is created, it becomes the source of inspiration for supply of labour, capital and also other

Figure 6.5

Urbanization and Economic Development

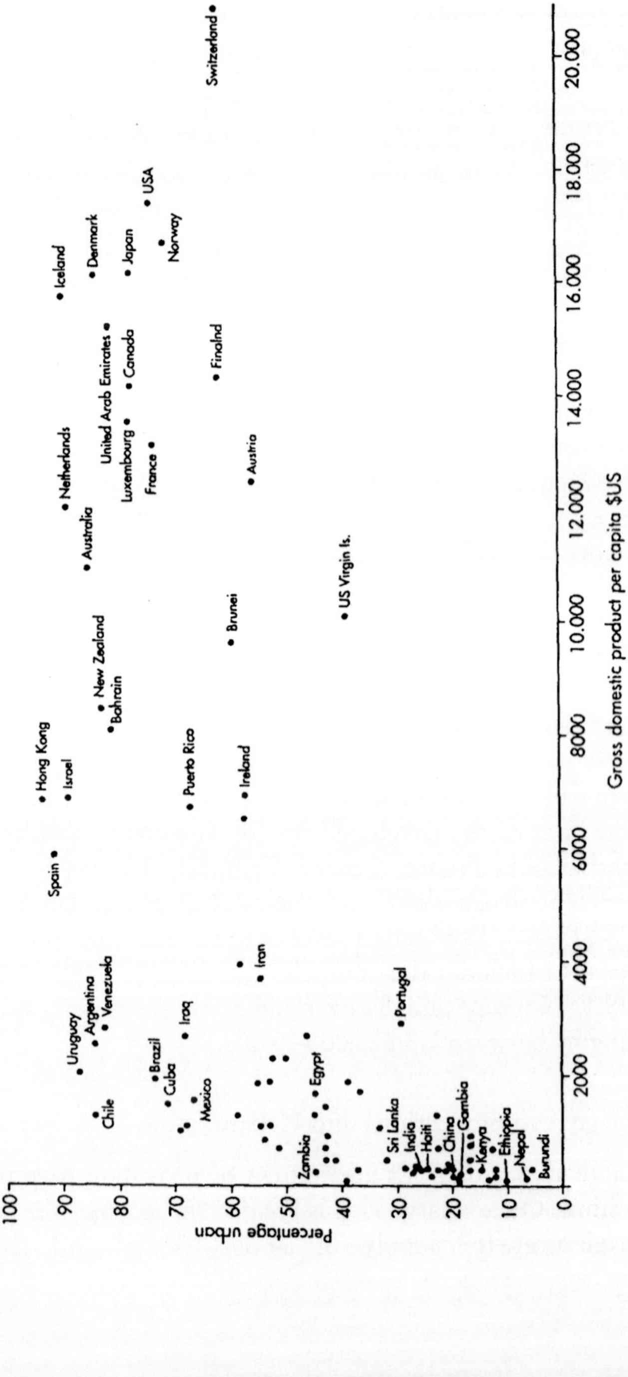

infrastructures initiating a rising spiral of urban development. Mexico City, Sao Paulo, New York, Shanghai, Delhi, Mumbai, etc., are agglomerations of volume where operation of economies of large scale is viable. It gives impetus to cities to grow fast. In Latin America nearly 25 cities have crossed the million mark, and cities like Buenos Aires, Sao Paulo, Rio de Janeiro and Bogota have an urban population of more than five million each. Nearly half of the world's urban population is concentrated in India and cities like Mumbai, Kolkata, and Delhi will reach a mark of more than 1.5 crores. The higher level of urbanization in individual cities typifies higher level of economies including commerce, transport, service sector and allied jobs associated with finance, public media, communication, education and health.

Political, Cultural and Social Causes

Many of the developing countries including India have been under foreign control until the mid-20th century. The rule of the colonial powers is well known for their exploitation of the local resources. It was both exploitative and extractive. It did not allow any sort of industrial development in the developing countries. There was a political change with the independence of these countries and the yoke of foreign rule came to an end because of the national ferver which was widespread in the Afro-Asian world. The political change consequently brought two significant characteristics in the cities of the Third World. The first was the end of exploitation which was rampant during the colonial rule and the second was the end of cultural division of labour (higher order jobs in the hands of the colonial power and social disintegration). The beginning of the national autonomy and democratic functioning in the developing countries, simultaneously gave rise to the industrial development and attraction for newer and higher jobs in the urban administration. The result was rapid urbanization. In Asia, large city population growth since 1945 has grown by almost

450 per cent in comparison with 160 per cent in Europe and North America. In Asia, there were 19 million-cities in 1950. There the centres generally developed as major centres after independence, and most of them have trebled their population since 1950. The 'gravitation' for city life is greatly encouraged by the nature of modern communication. Urban living standards have attracted people from neighbouring towns and villages. In India, metropolitan cities grew significantly as compared to the small and medium size towns. In Delhi, 89.95 per cent is the highest followed by Chandigarh having 89.09. The causes of such a large concentration are invariably after-effects of being national nucleus as node of commerce, administration, besides industrial and educational development. This has taken place mostly with "the break-up of all these constraints in the post-independence time, together with the stimulus of new national feelings".[11] Moreover, manufacturers from the developed world recently have invested with free hands and captured the markets in cities of the developing world which have undermined the local industries. This sort of economic chaos is also responsible for displacement of labour, of course, aimlessly to metropolises. Blind aspirations are now aroused among consumers, and they have migrated from their native villages and towns to meet these aspirations only to face sheer disappointment. This sort of migrational chains between country and town are set up to give rise to pseudo-urbanization. In India, the rate of net immigration into the cities between 1981-91 was equivalent to 20 per cent of the 1941 urban population.[12] Urban growth in Asia is taking place at a much faster rate and exceeded that of Europe during the last quarter of the 20th century. But the nature of modern metropolises is quite different and migrants coming over there have been facing frustration because of poverty, underemployment, lack of housing facilities and other minimum comforts of everyday life. They become unassimilated immigrants in metropolises by living in slum areas or 'shanty colonies' where life is neither rural nor urban. The immigrants collect their

shelters in extensive peripheral areas of settlements which now have formed at least a quarter of the total urban population. In Manila 35 per cent, in Kolkata 33 per cent, and in Jakarta 25 per cent of the population live in slums and uncontrolled settlements.[13]

Conclusion

Finally, the discussion about urbanization reveals that it is a highly complex process. It is not simply an idea based on inward migration. There are many levels operating in the contemporary world. The two may be briefly pointed out here. These include 'counter-urbanization', and 'concentration-deconcentration'.

Berry[14] in 1976, defined counter-urbanization as "a process of population deconcentration". It implies a movement from a state of more concentration of population to a state of less concentration of population. This process has begun in the central areas of metropolises which have become overcrowded. There has begun a tendency of dispersion and people have now preferred to live in open environment, free of pollution by congestion of buildings, transport traffic and vehicular movement. The CBDs (Central Business Districts) of the American cities began the population deconcentration process. The impact of counter urbanization was also felt in India's million-cities, and in Africa also. Berry pointed out that the increasing primacy of the former colonial capitals and explosive growth of squatter settlements and unemployment led to the growth of discontentment among urban dwellers who now have preferred to move outside.

Champion[15] shows disagreement with Berry's clean break with the reversing trend which had dominated the 20th century urban growth. According to him it might be a sort of new trend and may be termed as 'sub-urbanization'.

The process of 'concentration and deconcentration' dominates the developing world. The core regions are concentrated on capital cities and are very different from the industrial conurbations of the West. This type of concentration has attracted attention not only of geographers but economists, sociologists, demographers, planners and politicians too.

The ever increasing city under the process of urbanization either in the developed or developing world needs a balanced approach for achieving some sort of human well-being. In Brussels a Declaration was outlined by the World Environment and Resource Council.[16] Its main recommendations include:

1. Urban growth should be concrete in nature and should be accompanied by economic development of an area.
2. Residential units and their number within an area and facilities available for urban dwellers must maintain equilibrium.
3. There must be easy access and nearness for making use of facilities within and around areas of urbanization.
4. Convenience for movement in and around a city should be cheap, and there must be proper arrangement for parking vehicles at the city centre and also within residential sectors of a growing city.
5. A flexible plan should be prepared for future prospects of a developing city.
6. Regulations related to planning must be clear and practicable. Planning activities must produce results and have involvement of public participation.
7. Local population and administration must work in cooperation and with optimistic attitude "where there is a will, there is a way", should be the motto of projects and their completion.
8. There must be all care to avoid social distance. Open spaces, residences and public utility services must maintain

close association so that there may not incur unnecessary financial liabilities.

9. City centre should be joined from all parts of the city to provide services in such a way as to pedestrians and people who travel by vehicles may equally make use of them. Safety and security of consumers is a must in large cities.
10. Urbanization has industries in its roots. It is related with industrial establishments. Cities which possess factories have been facing acute problems of water, transport, labour, and above all, pollution care must be taken to keep cities free of pollution of air, water, sound, smoke, etc.

To sum up, urbanization is a process involving an increase in the population that is urban. The concept has two sides of the same coin, i.e., proportion of the growth of urban population, and a shift in the population from rural to urban areas. Urbanization is a way of life also reflecting in terms of complex division of labour, high level of technology, interdependence of economic functions and impersonal social relations.

Urbanization is an off-shoot of the Industrial Revolution. It created a demand for a large number of workers. This consequently is the initial cause for massive growth of cities and metropolitan areas. It has led to number of problems especially in million-cities. In India also, cities of Mumbai, Kolkata and Delhi have been facing numerous physical facilities problems of water, housing transportation and social distance. Besides these, nearly all lakh-cities and state capitals including metropolises have been suffering from ills of increasing urbanization such as crime and juvenile delinquency, alcoholism, drug abuse, shortage of housing or shelter problem, overcrowding, slums, unemployment and poverty. Air, water, noise, smoke, scrap and waste material have been polluting cities environment everywhere.

It is no use to repeat facts and figures of urbanization spatially. But this much can be enough to remind that nearly half a century ago less than 30 per cent of the world's population lived in cities, but by the year 2020 this will be over 55 per cent. Nearly two-thirds of the increasing level will be shared by the developing countries. Asia, Africa and Latin America will have three-quarters of the world's urban dwellers by A.D. 2020.

The crisis created by ever increasing urbanization can only be eased by adopting adequate measures. Some of the steps include systematic development of urban settlements of various orders, regional and city plans, redistribution of resource-based projects after surveying the needs, decentralization of the institutions – administrative, financial, cultural and educational – to areas of medium- and small-sized settlements, encouragement for private transport system, review of laws and regulations relating to land acquisition, land tenure and apartment ownership, and favourable, scope for provision of incentives to employers to build houses for employees. Above all, urban planning should be modified radically and be made for the benefit of the general masses and not for a few powerful groups with vested interests.

Notes

1. Oucho, J.O., *Urban Population Trends*, UNCHS Habitat Debate 7(2), 1-4, June 2001.
2. Kelly, A., and Williamson, J., "Population Growth, Industrial Revolutions and the Urban Transition", *Population and Dev. Review*, 1984, pp. 419-41, Vol. 10, No. 3.
3. Davis, Kingsley, "The Origin and Growth of Urbanization in the World", in the *Readings in Urban Geography*, (eds.) Mayer, H.M. and Kohn, C.F., Chicago University, 1959, pp. 57-68.
4. Carter, H., *The Study of Urban Geography*, Arnold, London 1972, IV Ed., 1995, p. 18.
5. Johnson, J.H., *Urban Geography*, Pergamon, London, 1967, p. 17.
6. Figures for Levels of Urbanization are based on the United Nations Population Report, 1995 and 2000.

7. Davis, K., op. cit., p. 68.
8. Johnson, J.H., op. cit., p. 17.
9. Mabogunge, A.L., "Urbanization Problems in Africa", in *Urbanization: National Development and Regional Planning in Africa*, Praeger Pub., 1974, p. 23.
10. McGee, T.G., *The Southeast Asian City*, G. Bell and Sons, London, 1967.
11. Carter, H., op. cit., p. 21.
12. Donald, J.B. and Zachariah, K.C., "Urbanization and Migration in India", *India's Urban Future*, (ed.) Roy Turner, Berkeley, 1967, p. 29.
13. Ulack, R.. "The Role of Urban Squatter Settlements", *AAAG*, Vol. 68, 1978, p. 535.
14. Berry, B.J.L., "The Counter Urbanization Process: Urban America Since 1970", in Berry, B.J.L. (ed.), *Urbanization and Counter Urbanization*, Beverley Hills, Sage Publishers.
15. Champion, A.G. (ed.), *Counter Urbanization*, Edward Arnold, London, 1989.
16. UNEP (United Nations Environment Programme) and Stockholm Env. Inst., OUP, New York, 1999.

7

Indian Urban Process

What is Urban?

India, primarily is a country of villages and most of the population of India is living in villages, hamlets or a small group of huts. Nonetheless important is a fact that our country is the largest urbanized nation in the world. Asoka Mehta, in an International Seminar on "Urbanization in India"[1] pointed out that at present, India is under the pressure of two forces – rapid rate of population growth and increasingly rapid rate of urbanization. Before going into these details our immediate concern is to know: what does the term 'urban', 'town' or 'city' imply as contrasted with 'village' or 'hamlet'? In other words we must be clear about the distinction between urban and rural.

Definition of an 'urban' area varies from country to country. For example, in Greenland a place with 300 or more people is called an urban area, while in Korea an urban area must have at least 40,000 inhabitants.

Difficulty in Case of India

In India, there is a difficulty of defining a town by numbers because several modifications were introduced to make the definition concrete on the Census Report of India. Moreover, latitude has also been given to Census Superintendents regarding settlements on the borderline of 'rural' and 'urban'. Through the decades 1901-51 'town' was defined by:

(1) every municipality of whatever size;

(2) all civil lines (not included within municipal limits); and

(3) permanent habitation with continuous collection of houses of not less than 5,000 persons (but decided as a town by provincial Superintendent).

In 1951, the above criteria remained the same but with a caution that places with a somewhat larger population than 5,000, and do not possess urban character (as decided by State Government in some states and Census Superintendents in others) may not be treated as towns.

Statistics-based criteria, therefore, had certain limitations prior to 1961. These were:

(i) There was an element of arbitrariness in the definition of town.

(ii) Decision about 'big villages' and 'small towns' rests largely on the discretion of Census Superintendents. It had many chances for lack of objectivity.

(iii) The aggregate urban population from decade to decade was based on individual judgement of scores of census officials.

(iv) The definition to include demographic data as well as administrative limits such as municipalities, notified areas, civil lines and cantonments suffers from lack of uniformity. The addition or deletion of municipalities may result into sudden increase or decrease in urban population.[2]

(v) The census definition had also emphasis on 'urban characteristics' like water, electricity, schools, post offices hospitals, etc. But there was no specific list available of these, and everything was left to the discretion of the census authorities.

Town as Defined in Census

Asok Mitra, the Commissioner of 1961 Census, defined 'town' on the basis of: (a) a density of not less than 1,000 per square mile; (b) a population of 5,000; (c) three-fourths of the occupations of the working population should be non-agricultural; and (d) the place should have a few pronounced urban characteristics and amenities as decided by the Superintendent of the State.

This definition too suffers from vagueness and discretion, and cases of elimination on the above basis had to be referred to the State Government for approval before being struck off the 1961 census list of towns. Similarly, all fresh cases of inclusion would be required to obtain the concurrence of the Registrar General's office.[3]

For 1971 and 1981 the census has used the same criteria.

Definition of an Urban Place by 1981 Census

(a) A place with a municipality, corporation, or cantonment or notified town area, or

(b) A place satisfying all the following:
   (1) Minimum population of 5,000.
   (2) 75 per cent male working population as non-agricultural.
   (3) Density of at least 1,000 person per square mile.

This concept too was vague because administrative status may have a population of less than 5,000 persons. Similarly, a large number of revenue villages may have 75 per cent male population engaged in non-agricultural occupations, but were not legally/administratively recognized as towns. The density too is unrealistically low in the Indian context and states like Kerala, West Bengal and Bihar had densities well over 1,000 persons per square mile. A much higher value (around 1,000 persons per square kilometre) would be more appropriate in the Indian situation.

UN Point of View

The above discussion shows that it is difficult to project a universally accepted cut-off point for areas of varied proportions of non-agricultural population and also varied densities and growth rates of populations. What follows is an arbitrary selection, but the basis which are used to define urban population should invariably be made clear by the countries in their respective context; *United Nations Demographic Year Book*, 1988 has cited the definitions of urban population for various countries.[4] Their analysis show much of varied ranges. For example, in Botswana, agglomerations of 5,000 or more persons including 75 per cent non-agricultural form urban places, while Argentina's urban places do qualify with only 2,000 inhabitants. Peru's urban centres include 100 or more dwellings.

In Canada, places of 1,000 or more persons having population density of 400 or more per square kilometre are urban, whereas USA has defined places with 2,500 persons as urban. In Japan, cities (shi) having 50,000 or more persons with 60 per cent or more of the houses located in the main built-up areas and 60 per cent or more population engaged in manufacturing, trade or other urban business qualify as urban. Besides this, a 'shi' can also be an urban which has urban facilities and conditions defined by the prefectural order. In former USSR, constituent republics designate city/urban locality on the basis of numbers of inhabitants and predominance of agricultural, or numbers of non-agricultural workers and their families.

What is evident from the *UN Demographic Year Book* is that every country has its own definition of towns and cities for census purposes. This means that for a definition which may be universally accepted, numerical value has very little value. A numerically small settlement may have urban characteristics: like density, markets, administrative functions – while, on the other end of the scale, a numerically large settlement may be a specialized centre either of mining, power-resource or agricultural research, etc. In case of India, it is not only 5,000 population which is essential for a town, but at the same time density over 1,000 per square mile plus 75 per cent of the adult male population engaged in work other than agriculture is required to qualify a settlement as a town. This suggests density and function both are criteria for a town. This may be more or less a reliable criteria to judge a settlement whether it is a town or not. In the real sense of the term, a town is what is implied by the local people when they call a locality a town irrespective of statistical standard.

Functional Status: A Reliable Test to Qualify for Town

In Indian Census 1991, the definition of urban was not basically changed and it was again based on density of not less than 1,000 persons per square mile, plus a population of 5,000 or more, and three-fourths of the occupation of the working population should be non-agricultural.[5] The identification of a place as urban by this process calls for massive tabulations in a country like India where the number of towns in 1991 was 3,696. In this context, it would be convenient to agree that all municipal areas are towns where urban functions including urban services and non-agricultural activities prevail over rural. In our Constitution much is left to decide by the respective states whether a place qualifies to attain a municipal status. Thus, it seems that there is no universal criterion for a place to be recognized as a municipal status. We have to be satisfied by the fact that a place where secondary and tertiary functions and professional services dominate over primary ones, and two-thirds of people are engaged in non-agricultural occupations, that place is a 'town'. And, invariably it must have shops, banks and institutions providing amenities like health, education, culture and entertainment.

On a world scale above 5,000 people may be acceptable simple numerical index, and there is less doubt on the point whether a centre is urban or non-urban. But above 10,000 population there seems hardly any doubt about the status of a centre as a town. If any misunderstanding crops up, then it is better to accept the opinion of local people whether they themselves consider a locality, a town. Defining a town by scholarly exercise would not be a meaningful effort towards understanding the nature of urbanism.[6]

Global Perspective

By the end of 20th century, problems of definition have increased manifold. There has been undoubtedly tremendous growth of urbanism and new terms like conurbation, metropolis and megalopolis were introduced in the Western world. City population everywhere overflowed to usurp countryside and there appeared 'suburbs' all around a metropolis. A new term has been coined to reflect the change, and the 'metropolitan village' came up to house city workers who have invaded the countryside.

Urban functions too remained less reliable when a small village was found to perform area-serving role by its small shop, post office, school, dispensary and an institutional community centre. Being a village, it was not less active than a town for a rural countryside. Thus, a distinction between urban and rural has lost any real meaning almost everywhere.

Another problem is inherent in delimiting the area of a town physically or administratively. If a city is administratively bound by municipal regulations, its physical extent may cover larger areas, and conversely, the administrative area overbound the physical extent. It is not necessary that both administrative bound and physical extent coincide. It results into arbitrary division between rural and urban, and it becomes difficult to point out a crucial break between the two. In reality, the common denominator for definitions seems non-existent. Therefore, the recommendation of the UN, based on size is acceptable where the population above 5,000 forms a town.

How Many Live in Towns?

To make urbanization clear and understandable, an important fact is to estimate how many of the world's people live in towns and cities. In developed countries, approximately six persons out of ten live in towns. In Britain, four out of every five are city dwellers. On the contrary, the fact about the developing countries is just the opposite where seven out of ten people live outside cities and towns. In India, only 25 per cent population live in towns.

The urbanization process in the Western and Orient worlds may be shown by a graph given below:

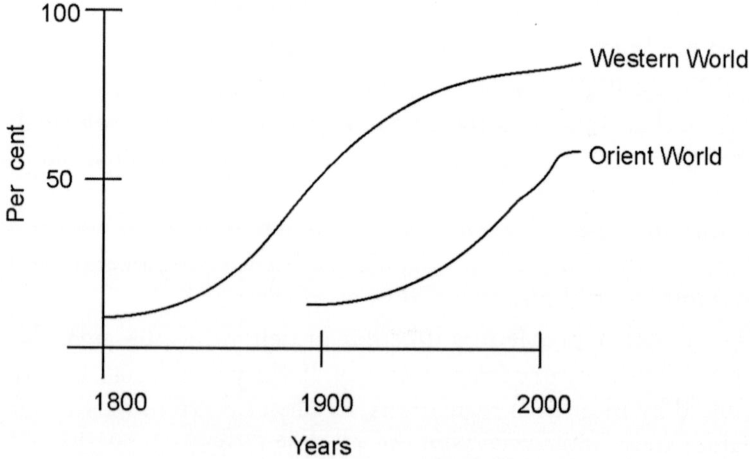

The graph is concave in the beginning and convex in the 20th century in case of the Western world, whereas the Orient world is represented by a concave trend during the 20th century, and only at the end of the century and in the beginning of 21st it takes a bit of convex turn. The figures of percentage show rate of urbanization over a given period in its increasing trend in case of the Western world over the Orient.

The spread of urbanization is very uneven over the world surface. Only a few regions show extreme urbanization. The figures by continental regions are given below:

Table 7.1

UN Classification: World Urbanization, 1950-1970

	% in the cities over	
	5,000	*100,000*
World	46	28
Oceania	90	75
North America	80	65
Europe	70	35
USSR	55	30
South America	45	32
Central America	40	25
Asia	25	15
Africa	15	10

The high figures for Oceania (Australia and New Zealand), and North America show great cities therein. But perhaps it is surprising that Europe is third with nearly three-fourths of its people living in towns of over 5,000.

Levels of Urbanization

It is estimated that by the year 2050, most of the world would be urbanized. The countries of the developed world will be facing decreasing demand for agrarian labour but an increase in demand for technical sector workers of skilled knowledge.

But in older settled countries where the economy is being characterized even today as semi-industrialized, urban population ranges between 40 to 60 per cent. There, the level of urban order is guided not by metro centres, but people occupy medium and small-sized towns. Of course, there has begun industrialization, but only a few industrial nodes appear besides market towns.

World in its broad framework has two distinct levels of urban milieu: one, highly urbanized, and the second one is characterized by less urbanized.[7]

High Level of Urban Order

This includes the developed countries like Australia, New Zealand, Japan, Brazil, Venezuela, Eastern USA, Argentina, Canada, etc. Towns in these countries have grown into 'metro' and 'mega' centres and mostly possess coastal location.

Less Urbanized Order

This order is seen in large areas of Asia, Africa, and South America.[8] Urban population of these areas is facing a crisis of only a few centres with giant metropolises versus large number of small towns which are characterized by market-centres.

Levels in India

Indian urban process is typically different either from the developed or underdeveloped world. This is because of the fact that in India it is not an easy task to identify the hierarchical level by regions. Since independence, there has been taking place a newer phenomenon of growing capitals challenging primary metropolises.[9] These include cities like, Jaipur, Ahmedabad, Bangalore, Hyderabad, etc. These may be termed as metros of second order. At the same time, medium and small towns in India have been facing the problem of stunted growth. Consequently, urban levels in India is the process of regional economic development confiscated largely by metropolises and urban centres of one to ten lakh population.[10]

Thus, there appear three distinct levels of urban order in India:

(1) Primary metropolises.
(2) Secondary metropolitan centres.
(3) Medium towns and small urban places.

Primary Metropolitan Areas

These include largely colonial cities of pre-independence time such as Kolkata, Mumbai, Chennai and also Delhi. These have been dominating India's economy since early 19th century. Delhi too became the national capital in 1911 and after the independence its growth has been spectacular. Now, it has almost overshadowed the colonial cities.

Secondary Metropolitan Centres

Some of the states have fully developed urban system characterized by their own million cities at the apex. They are exclusive cases of urban primacy. But at a lower level, the lakh cities (ranging between one to ten lakh population) play an important role in the Indian urban system. There were over 225 such cities in India in 1991. They formed a secondary metro level.

Medium Towns Forming the Third Urban Level

These have an important link by their function. Their role in the urban system cannot be minimized. They play roles of both ends – metro, as well as, small market towns. Medium town level is comprised of nearly one-fourth of the total number of towns, and also total urban population.

However, at the base of the Indian urban system, there are nearly 60 to 70 per cent towns of India reckoned as small agricultural and market towns.

What is Emerging Out of the Process?

The process of Indian urban scene reflects some important trends. In our country industrialization is a feature which began typically after independence. Thus, pre- and post-industrial processes have grown under different economic and political environs. This has given rise to two different patterns among urban centres. These two distinct aspects are known in urban terminology as (a) urban agglomeration, and (b) urban cluster.

The Census of India recognized in 1951 'town group'. This is actually a phenomenon very similar to urban agglomeration. In our country, at present, there are nearly 30 such agglomerations. Agglomeration is the tendency where in a number of smaller towns agglomerate around a major city, may be million-city. This ultimately becomes a contiguous urban area.

Recently another pattern which has emerged is known as 'urban cluster'. There are nearly twenty clusters at present having as many as 150 lakh-cities in India. The phenomenon of urban cluster is defined as the tendency of a number of cities to locate within a radius of 75-100 km from another major city acting as a focal centre for the surrounding cities. This phenomenon is quite distinct from that of being agglomerated one.

Indian urban process also reveals the spatial overlapping of different levels.[11] The process represents juxtaposition of old and new, small and big, simple and complex and also ancient and modern. There has been a physical variability evolved because of terrain of plains, plateaus and hills. New relationship have come up by todays complexities of urban functions and life.

Notes

1. International Seminar on "Urbanization in India", sponsored by Kingsley Davis, R.L. Park and Catherine Bauer Wurster at Berkeley, California in 1960.
2. *Census of India 1951*, Vol. IV, Part I, p. 31.
3. *Census of India 1961*, Vol. I.
4. United Nations 1990: *UN Demographic Year Book 1988*, N.Y. United Nations.
5. *Census of India, 1991*, Part I.
6. Jones, E., *Towns and Cities*, OUP, London, 1966, p. 5.
7. Davis, K., and Hartz, Harold, *The Pattern of World Urbanization*, New York, 1966.
8. Mabogunge, A.L., "Urbanization in Africa", in *Urbanization, National Development and Regional Planning*, Praeger Pub., 1974.
9. Dutta, K., "Urban Zones of India", *The National Geogl. Journal of India*, Vol. 13, 1967, pp. 97-109.
10. Rao, V.L.S. Prakasa, *Urbanization in India: Spatial Dimension*, Concept, New Delhi, 1983, pp. 24-43.
11. Raza, M., et al., "Spatial Organization and Urbanization in India", in R.P. Misra and K.V. Sundaram (eds.), *Rural Area Development: Perspectives and Approaches*, Sterling, New Delhi, 1979.

8

Urban Plan, Structure and Morphology

Urban morphology comprises the structure of a city and pattern or plan of its development. It is actually the layout of a city both in its historical as well as geographical contexts which gives it an individuality. Therefore, the internal pattern or structure of each city is "unique in its particular combination of details".[1] Combinations involving structure of most American cities have business, industrial and residential districts. The cities of the Western world in their structure display generally city centre or downtown, Central Business District (CBD) including shopping centre, industrial estate, housing estate giving it a spatial framework in order to make sense of the environment in which people live and work.[2]

In case of an Indian town, E. Ahmad has identified some of the components of urban morphology as site characteristics, historical background, sky-line, green open spaces, water bodies, physical and cultural dominants.[3] In combination these elements form the 'urban landscape' which is actually the soul and spirit of physical morphology of a town.

Speaking precisely, morphology of a town is a geographico-historical interpretation of its site, situation or modality and existing layout and arrangement of houses as well as streets and roads. It also includes within its purview the development of different parts of the town and analysis of its boundary in different phases of history as well as explanation of existing land use. Urban morphology or a town's anatomy and physiology are mutually interrelated.

The town is both a historical and geographical fact. Its morphology represents various elements which form part of its structure, plan and growth. Its relief and terrain on which its nucleus seeks origin form a base. Its expansion from the nucleus shapes its morphology through streets and roads, houses and buildings and finally develops its functions as a trading and commercial centre with all the complexities of its administrative and cultural services. Its plan, during various phases of history may change to cope with the changing urban-scene. In India, the town plans represent a sequent occupance of settlement by their inhabitants during the course of past history right from its origin to the present day.

Morphology of towns in India, therefore has distinct phases like ancient, medieval and modern layouts including sprawl with the rapid increase in population after independence.

Ancient Urban Morphology

Most ancient settlement in the Indus Valley had typical morphology known as 'grid-iron' of main streets running north-south and east-west dividing the town roughly into blocks of equal size. The rectangular plan of the urban morphology was designed to conform with the needs of some sort of ceremony – religious or secular or both – in which the terrace or terraces played a dominant role, and to which processional access was required.[4] In the Vedic period, the town plans and their morphology represented "rectangular layout with its sides oriented to the four quarters and intersected by two avenues terminating in four gateways",[5] the centre being occupied by a temple or palace, tank or garden. Towns in ancient India had their typical characteristic of morphology which has had its indelible marks of religion and culture even in today's civic planning and expression.[6] The morphological pattern of quite a few towns of India represents the articulation of streets, siting of public buildings and monuments adjusted to the direction and position of their initial nucleus – 'temple'. Udaipur's morphological nucleus is the Jagdish temple – temple of the 'Lord of Universe' –, and it is sited perfectly where the principal street of the city is articulated with the Sun-Gate in the east in a manner to allow first rays, of the Sun-god be enshowered the idol.[7]

Medieval Morphology of Towns

The grid plan morphology of the Indus Valley (about 3,000 B.C.) later on was adopted by the Greeks. Hippodamus was a town planner and in 500 B.C. he rebuilt Miletus on the grid morphology (Figure 8.1) after it was being sacked by the Persians. The grid morphology (Figure 8.2) prospered further under Roman rule and in north-west Europe. Roman settlements also had the grid pattern.[8] The Roman towns were originally garrison towns rather than trading centres. The influence of Roman grid plan was far and wide, and quite a good number of towns in the northern plains of Italy and southern France had the Roman legacy. Britain too had significant influence of the Roman grid plan on morphology of many.

Bastides

The convenience of exact measurement is the main cause of medieval town planning. It was represented in its best form in southern France where 'bastides' were planned. The most

Figure 8.1

Map Showing Street Plan of Miletus Morphology

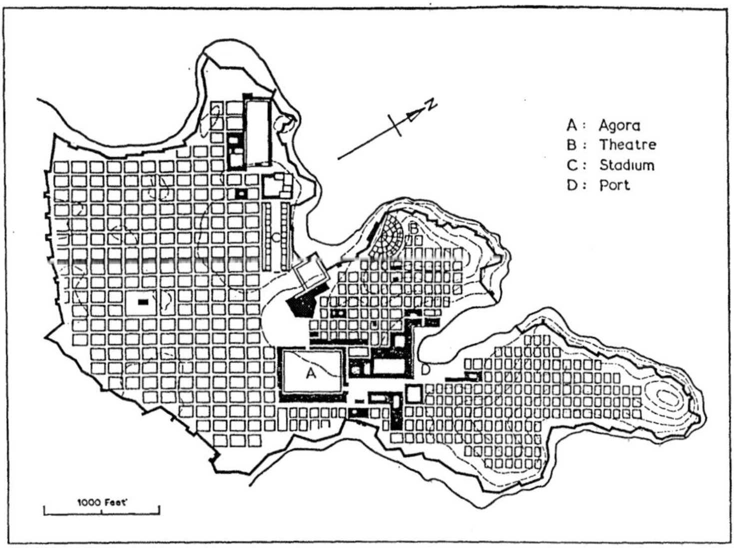

Greek Town Planner – Hippodamos.

Figure 8.2

Roman Town Plans

(areas in black are grid morphology under Roman rule)

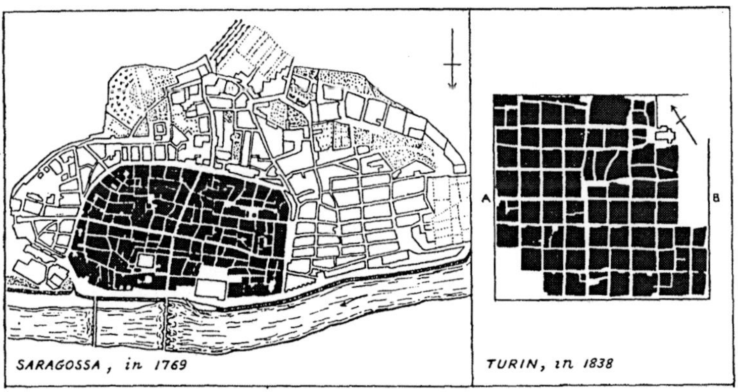

Figure 8.3

Bastide Town Plan (South-West France)
Monpazier

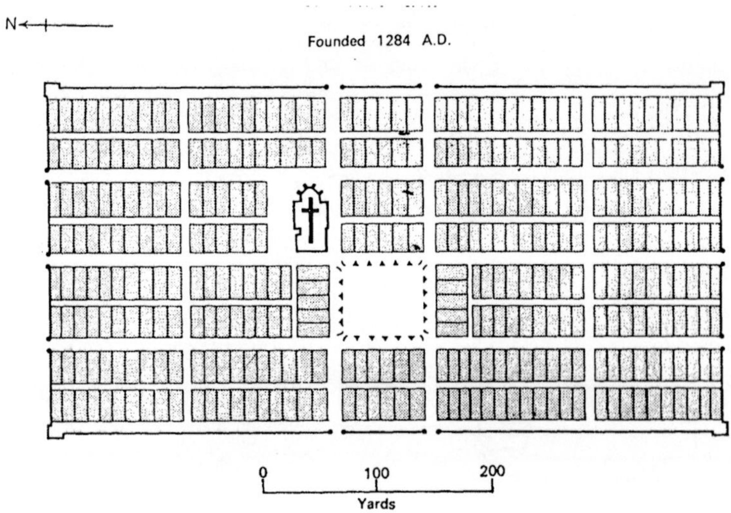

Grid Plan: Regularly arranged around a central market place.

remarkable is Montpazier erected in 1284 (Figure 8.3). It was designed as a rectangle 400 × 200 metres with two large squares near the centre for the cathedral and market.

Medieval Town Plans

Morphological pattern of the medieval times besides grid pattern was considerably influenced by cellular growth. Brunswick consisted five nuclei around the original 'burg' of Dankerwarderobe. Alstadt founded around two churches, Koningsberg castle erected in 1255, and three small settlements were added in the Altstadt. In these and many towns of eastern Europe, cellular growth formed an important aspect of their morphology; and was related to the fortress and even to fortified churches.

In India, the towns of medieval origin in Madhya Pradesh, Maharashtra and Rajasthan generally have four features signifying their morphological character: the castle or fortress, the temple, the tank or water bodies, and the wall enclosing the separate cells of communities of social hierarchical order, the lowest being at the fringe or even outside the wall. Agra, Dhar, Sikri, Golconda, Bijapur, Pune, Delhi, Mander, Chittorgarh, Jaipur, Udaipur, Ahmadnagar, Aurangabad, etc., were some of the towns having medieval plan-based morphology. Most of them now have a changed urban landscape because of the superimposition of the post-independence development. Medieval towns sought their sites invariably on high mounds or by the sides of an isolated hill or in a naturally fortified depression. Besides the advantage of the natural defence, the availability of water is also responsible for their irregular morphology. Some of the towns are squeezed between high mounds and water-bodies at least from two sides. Their irregular, tortuous and narrow streets near the centre or core also have distorted the shape or layout.

Modern Development and Changed Pattern of Morphology

Out of many changes brought about recently, most important has been in the nature of manufacturing. Both heavy as well as lighter industries of modern towns, reshape their ground plan. The tertiary sector of the economy and diversity of jobs have altogether changed the urban milieu. The increase in service activities has stimulated the growth and plan of medium-size towns, and has also encouraged the extension of large towns. In India after independence, developmental plans have been executed in all parts of the country. In cities, the force of 'gravitation' is greatly encouraged by the nature of modern communications and an increased awareness of urban living standards. People from surrounding countryside began to pour into cities in search of high-income employment and white-collar jobs. The change in social order and population increase have their impact on cities' plan, layout, and morphology. The force or gravitation may be outward also, and people from the congested city areas have now started moving out to settle in suburban areas. The process of out-and-in migration has been constantly changing morphological patterns of cities in nearly all parts of the world. The older, more central, buildings in many American cities have undergone change as a result of the social leap-frogging.[9] The best fashionable districts having high-rent areas migrated outwards (Figure 8.7B) in Boston, Seattle, Minneapolis and San Francisco.

The changed morphological pattern within cities both in the developed and developing world is largely because of specialist land uses. The uses of land by certain activities require specialized facilities in terms either of sites or by human enterprise. Clothing industry, utensils and ornaments' craftwork, hardwares, high-class residential areas, etc., seek separate nuclei in various directions in the cities. The cohesive morphology of the gone-by times, consequently is being disintegrated into nuclei. The entire pattern has now evolved as a changed urban landscape. But Harris and Ullman point out, the nuclei have been in existence from the time of origin of the city,[10] persisting urban growth has filled in around them. In London, 'The City' and Westminster is an example originating at separate points – one as centre of finance and commerce and the other as a political centre.

Morphology of cities in India, in case of their modern urban scene, is the legacy of the British rule. Indian cities even after five decades, display duality in their morphology – the indigenous pattern as well as an alien pattern.

'The city unit' including areas around its nucleus form the indigenous oriental type of common patterns visible in its uncontrolled growth and provide a mixed land use. They consist of numerous foci of activity flanked by irregular street plans nearly from all sides by narrow, tortous, crooked and at places blind-alleys and lanes. The indigenous city unit is deeply ingrained by phenomenon of caste and community quarters living in separate localities or residential blocks. The central parts are mostly occupied by higher castes and business communities while the lower and poorer people are largely confined to the outskirts.

The alien or European pattern has developed into the civil lines, the cantonment and the railway colony. Here the areas are monotonously planned in European style with bungalows, barracks and residential quarters along straight broad roads. "The Civil Lines of the city of Allahabad were situated to the east of the New Cantonment and were established on an extensive grid plan cut through by the main route which was related to the axis of the old Mogul city. Within the area were all the standard representatives of English culture in India: The Government Offices, the Law Courts, the Hotel, Hospital and the Allahabad Club. It was neatly segregated: to the north was the river Ganges while the New Cantonment was to the west: to the south were the railway lines and to the east Alfred Park provided a break."[11] (Figure 8.4) The railway thus completely shuts off the crowded and irregular Indian city from the broadly planned rectangular Cantonment and Civil Lines, a district of large bungalows and public offices in spacious compounds and gardens.[12] Modern towns in India "represent either conflict or blending of indigenous features and hybridized European features".[13] It is a fact that initial plan of a city is largely the product of the cultural and social characteristics of the group which lays it out. The two cultures of colonizer and colonized continued side by side, certainly interacting but engendering a distinctive urban form made up of the two elements.

In South Africa, ethnic segregation within the city of Cape Town is based on a complex of social, economic and racial motives.[14] The main groups of White, the Coloured, the Black

Figure 8.4
Allahabad, 1931 (Internal Structure)

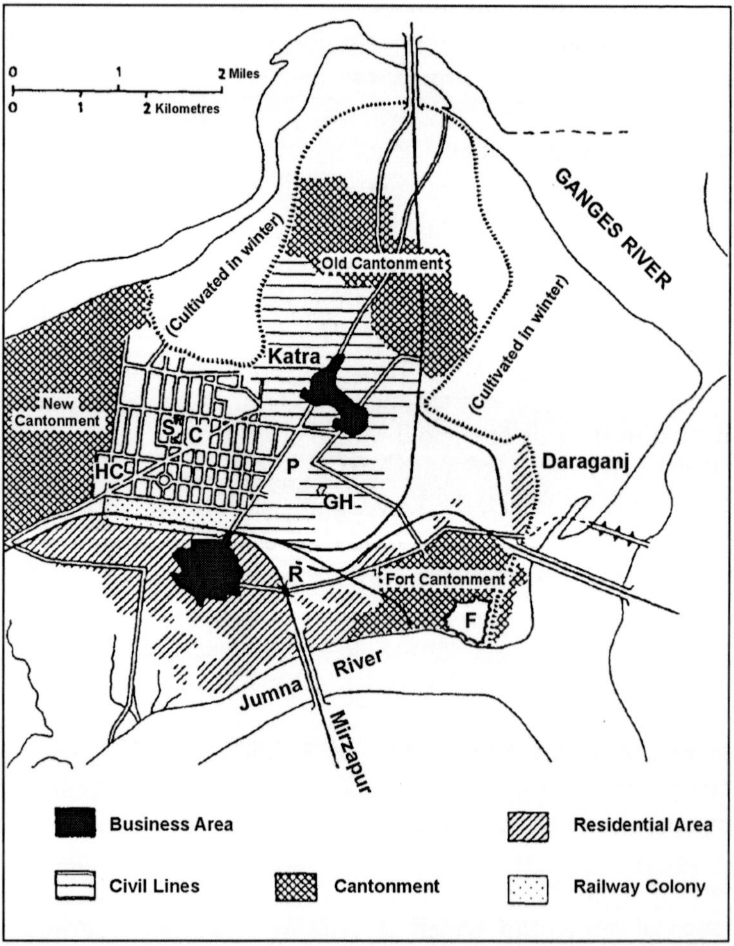

Source: Spate and Ahmad – *Geogl. Review*, Vol. 40, 1950.

Figure 8.5
Apartheid City in South Africa

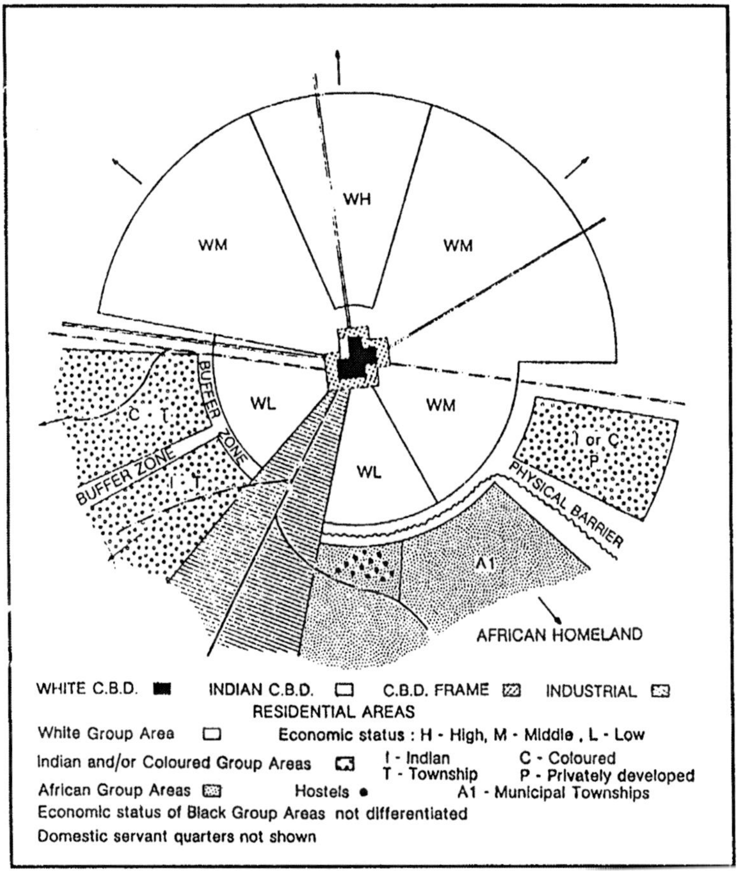

Source: R. Davies, 1981, *Geogl. Journal*, Vol. 71, 1981, Suppl. Issue 2.

or Bantu (the Indian) were allocated consolidated areas which ideally were separated by marked physical barriers or by buffer zones of unused or non-residential land. Contacts and mixing at the margins were prevented, and travel among groups was also minimized. This naturally gave rise to sectoral form of the city. Figure 8.5 is an idealized diagram or model of a morphology representing an apartheid city.

It is clear from the aforesaid discussion that morphology of a city is the product of both historical and geographical processes. Its site, situation, nature of terrain, spatial limits of sprawl, water bodies, etc., are components determining the geographical environment. At the same time, equally important are its age-old streets and roads, buildings, populations of various social groups and its historical lineaments and legacy of the rulers responsible for shaping and reshaping the morphological patterns.

Theoretical Explanations of Morphological Pattern of a City

The forces underlying the pattern of land use, process of urban growth and accessibility within and outward of a city can be generalized by means of a number of theories. It is true to a large extent that each city possesses a unique combination of various use of land, but to some degree a common pattern is visible. The commonly referred patterns are concentric, sectoral and the multiple nuclei. They are known as models of city structure or theories explaining urban morphology.

*The Concentric Theory**

The concentric model was devised in 1923 by E.W. Burgess.[15] He was a sociologist. The idea behind the concentric model is

* Concentric model of Burgess represents in (A) general schemes of urban land use based on Chicago in 1925; and (b) represents generalisations from it for all rapidly growing industrial cities.

Figure 8.6A
Concentric Theory of Urban Structure

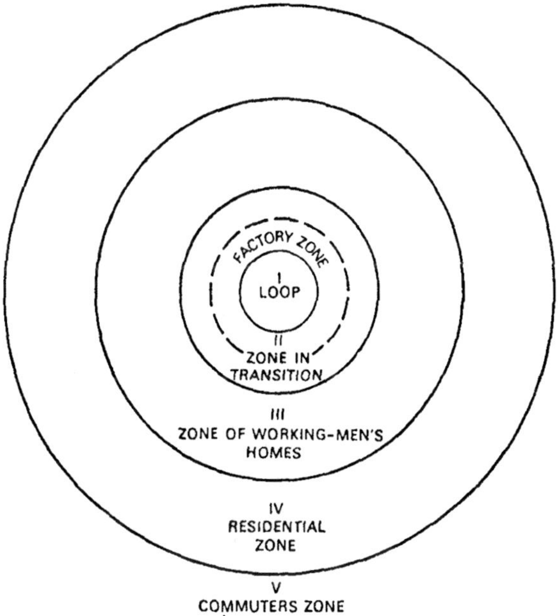

that the development of a city takes place outwards from its central area in a series of concentric circles to form zones. The model therefore is also known as concentric zonal model. According to Burgess, the American city should take the form of five zones. These zones begin with Zone I as Central Business District (CBD), the focus of the city's social, commercial and civic life. CBD is also the focus of transportation. Burgess identifies its two parts: (i) the downtown retail district, and (ii) the wholesale business district encircling the downtown.

Zone II is the 'zone in transition' surrounding the CBD. It is a zone of residential deterioration of older private houses consisting of largely subdivided dwelling units. The transition area is occupied by immigrants and infested by 'vices'. In this

Figure 8.6B

Urban Areas in Chicago

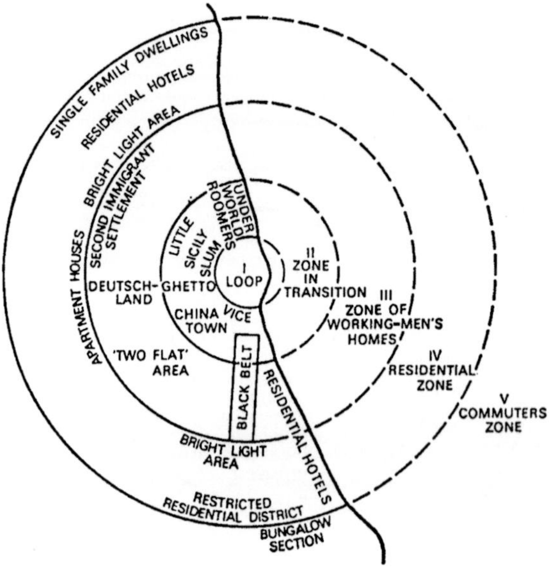

after E.W. Burgess

zone rotten business and light manufacturing from Zone I have encroached upon residential areas. Some of the parts of this zone are likely to be found in the city's slums or areas of poverty and crime.

Zone III is the third ring made up of the houses of 'working-men's homes'. This is the zone of old residential buildings occupied by stable social groups of working class families. These are families of people who have moved out of Zone II to live near their place of work.

Zone IV concentric space still farther from the centre is occupied by spacious dwellings. Here, middle-class groups of native-born Americans live. These people are likely to be proprietors of small businesses, professional people, clerks and salesmen.

Final and beyond the city limits is Zone V of small cities, towns, dormitory areas to make up the commuters' zone. From the city centre it is almost at the distance of one hour's travelling time. This zone may still be an open country. Most of the people of this zone seem to commute daily for their livelihood in the CBD.

Criticism of the Concentric Theory

Burgess' theory is popular and widely used by current authors with a few modifications. But the concentric zonal theory is severely criticized on the grounds of local topographical features which affect the location of residential areas. This type of criticism seems invalid because Burgess himself pointed out that zonal distortions may result from variations in relief features. Davie[16] was the most active critic of the theory who exhibited against the theory in several ways: (i) CBD's size irregular and often rectangular than circular, (ii) areas of commerce and business extending radially along streets from the CBD, (iii) industrial units lying along lines of transportation and near water or rail, (iv) low-grade housing near industrial and transportational areas in every zone, and (v) finally, concentric zoning lacking universal pattern.

The theory of Burgess was not appropriate in case of treatment of wholesaling. Besides the edge of CBD, the wholesaling may be most often found adjacent to the side with maximum railroad availability. Similarly, heavy industry in the modern city does not take the form of concentric belt just outside the CBD, instead, it tends to form wedgelike areas along transportation lines which follow river valleys, lake or ocean fronts.

In the historical context too, the theory of Burgess seems untenable. The cultural areas along with buildings, streets and railroads developed during historical phases cannot be easily moved from their old location. The theory was particular in time and place, and by the late 20th century it was outdated and limited only to large Western industrial cities. Sjoberg[17] negated the concentric scheme for the 'pre-industrial city' in which privileged classes – the elite, gather at the centre because of governmental and religious buildings' nearness. In feudal cities, religion and politics had far more status than the economic – the main market of the centre being subsidiary to religious and political structures.

Merits of the Concentric Theory

Quinn, the chief supporter of the Burgess theory, says: common-sense observations tend to confirm the theory.[18] Urban-gradients' researchers indicate the probability of the concentric structure around the dominant retail area in various cities. Local irregularities may violate the symmetry of concentric ones, yet Quinn opined that most cities conformed at least roughly to the Burgess pattern. Haggett and Chorley too had appreciation about the contribution of Burgess's model which according to them was a normative model, 'a simplified structuring of reality presenting supposedly significant features of relationships in a generalized form.'[19]

To conclude, Burgess' model was plainly introduced to illustrate the expansion of the city in its comprehensible manner by a series of concentric circles designating both the successive zones of urban extension and the types of areas differentiated in the process of expansion.

The Sector Theory

The Concentric theory of Burgess was based on the conditions of American cities in 1920. Since then, as Homer Hoyt observed, picture of cities had changed and therefore, he advanced in 1939, the sector theory. His idea was that because of rise of automobile, access to the downtown had been improved and lot of shifting of uses in the CBD had arisen. On major routes of transportation sectors of specific land use were

Figure 8.7A
The Sector Theory

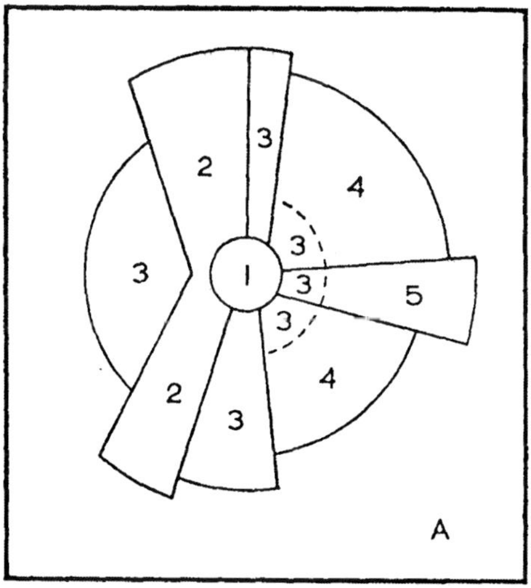

1 : CBD
2 : Wholesale and light manufacturing
3 : Low-class residential
4 : Middle-class residential
5 : High-class residential

likely to grow with the expansion of city. Residential land uses tend to be arranged in wedges radiating from the centre. (Figure 8.7A) Hoyt's theory, of course, deals only with residential land use. Rent areas in cities tend to conform to a pattern of sectors rather than of concentric circles. (Figure 8.7A) The highest rent areas tend to be located in one or more sectors of the city. But various rent areas are not static. High quality residential areas tend to migrate outward in the sector, older houses remaining behind to become medium-quality areas (Figure 8.7B). The movement of the high rent area is important because it has tended to pull the growth of the entire city in the same direction. The net result of urban growth is that a zone of

Figure 8.7B

Shifts in Location of Fashionable Residential Areas

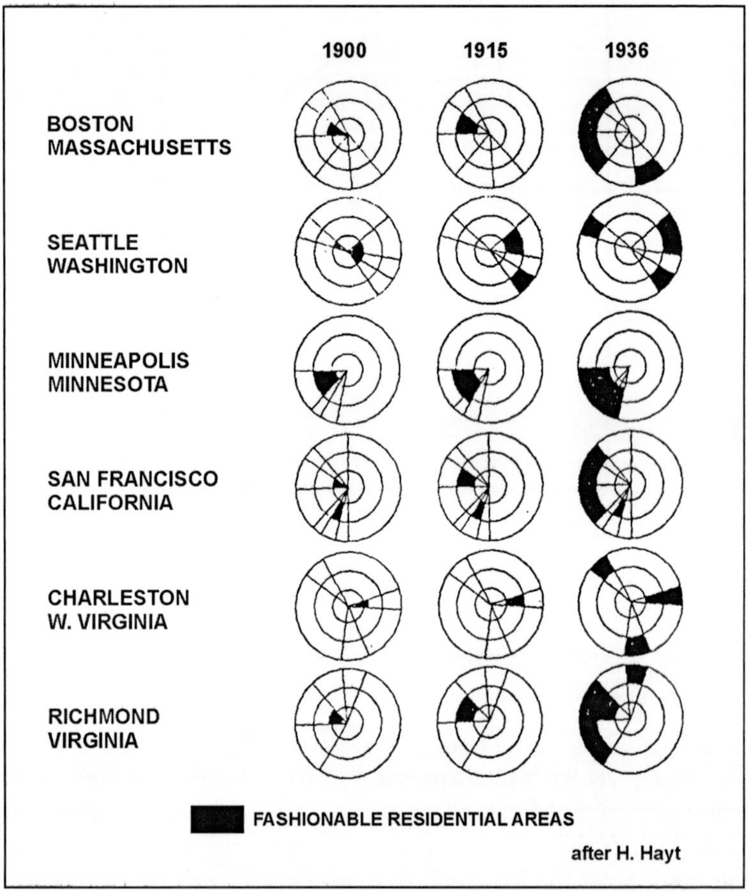

Figure 8.8
The Structure of a Hypothetical British City

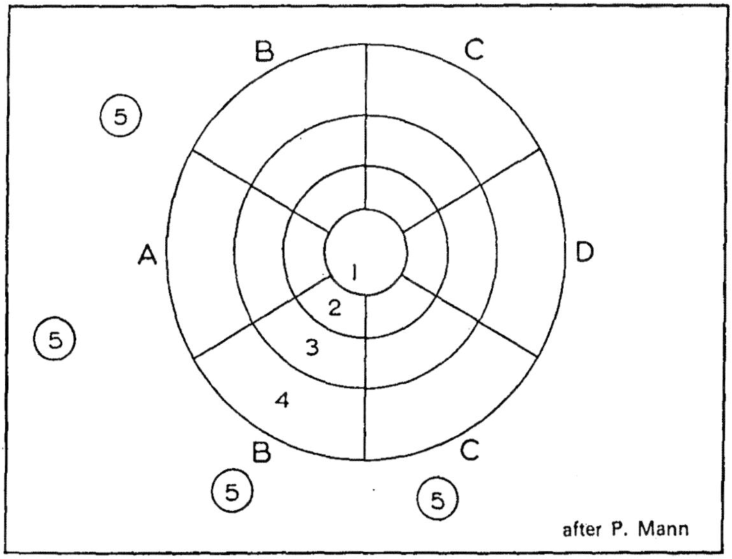

high-class housing tends to be located on one side of a city rather than in the continuous ring. At the same time, the age of buildings is more likely to show a concentric arrangement.

Peter Mann's Views

Peter Mann (1965) expressed that the sector and concentric theories show the possibility of the coexistence, and Hoyt's sectors are just a refinement rather than a radical alteration of the concentric mode.[20] Mann suggests that urban structure of the typical medium-sized British city shows internal differentiation but not complexities as seen in a conurbation (Figure 8.8). His model assumes a prevailing wind from the west attracts location of best residential area on the western fringe of the city, on the opposite side from the industrial and lowest working-class sector. In other words, the diagram showing shifts in the location of high-rent residential areas, illustrates

Figure 8.9
Sector Analysis

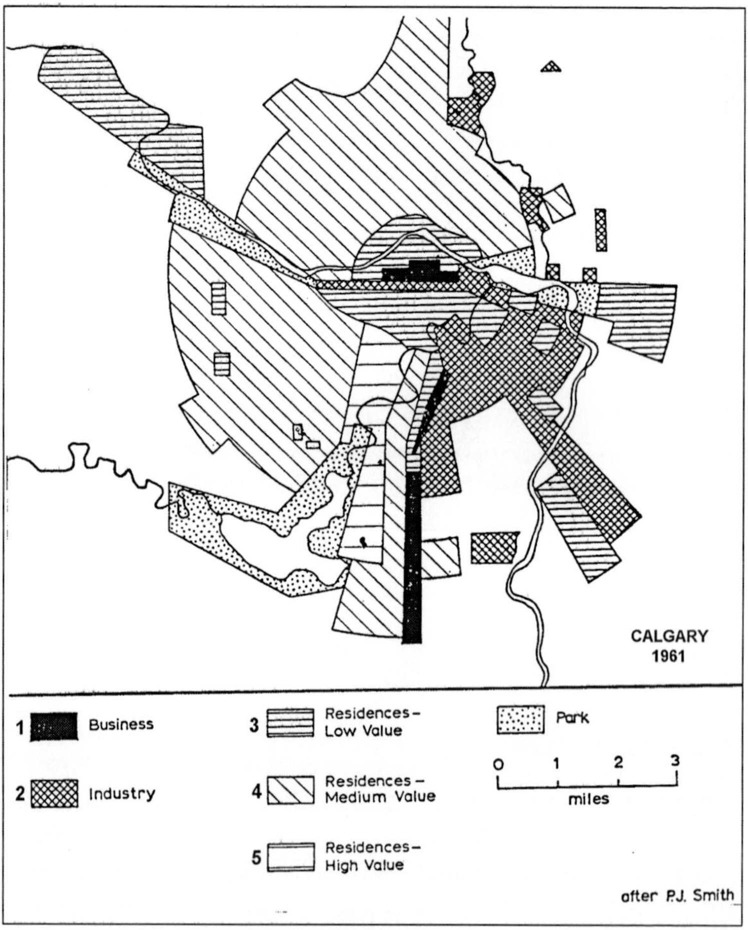

elements of both a concentric and a sector structure (see Figure 8.9).

Hoyt's theory is based on a vast amount of empirical work. The data for the theory were collected for 64 cities in America by the Works Progress Administration. The data of these small- and medium-sized cities were supplemented with surveys of New York, Chicago, Detroit, Washington and Philadelphia. Thus, it amounts in large part, to an empirical generalizations. Nevertheless, the theory has not gone unchallenged.

Walter Firey's Criticism of Hoyt's Theory

Walter Firey carried out a land use study of central Boston.[21] In his study he explored the role of social factors in shaping urban land use. On this basis, he contradicted various aspects of sector theory. According to Firey, there is little validity of comparing the result of work in a number of cities when relief, location on a waterfront and other factors affected the sector pattern of some cities. He also criticised cartographic approach on the ground that maps can only give clues to theories. This needs to be worked out in terms of abstract concepts. Hoyt has not sufficiently considered the roles of cultural and social systems in conditioning land use. Wealthy residents can choose to live anywhere and may not follow the 'normal', either sector or concentric pattern.

The Multiple Nuclei Theory

Urban development and growth of a city in different parts of the developed and developing areas is not a simple phenomenon which can be explained by geometric designs – either concentric circles or sectors radiating from the centre. Its land use too, is not simple and singular. It represents intermingling of various functions like commercial, industrial, cultural, administrative and social. As a result, morphology of a city

Figure 8.10
Multiple Nuclei Theory

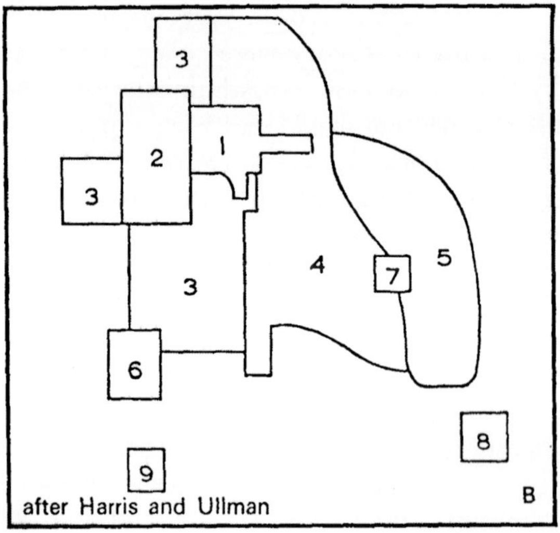

Central Business District	1	Heavy Manufacturing	6
Wholesale Light Manufacturing	2	Outlying Business District	7
Low-class Residential	3	Residential Suburb	8
Medium-class Residential	4	Industrial Suburb	9
High-class Residential	5		

cannot be unicentred. Its evolution cannot be the product of a zone or sector. Various types of land uses and their patterns develop often around several separate nuclei. Chauncy D. Harris and Edward L. Ullman suggest multiple nuclei for accommodating growth of residential, business, industrial or other elements taking place in cities during the course of time from their inception to the present day (Figure 8.10).

The rise of separate nuclei has been due to factors which influence the distribution of human activities within a city. The various factors may be of four categories:

(a) Certain activities require specialized facilities, for example, CBD can function at the point where maximum accessibility is available.

(b) There are also group of activities which prefer cohesion. Clothing industry is clustered in the densely packed inner districts of large cities. They profit from cohesion.

(c) Certain activities are detrimental to one another, and generally seek separate sites. For example, heavy industry and high-class residential areas do not prefer to be near-neighbours.

(d) Certain activities are unable to pay the rents of most desirable sites: residential areas of low-income residents or bulk storage facilities have to seek nuclei in remote corners.

The above factors, and also factors of social, cultural and economic significance give a peculiar urban landscape with separate nodes. Nuclei may be of two categories – those which take their shape at the time of city's origin, and some nuclei develop with the growth of a city. Nuclei existing at the time of origin of the city have a long history behind them. The areas around them have been covered by land uses during the course of growth of a city. London at the time of origin had 'The City', and Westminster as separate nuclei, the former being a commercial-financial node, while the other a political centre. Harris and Ullman cite an example of Chicago as the second category. It developed simultaneously with the growth of heavy industry in the heart of the city, and further migrated to the Calument district where it formed a new nucleus. In India many cities like Delhi, Mathura, Varanasi, Patna and Mumbai have numerous nuclei of antiquity, and their intermittent gaps were filled in by land uses during their historical development. Thus, the history is an important factor shaping the form of urban development. But this fact should not be overlooked that economic and social factors are also operating.

The multiple nuclei theory reveals two significant observations based on historical and site elements of morphology. One is that the theory produces a model involving complexities of urban structure which may not be easily and immediately discernible because of historical stratification of land uses during the process of urban growth. Although most cities have only one CBD they have a series of sub-centres around nuclei.[22] These are less specialized but enough to provide needs of smaller sections of the city. Second observation which is more significant, is about the probability of elements of the concentric and sector models present in its depth. Nothing new is involved conceptually in the multiple nuclei, and, it should not be given the status of a theory. Actually, land uses around nuclei and in between areas filled in, they display land uses intermixing of concentric and wedge areas. The multiple nuclei approach should be looked upon "as a guide to thought about the structure of the city, rather than as a rigid generalization about urban form".[23]

Morphology of Cities in India

Generally, urban morphology of towns in India shows dual structure. It is either blending of indigenous features and Western-style structure or hybridized European features. Kolkata is similar to a Western city functionally, but it is more compact than any of the west-European city of the same population. Allahabad was and is still densely populated to the south nearer the Jamuna river. It is unplanned having maze of narrow streets in complete contrast to the Civil Lines which is established on an extensive grid plan. The railway area acts as an effective divide blocking access to the north. It completely shuts off the crowded and irregular city from the broadly planned rectangular cantonment and civil lines (see Figure 8.4).

The impact on morphology of cities in India is purely social. Society in the 19th century had a distinctive character and organization of its own. Thus, morphology or forms of the towns in India reflect faithfully ethnic and social distinctions. The social areas of Third World cities are basically characterized by the degree of modernization, and consequently, there is visible in the urban landscape patches of both 'traditional' and 'modern' areas.

In most of the cities in India, there is found a dual structure, and their morphological pattern may conveniently be divided into 'local' and 'foreign' lineaments. The old city of Delhi, for example, was a walled city with a moat. The walls and moat have now given way to post-independence development. But the 'remains' in the form of residential and commercial areas reflect high density of buildings, irregular pattern of streets flanked by narrow lanes and uncontrolled growth of mixed land use. The residential units of the indigenous city, mainly the 'Chandni Chowk' and 'Sadar Bazar area' are deeply ingrained by caste and community quarters. Outside the old city, and, beyond the Daryaganj area, there lies a spacious area of the European-style buildings with a core in the Connaught Place. It is further extended including the Parliament area of European-style bungalows, modern shops and offices, the Central Business Circular Area with modern departmental stores and supermarkets. The entire facade represents the British legacy. If someone closely examines the morphology of Indian cities, it would not be a surprise for him to find that over one city, another of entirely different urban scene is being superimposed. Besides a mixed land use, a new type of layout is being grafted along an indigenous one.

After several decades of the country's freedom and alienation, the most ubiquitous factor is continuation of the western way of urbanism in political, economic, cultural and social life in urban centres of India. These influences are subtle in medium-sized towns but dramatic in metro cities.

Most of the cities which were formerly under the princely states' rule had a wall indicating the need for protection. The wall now is being demolished to give place for new business markets flanked on both sides by spacious roads and multi-storied buildings used as offices, financial and commercial establishments and even for residential purpose in some cases.

Figure 8.11
Cairo (Egypt)

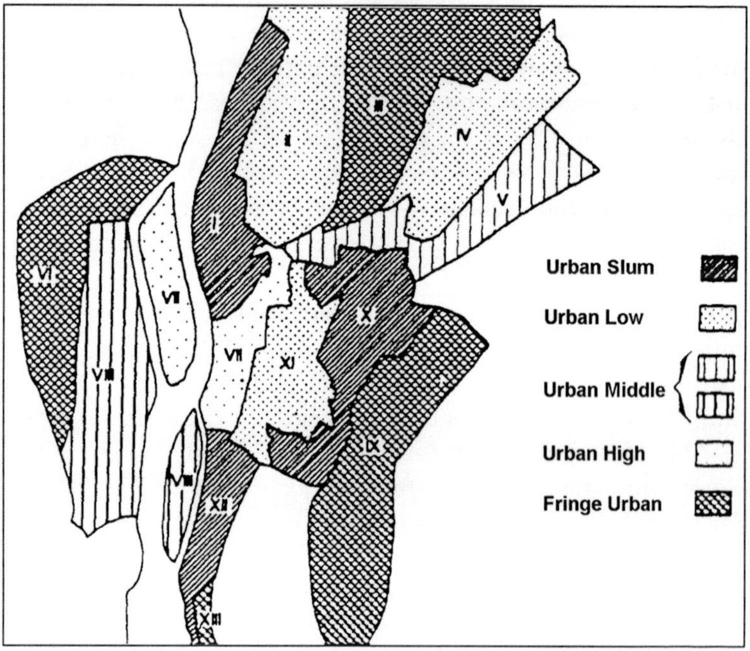

"With the change in the concept of security, the city wall appears to be an anachronism. In Jodhpur, in view of the futility, it is now being demolished at various places to give way to roads and to provide more space for shopping centres."[24] The same is the case in Udaipur where the city wall is now being demolished for the development of the central business area where banks, financial institutions and retail stores find sites in buildings erected on both sides of the roads radiating east, north and westward from the gates of the demolished wall.

City Morphology in the Developing World

City morphology in the developing world is the product of the cultural and social characteristics of the group which lays it out.[25] In India, it is the impact of English colonialism which largely has its stamp on urban landscape. Here the two cultures – indigenous and western – continued side by side to produce a distinctive urban form made up of the two elements. The major spatial elements of the morphology of Indian urbanism may be broadly represented by (a) garrison, (b) civil administration developed by the British 'to run' the country, and (c) the indigenous city followed by the colonial grafting on of the newer parts. These features have already been discussed previously. Nevertheless, social areas of the Third World cities represent the degree of modernization, and also, the existence of both 'indigenous' and 'modern' areas.

Cairo's medieval community is coextensive with the city and runs all the market activities. But away from it is a dark and dense residential-cum-commercial quarter, mud splattered and garbage strewn, penetrated by winding, narrow, dirt paths terminating at the gate '*cul-de-sac*'.[26] In contrast is the westernised central business area. Between the old city – heart of the city (Cairo community) and the westernised CB area is a 'transitional belt'. The old city's slums have location neither at the inner-belt nor at the periphery but rather related to the oldest sections. Cairo's morphology represents nuclei arrangement coexisting the three types of population – rural, traditional urban and the modern industrial urban (Figure 8.11).

In her another contribution, Abu-Lughod identifies six fairly distinctive and co-existent urban arrangements making up the morphological pattern which is practically a mixture of concentric, sectoral and nuclei models. This situation is illustrated in the study of Rabat in Morocco.[27] The six arrangements include: (i) Medina core, (ii) modern appendage in European style, (iii) rapidly growing uncontrolled settlements, (iv) peripheral suburbs or built-up areas of outward growth occupied by both middle and upper class, (v) rural fringe of underdeveloped rural land as wedges, and (vi) transitional

Figure 8.12
City in the Developing World – Rabat (Morocco)

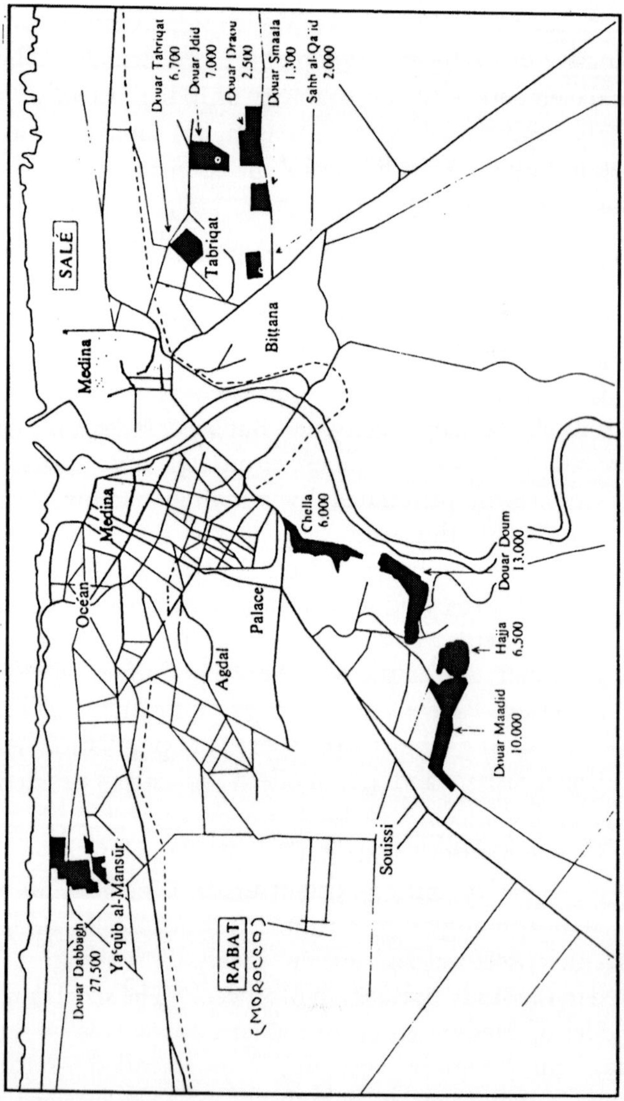

After Abu-Lughed, 1980.

working class zone between Medina core and modern appendage. Figure 8.12 of Rabat represents more or less the same arrangement.

Sector occupying the periphery in the developing world shows uncontrolled settlements of squatter population. At least one quarter, and often one-third or even more of the total urban populations in most primate cities are squattering there because of huge urbanward migration. About 35 per cent of the

Figure 8.13

Change in Urban Land Use

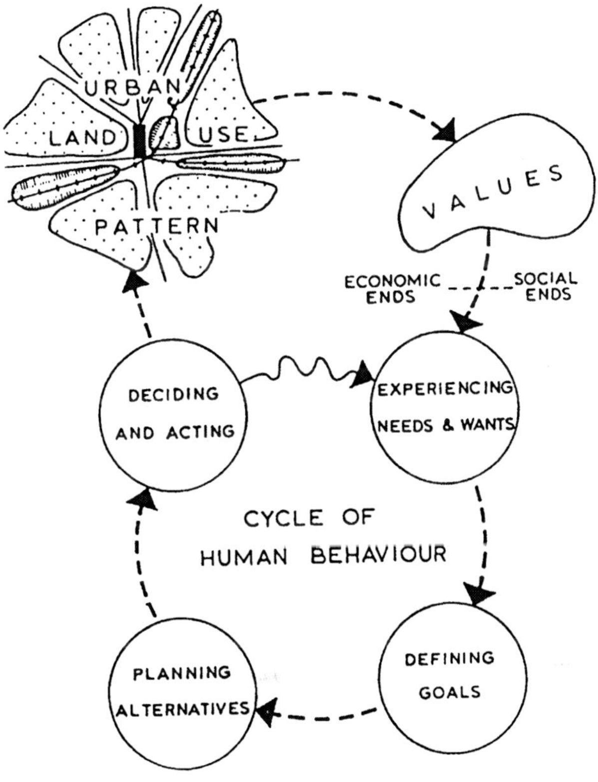

The sequence of action and the influence of values in bringing about a change in the urban land use pattern (after F.S. Chapin, 1965).

people in Manila, 33 per cent in Kolkata, 45 per cent in Jakarta, and 46 per cent population in Mexico City live in slums and uncontrolled settlements.[28] These are illegally occupied areas where spontaneous or uncontrolled dwellings produce social problems. Economic activities have polluted the physical environment and relations among the dwellers have created crime-bound problems for civic authorities.

Conclusion

The above chapter has sought to analyze the land use of a city on its core, the central business area, on fringe and in between the centre and fringe. The discussion is based on assumption of three situations, viz., concentric pattern of land use, sector or wedge-like arrangement, and also land uses in the form of numerous nuclei developed through various thoroughfare or axial lines of transportation radiating from the centre. Urban history of origin and growth shows that none of the above three notions analyzes fully the dynamism of urban structure.

There are various forces underlying the contrasts between the centres and the peripheries of cities.[29] 'Centrifugal forces' have driven out certain land uses from city centres because of the increased land value and the congestion associated with a central location. There is also another force, 'centripetal', which attracts specialized land uses in city centres because of their accessibility to consumers and proximity to closely related activities which can be obtained there.

An idea of 'gradient analysis' too distorts any single arrangement of land use, and therefore, no one theoretical explanation can be held valid for the reality behind the morphological pattern evolved. Many features of a typical city tend to vary in a logical sequence at increasing distances from the centre. Berry[30] has illustrated the sequence by means of graph and equations can be calculated describing the graphs

(Figure 8.13). Gradient analysis, of course, takes into account both concentric and sector models. Burgess in his model has referred to the various social and economic gradients produced by the growth of a city. Similarly, conditions at various distances from the city take form of sectors along the line of a highway.

The models as expressed above to analyze urban land use are primarily based on human ecology. But the notion of human ecology is like a closed-lane because human behaviour is unpredictable. To some extent, economic models contribute to explain urban structure. The coherent framework of a city does not conform to any set of theoretical structure. Organic city life and activities in and around cities depend now on the behaviour pattern of individuals and institutions and firms. Chapin[31] has illustrated urban land use pattern based on dynamics of human behaviour (Figure 8.13). The figure indicates the sequence of action and the influence of values in bringing about a change in the urban land use pattern.

Transportation system and social variations in the cities of India show much flexibility rather than steep gradient. Thus, morphological pattern of cities in India follows axial growth rather than concentric, sectoral or nuclei. Because of rich historical background, cities of India show simultaneously land uses around the centre, along radiating highways, in sectors and also on the city-fringe in suburbs.

Notes

1. Harris, C.D. and Ullaman, E.L., "The Nature of Cities", in *Readings in Urban Geography*, (eds.) H.M. Mayer and C.F. Kohn, Chicago, 1959, p. 282.
2. Carter, Harold, *The Study of Urban Geography*, Arnold, London, 1995, p. 125.
3. Ahmad, Enayat, *Geographical Essays on India*, Patna, 1954, p. 267.
4. Piggot, S., *Prehistoric India*, Penguin Books, 1950, p. 164.

5. Havel, E.B., *The History of Aryan Rule in India*, New York, pp. 23-24.
6. Mukerjee, R.K., *Man and His Habitation,* London, 1940, p. 259.
7. Meena, Namonarain, unpublished M.A. Dissertation on "Udaipur Morphology", Udaipur University, 1966.
8. Houston, J.M., *A Social Geography of Europe*, Gerald Duckworth, London, 1953, p. 167.
9. Johnson, J.H., *Urban Geography*, Pergamon, London, 1967, pp. 168-169.
10. Murphy, R.E., *The American City: An Urban Geography*, McGraw Hill, New York, 1966, 2nd ed., p. 303.
11. Carter, H., op. cit., p.345.
12. Spate, O.H.K. and Ahmad, E., "Five Cities of the Gangetic Plain", *G.R.*, Vol. 40, 1950, pp. 260-78.
13. Turner, R. (ed.), *India's Urban Future*, 1968, p. 50.
14. Davies, R., "The Spatial Formation of the South African City", *Geo Journal*, Supplementary Issue 2, 1981, pp. 59-72.
15. Burgess, E.W., "The Growth of the City", in Park, R.E. and Burgess, E.W. (eds.), *The City*, Chicago University, Chicago, 1925, Ch. 2., pp. 47-62.
16. Davie, M.R., "The Pattern of Urban Growth", in G.R. Murdock (ed.), *Studies in the Science of Society*, Yale University Press, New Haven, Conn. 1937, pp. 133-161.
17. Sjoberg, G., *The Pre-industrial City: Past and Present*, New York, 1965, p. 97.
18. Quinn, J.A., "The Burgess Zonal Hypothesis and its Critics", *American Sociological Review*, Vol. 5, 1940, pp. 210-218.
19. Haggett, P. and Chorley, R.J., *Model in Geography*, London, Methuen, 1967, p. 22.
20. Mann, P., *An Approach to Urban Sociology*, London, 1965, Ch. 4, p. 96.
21. Firey, W., *Landuse in Central Boston*, Cambridge, Mass., 1947.
22. Harris, C.D., "Suburbs", *American Journal of Sociology*, Vol. 49, 1943, pp. 1-13.
23. Johnson, J.H., op. cit., p. 172.
24. Kumbhat, P.C., in *Essays in Applied Geography*, Sagar, M.P., 1976, p. 194 and 195.
25. Carter, H., *An Introduction to Urban Historical Geography*, Edward Arnold, London, 1983, pp. 114-29.

26. Abu-Lughod, J., *Cairo: 1001 Years of the City Victorious*, Princeton, N.J., 1971, p. 190.
27. Abu-Lughod, J., *Rabat: Urban Apartheid in Morocco*, Princeton University, N.J., 1980.
28. Ulack, R., "The Role of Urban Squatter Settlements", *A.A.A.G.*, Vol. 68, 1978, p. 535.
29. Calby, C.C., "Centrifugal and Centripetal Forces in Urban Geography", *A.A.A.G.*, Vol. 23, 1933, pp. 1-20.
30. Berry, B.J.L., "The Spatial Organization of Business Land Uses", in Garrison, W., et al., (eds.), *Studies of Highway Development and Geographic Change*, University of Washington Press, Seattle, 1959.
31. Chapin, F.S., *Urban Land Use Planning*, Urbana, Illinois University Press, 1965, p. 30.

9

Classification of Towns

Urban centres are numerous, and these vary in their size, functions, location and in their social composition, culture and heritage too. It is therefore worthwhile to classify towns into categories for better understanding about their role in the regional and national context. In India, the problem of classifying urban centres is not an easy task. This is because of several reasons. First, the number of towns in India is too large to handle on some viable grounds. The size of towns has a wide span ranging between 5,000 to 10,000,000, and this might not characterize town's personality by breaking these into subjective or arbitrary classes. Second, the towns of India have a long historical background and have been under various regimes dating back thousand years from birth of Christ to the present era of democratic set-up. Finally, the data about functions and economy of Indian cities have not yet been standardized because of the absence of a suitable urban agency to deal with these. Under these circumstances classifications and categorization of urban places in India differ from state to state and from author to author.

There may be several methods, ways and means to classify urban centres. Site and situation of towns, population, size and functions, their social and cultural environment, etc., are some of the recognized bases to put them into groups. Out of all the bases of classification, the variable of 'function of a town' is widely accepted and reliable too. 'Reliable' in the sense that town itself is defined as an unit characterized by non-agricultural activities. Non-agricultural activities include administrative, industrial, commercial, cultural, etc. It is rarely that a town is 'mono-activity' centre. Often towns develop diversified activities and are known to posses multifarious functions like economic, administrative and cultural. Nearly all towns are supposed to provide various services like health, education, municipal (water, electricity, sanitation), transportational and marketing. Therefore, it is not worthwhile to classify urban places into a single particular function.

Aurousseau's Attempt

Here some of the most significant classifications have been discussed. In 1921, M. Aurousseau[1] classified towns into six classes: administrative, defence, culture, production-towns, communication and recreation. His classification though a simple one, however, suffers from the defect of over-generalization. To classify a town into one major category, generally neglects the role of other classes. The cut-off point of one-class is decided by the arbitrary percentage, and therefore it is subjective. Economic activities too are neglected. These are important in the sense that a town also caters for the need of people residing outside its municipal limits. Various classes of functions as suggested by Aurousseau create confusion in the sense that both functional and locational characteristics are mixed; for example, under communication-class group of towns performing function of 'transfer of goods' are put. Towns with tidal-limit, fall-line-towns, bridgehead towns point out attribute of location in performance of their function. It is thus doubtful that such towns are exclusively communicational, and not locational. Similarly, pilgrimage centres are cultural towns, but these equally are significant in their geographical location on mountainous terrain, in valleys or on banks of rivers. University-town is also a misnomer because this type of adjective cannot be its function but only a single quality among its over all urban milieu. But Anuousseau's classification marks a significant stage and provides a springboard for sophisticated methods. It is actually a comprehensive scheme bringing together polygonal functional urban activities to classify urban centres.

Harris's Classification

Chauncy D. Harris[2] remedied the deficiencies of the former subjective and common-sense-judgement-based classifications. He was able to identify quantitatively dominant function out of multifunctional character of cities. He used employment as well as occupational figures reduced to percentages to indicate cut-off points for urban activities varying in importance. His classification is based on the fact that some activity-groups employ many more persons than others do. For example, USA's 27 per cent employed persons of the total urban employment are in manufacturing, while wholesale trade has about 4 per cent. Thus, it is obvious that some functions should be assigned higher percentages than others. From analyzes, he was able to set up limits for each of his types as shown in the Table 9.1.

Harris's classification suffers with some grave defects and cannot be universally viable. He used metropolitan districts as functional units because the industry-group data such as those published now were not then available when he did his research. Consequently, number of cities which were too small to have metropolitan districts were left unclassified. In his

Table 9.1

Criteria used by Harris in Functional Classification of Cities of USA

Types	*Principal Criterion*	*Secondary Criterion*
Manufacturing Cities (M' subtype)	Employment in mfg. equals at 74% of the total employment in mfg. + retailing + wholesaling.	Mfg. and mechanical contain at least 45% of gainful workers (occupation figs.)
Manufacturing Cities (M subtype)	At least 60% of total employment in mfg. + retailing + wholesaling	Mfg. and mechanical contain between 30% and 45% of gainful workers.
Retail Centres (R)	In retailing at least 50% of the total employment in mfg. + wholesaling + retailing	At least 2.2 times of wholesaling alone.
Diversified Cities (D)	Employment in mfg. + wholesaling + retailing is less than 60%, 20% and 50% respectively of the total employment in these activities.	Mfg. and mechanical contain between 25% and 35% of the gainful workers.
Wholesale Centres (W)	Employment in W at least 20% of the total employment in M + W + R	At least 45% as much as in retailing alone.
Transport Centres (T)	Transport and communication at least 11% of the gainful workers, and workers in transport and communication equal at least one-third the number in mfg. and mechanical.	At least 2/3 the number in trade.
Mining Towns (S)	In extraction of minerals for more than 15% of the gainful workers (for cities of more than 25,000 pop.)	–
University Towns (E)	Enrolment in colleges – (university, technical institution, liberal arts colleges and teachers' colleges) at least 25% of the pop. of the city.	–
Resort and Retirement Towns (X)	No satisfactory statistical criterion was found.	–

Source: Abridged from, (*Geog. Rev.*, Vol. 33, 1943, Table 1).

article referred here (*Geo. Rev.* Vol. 33, Table 1) he did not include a list of urban centres and the categories to which they belonged. Carter labelled Harris's classification as subjective because the decisions to access or delete with a minimum number or cut-off points seem to be a personal one and were set by simple empirical means. Under the class of 'Transport and Communications', workers engaged in telephone and telegraph services were omitted simply on empirical grounds which was nothing more than a subjective decision. Duncan and Reiss tried to revise the problem of functional specialization by using the lowest value of supper decile or quantile groups. This revision is advantageous in the sense that it made an allowance for the different size-classes in the classification.

Howard Nelson's Classification

Nelson[3] further removed the shortcomings of the classifications of those of Harris and others by using a stated procedure that could be objectively checked by other workers. He decided to base his method of classification entirely upon major industry groups as listed in the 1950 Census of Population for standard metropolitan areas, urbanized areas and urban places of 10,000 or more population. He omitted the little significance groups like agriculture and construction, and finally, arrived at the nine activity groups.

The problem of city specialization, and also the degree of specialization above the average was solved by giving margins of different degree to different size classes. He did find a definite tendency for the percentages employed in some activities vary with city size. The question – 'When is a city specialized?' was solved by using a statistical technique – the Standard Deviation (SD).

A city can be specialized in more than one activity and to varying degrees. Thus he showed for each city all activities that qualified for plus 1, plus 2, or plus 3 SDs above the mean. Table

Table 9.2

Nelson's Nine Activity Groups (1950)

	Manufacturing	*Retail Trade*	*Professional Service*	*Transportation and Communication*	*Personal Service*	*Public Administration*	*Wholesale Trade*	*Finances Insurance and Real Estate*	*Mining*
	Mf	*R*	*Pf*	*T*	*Ps*	*Pb*	*W*	*F*	*Mi*
Average	27.07	19.23	11.09	7.12	6.20	4.58	3.85	3.19	1.62
Standard Deviation	16.04	3.63	5.89	4.58	2.07	3.48	2.14	1.25	5.01
Average Plus 1 SD	43.11	22.86	16.98	11.70	8.27	8.06	5.99	4.44	6.63
Average Plus 2 SD	59.15	26.49	22.87	16.28	10.34	11.54	8.13	5.69	11.64
Average Plus 3 SD	75.19	30.12	28.76	20.86	12.41	15.02	10.27	6.94	16.65

9.2 indicate averages and SD in percentages for selected nine activity groups (1950) as developed by Nelson.

Suppose, any city which is classified as Pf 2F, it means that it has 22.87 or more but less than 28.76 per cent of its labour-force employed in professional service and 4.44 or more but less than 5.69 per cent employed in finance, insurance and real estate. In short, the table indicates, the number of SDs shows the degree to which the urban centre stands out for the activity in question. A city which does not fall even under 1 SD, average in any activity appears as diversified D, in Nelson's classification.

Classification of Cities Attempted by Some of the Indian Authors

Generally cities and small towns have been classified in the Census Reports of India on the basis of their population size.[4] It is a simple classification and is easy to understand. Class I cities are of one-lakh and more population, Class II towns range between 50,000 and 100,000, Class III have population between 20,000 to 50,000, Class IV between 10,000 and 20,000, Class V between 5,000 to 10,000 and at the bottom of the various groups are small towns having less than 5,000 population.

The ranking into various classes of towns is actually not a classification but a grouping without any consideration to their components assigning them a town-status. There are number of villages in India having more than 5,000 population. It is an arbitrary attempt to classify settlements as town or village on the basis of population. Truly speaking, towns have a different sort of environment created by people as well as their activities like economic, social and cultural forming their base for existence. Boundaries set between settlements demographically are arbitrary and illusory. Towns exist to cater for various sorts of needs not only locally but also has its clientele in its surrounding area for social, cultural and above all, economic interaction.

Indian authors taking into account weaknesses of the Census classification, preferred economic activities as the basis for grouping them into major and minor groups. The economic activities of primary, secondary and tertiary are included to determine their respective role – dominant or of minor importance, and also to their degree of extent. This problem of objectivity about a town's functional role and also the scale of measurement was dealt statistically by various authors in their own way. Janaki[5], Amrit Lal[6], K.N. Singh[7], Prakasa Rao[8], O.P. Singh[9], Rafiullah[10], Mahamaya Mukerjee[11], Qazi Ahmad[12], Anant Padmanabhan[13], Asok Mitra[14] and many others classified towns in their own regions. None of these classifications is inherently superior or inferior to the others. But all of these explain the functional role of towns in their regional perspective.

Prakasa Rao considered the variables of urban services and amenities, bus-transport and clientele area of a town to assign it a numerical grade. Fariullah preferred Weber's method of ranking various functions of a town. Tiwari[15] went further to classify towns of M.P. by using IBM 7044 computer-method and analyzed them on the basis of multi-variable. O.P. Singh reviewed the functional analysis of central places of India. He distinguished between functional specialization and functional hierarchy. Pothana[16] analyzed the economic base of the towns of Andhra Pradesh. Mahapatra, Tripathi and Sinha[17] attempted a detailed functional economic base of small towns of Orissa. Raza[18], Agarwal and Mondira Dutta examined the dominance of the functions of the metropolitan centres in the Indian space economy.

A Case Study of Mitra's Classification of Indian Cities

Asok Mitra, a former Registrar General of the Census of India, attempted a comprehensive classification of all urban places in

India. He grouped the seven industrial categories* of workers into three broad groups:

(a) *Manufacturing Town* (percentage of workers in III, IV, V and VI put together is greater than the percentage in VII+VIII or in IX).

(b) *Trade and Transport Town* (percentage of workers in VII+VIII is greater than IX or in III+IV+V and VI put together).

(c) *Service Town* (where percentage of workers in IX is greater than workers in III+IV+V+VI or percentage in VII+VIII).

Degree of specialization in each of the three basic groups (a, b, and c) was identified by a triangular method on a graph. The three sides of an equilateral triangle represent three groups by 100 value as shown in Figure 9.1. The values of all the three groups are then plotted, and a point for each town within the triangle's perpendiculars was located. Three circles from the incentre point (33 1/3) are drawn proportionately to represent 40, 45 and 50 values respectively. These show increasing tendency for specialization. The points within the first circle show highly *diversified* functions; points between first and second circle are *moderately* diversified; points between second and third represent *specialized* predominant function; and the points outside the outer (third) circle show *highly specialized* predominant function.

The classification of 2,528 towns** shows that as many as 736 were agriculture, (total number of workers exceeding the number of workers in three non-agricultural groups), and out of 1,792 non-agricultural towns, 655 were manufacturing towns, 708 as trade and transport towns, and 429 as service towns.

---

* (I Cultivation, and II Agricultural labour are left, being a representation of Agricultural sector.) Seven Categories are: III Foresting, Fishing, etc., IV Household Industry, V Manufacturing, VI Construction, VII Trade and Commerce, VIII Transport, Storage and Communication, and IX Services.

** Towns and Cities included in both the 1961 and 1971 Censuses.

Figure 9.1
Classification of Indian Cities

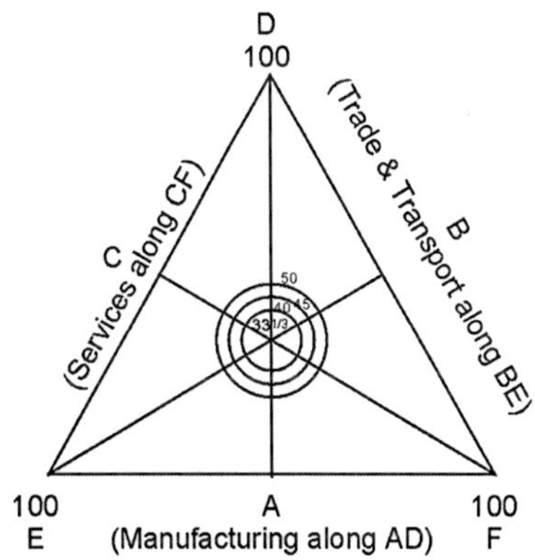

The Figure 9.2 shows the classification of one-lakh cities. There are 80 manufacturing cities, 78 trading and 81 are service cities. Table 9.3 given below shows their seven categories and there degree of specialization:

Table 9.3

City type	*Code*	*Degree of Specialization*				*Total Cities*
		FHD	*FMD*	*PFA*	*PEHA*	
		Number of Cities				
1.	MMt	17	28	9	26	80
2.	MA	2	2	2	2	8
3.	MMg	–	–	1	1	2
4.	MP	–	–	–	1	1
5.	TTg	22	35	18	3	78
6.	TTt	–	1	3	5	9
7.	SS	8	15	12	6	41
Total		49	81	45	44	219

(Courtesy: R. Ramchandran *Urbanization and Urban Systems in India*, pp. 183-186, Oxford, New Delhi, 1999).
FHD = Diversified, FMD = Moderately Diversified, PFA = Specialized, PEHA = Highly Specialized

Figure 9.2

Classification of One-Lakh Cities

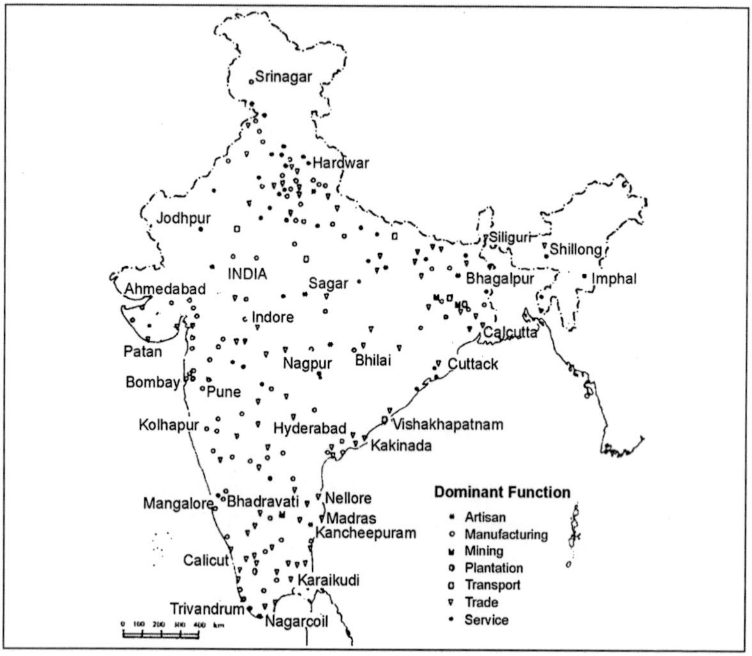

The Figure 9.2 shows that 219 on lakh cities (1981) fall into seven categories (Table 9.3). The cities showing specialization in manufacturing (80), trade (78) and service (41) are by far the most numerous. Some of the leading manufacturing cities with high degree of specialization are Ahmedabad, Surat, Jamshedpur, Ulhasnagar, Ludhiana, Salem and Solapur. They are widely distributed from north to south and west to east. The trade cities too show high degree of specialization but of lower level than manufacturing and/are distributed all over India. The service type of cities with specialization of high order are mostly new towns such as Chandigarh, Gandhinagar, Bhubaneswar, etc.

Mitra's classification, on the whole, brings forth the major categories and their specialization degree of cities. It distinguishes the three broad functional categories of manufacturing, trading and service (administration) among cities. Majority of cities show no clear specialization in one economic activity and have diversified economic base. The diversified city with multiple functions constitutes the most common and representative type of cities.

Conclusion

System of classification whether statistical or non-statistical is a scientific enquiry into the character of urban places. Some of the major problems are selection of bases for the classification. It depends upon objectives for which the classes are identified. Another problem is the unit whether small towns or metropolitan areas or some other form of urban places are to be classified. Various forms of urban units differ in their character, and thus, these should be classified on various grounds or methods. There is no sense in classifying a country-town or a million-city by a single methodology. Urban places can be distinguished on the basis of single variable or multiple variables. The only safeguard which may be taken is to save the process including interval scale measurement by arbitrariness. Urban places differ in their historical, environmental, social and economic attributes which can only be followed, provided one is capable of making it clear at the outset for what the classification is being attempted.

Statistical classification of towns and cities are mechanical and are unable to throw light upon specific behaviour of urban centres. Individuality of a city is reflected in its total environment. Its soul lies in its air, water, soil, energy and vegetative-cover which provide a real life to people. Interaction among these is not a subject of measurement – it can only be felt. The feeling about a town is a mental process and needs no classification or a label of a proper noun. Its quality or its quantitative scale on whatsoever methodology it is determined, will be merely a logical exercise and might be miles-and-miles away of meaningfulness and practical utility. Classification simply for the sake of groupism carries no meaning. Identification of town's character lies in its environmental probe.

Notes

1. Aurousseau, M., "The Distribution of Population: A Constructive Problem", *Geogl. Rev.*, Vol. 11, 1921, pp. 563-93.
2. Harris, C.D., "A Functional Classification of Cities in the United States", *Geogl. Rev.*, Vol. 33, 1943, pp. 66-89.
3. Nelson, H., "A Service Classification of American Cities", *Eco. Geog.*, Vol. 31, 1955, pp. 189-210.
4. *Census of India*, 1961, 1971, 1981.
5. Janaki, V.A. and Sayed, Z.A., *The Geography of Padra Town*, Baroda University, 1962.
6. Lal, A., "Some Aspects of Functional Classification of Cities", *N.G.J. of India*, Vol. 5, 1959, pp. 12-24.
7. Singh, K.N., "Functions and Functional Classification of Towns in UP", *N.G.J. of India*, Vol. 5, 1959, pp. 121-48.
8. Prakasa Rao, V.L.S., *Towns of Mysore State*, Asia Pub. House, 1964.
9. Singh, O.P., *A Study of Central Places in U.P.*, B.H.U., Varanasi, 1969.
10. Rafiullah, S.M., "A New Approach to Functional Classification of Towns, *The Geographer*, AMU India, Vol. XII, 1965.
11. Mukerjee, M.M., "Functional Association of Towns in Bihar, India", 21st Geogl. Congress, 1968.
12. Ahmad, Q., *Indian Cities: Characteristics and Correlates*, University of Chicago, 1965.
13. Padmanabhan, N. Anant, "Functional Classification of Urban Centres in Madras State", *Bombay Geogl. Magazine*, Vol. 13, 1965.
14. Mitra, A., *Functional Classification of Indian Towns*, Institute of Economic Growth, Delhi, 1973.
15. Tiwari, P.S., "Functional Pattern of Towns in M.P.", *N.G.J. of India*, Vol. 14, 1968, pp. 41-54.

16. Pothana, V., "Economic Base and Location of Towns of Andhra Pradesh: A Regional Analysis", *Indian Journal of Regional Science*, Vol. 8, 1976, pp. 71-76.
17. Mahapatra, P.K., Tripathi, S.N. and Sinha, B.N., "Economic Base of Small Towns in Orissa Coastal Plain", in R.L. Singh and Rana P.B. Singh (eds.), pp. 155-160.
18. Raza, M., Agarwal, Y.P., and Khurana, Indu, "Economic Base and Commodity Flaws: A Case Study of the Indian Urban System", *N.G.J. of India*, Vol. 26, pp. 157-73.

10

Small Towns

Concept of Small Towns

As it is evident from its title, 'small town' is some place where urbanity has not yet reached in its full vigour. It may also sound relatively smaller in size by area and also by population residing within it. But the concept is not fully clear simply by its demographic status or by its areal occupance. There are special small urban settlements within hills providing facilities or resorts. Similarly, there are towns near or adjoining to mining areas. These cannot fulfil the underlying concept involving functions of urban centre termed by urban geography as 'small town'. Population and areal occupance may be components of small town but these do not carry the entire ecology of small towns.

As pointed out by Moonis Raza, "small-towns occupy an important position in the urban-rural continuum"[1] of India. Let us examine the statement in the context of our country which is overwhelmingly rural. In our country space-organization warrants a mid-way settlement to cover vast agrarian landscape and a city. This is because of the fact that only through a mechanism of the hierarchical system agro-production forces could respond favourably. Our country which is primarily agricultural, necessarily requires settlements to bridge rural and urban functionaries. A village which is actually a centre of production of food products cannot singly handle the distribution and marketing of the same. Cities which are centres of administration, finance and commerce, and socio-cultural institutions, health and education are too busy to perform as a base for collection and subsequent distribution of agricultural products of the surrounding region. It is actually this rural-based function which links small towns with the countryside. Originally, small towns might have been rural centres, but in due course of time they gradually have assumed urban character by virtue of their nodality, function and services – local as well as central. On the core of urban built-up area there is generally developed an outer fringe where urban shadow begins to appear and countryside dispersion gradually disappears (Figure 10.1). As observed by Mukerjee, small towns in India are 'rurban' centres, their main function being "collecting the agricultural produce from the entire region and distribution and directing and coordinating the sale of imports and manufactured goods".[2]

Small towns possess a unique binomial status of acting as a bridge between villages and cities. They provide to villages 'a sort of resort' activity during their off-period from agricultural operations. Farmers visit nearby larger urban centres for having a change from their routine life and have a pastime. On the other side, cities being overcrowded have become unwieldy and too convenient to be a place for comfortable living. Small towns may provide a new ground for metropolitan cities. Small towns should be developed at a reasonable distance by free ways from big urban centres to reverse the process of present trends of migration.[3]

Small Town Defined

Small town is neither a village, nor a city. It is an economic parlance representing the area providing liaison between rural

Figure 10.1
Town-Countryside Unision

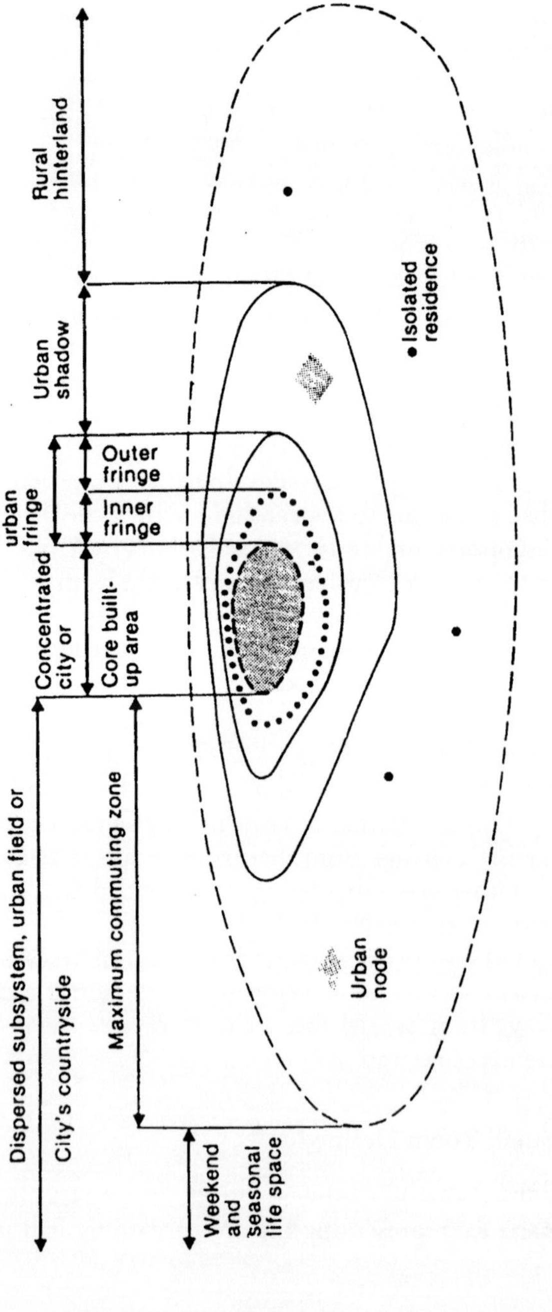

centres and urban places of significance. It is here that the forces of demand and supply converge. Geographically, it varies from a well defined village to a metropolitan centre. It may be compared to a spatial organism with fixed functions, behavioural patterns, growth process depending upon the nature and extent of the region and linkages in terms of transport and communicational network.

In the developing world, small towns are neither traditional in their structure, nor do they represent modern settlement milieu. But they are empowered functionally by both the city and the country. Small towns have a unique way of life governed by their size, site, demography, social ecology and economy. Unlike villages, small towns are bigger, have better links with their surrounding countryside but are having weaker community affairs and social set-up.

Demographic Dilemma

So far, small towns have been identified in the census on the basis of population. The demographic concept of small towns is in vogue for the past several decades. The census organization has consistently recognized ten categories of settlements ranging from the population of less than 500 to more than 1,000,000. In this array of settlements, a small town is lost in oblivion. In India, there are towns too with population of less than 10,000. In between the array of 5,000-10,000 it is very confusing and non-scientific to identify the census bound small town (5,000-9,999). It may be a village, and at the same time, a town.

In this connection, the statement of Moonis Raza may again be recalled who supported the continuum with three-fold arrangement and not two break points. Formerly, there have been 'shahar' (city), 'kasba' (town) and 'gaon' (village) to be used practically for all purposes. This array of three has

Figure 10.2

Small Towns (% of Total Urban Population)

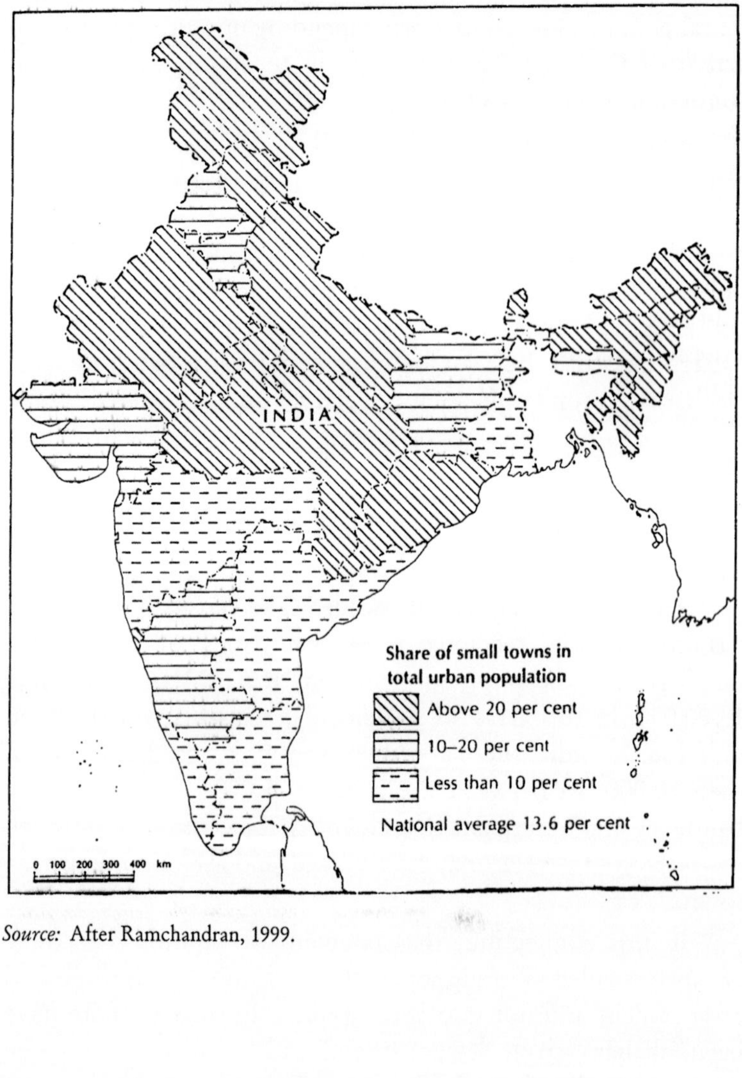

Source: After Ramchandran, 1999.

emerged through a historical process spread over millennia. The break point of two, i.e., village and city, does not fit into the overwhelming rural economy of India, and is unable to integrally link the surrounding smaller rural settlements with the larger settlements designated as 'shahars'. It is by the exploitative economy during the colonial rule that the three-point system was disrupted, and the 'kasbas' – small towns in the real sense were destroyed or considerably weakened.[4]

However, demographic criterion for the recognition of the significance of small towns cannot be held valid. They act as vital links between various grades of lower status and full-fledged towns of the region (Figure 10.1). Small towns represent a sort of unison between town and countryside. Thus, there are two aspects of town function. They are, of course, interrelated, but are quite different. Together they are the determinants of growth. The product of that growth is the population of the small town. But population size alone could

Figure 10.3A

Hierarchical Urban Order

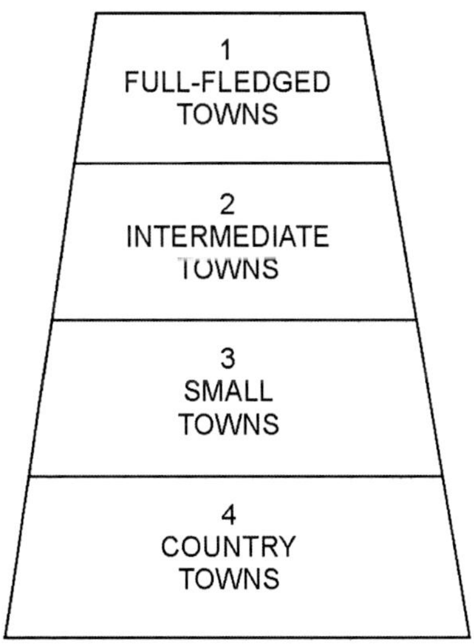

Table 10.1
Hierarchical Order of Towns: Lowest Level of Services-INST

	Hierarchical Order	*Services (Threshold)*	*Institutions (Threshold)*
1.	Full-fledged	Wholesale-retail marketing, Administrative, Educational, Judicial, Health, Transportational and other miscellaneous civic services Secondary institutions	Markets, Banks, College, Courts, Hospitals and Cultural and Social Institutions, Industrial Establishments.
2.	Intermediate Towns	Marketing, Limited central services, Health services, Primary industries	Markets, One or Two Banks, High Schools, Health Centres, Civic Institutes
3.	Small Towns	Marketing, Limited civic services, Agricultural and Primary industries	Small Market, School, Dispensary, Community and Civic Centre
4.	Country Towns	Agricultural and Primary industries	A few shops, Junior School and Civic Centre

not be reflected in its more important function – i.e., 'centrality'. It is, according to Christaller, the degree to which the town served a tributary area which is important rather than population. Small towns act as central places for the countryside; that they come into being to carry out at a central, accessible place the tasks which the life of the countryside creates.[5]

Rural-Urban Behaviour in Small Towns

In a country like India where agriculture and other primary activities engage more than 70 per cent population, role and behaviour of small towns form significant part of people's life. There, people from countryside come to take advantage of various services and economico-cultural institutions. A large number of administrative institutions and wholesale establishments provide the farmers multiple services of wide range functions.* An identification of the characteristic functions and services at different hierarchical level was attempted on the basis of empirical observations.[6] It may provide an idea of rural-urban travel behaviour of villagers from countryside to small towns in the region. The list is being tabulated and generalized on the basis of several studies, and it can be held sufficiently appropriate at the national level in India. But it should not be taken as final and complete. The regional differences can only be identified through systematic field observations.

The movement of people from countryside to small towns has several options. In reality in India there is no village which is exclusively attached to a particular town. Empirically its has been ascertained that people from each village visit five to ten towns of the surrounding countryside. Even for a single purchase or for utilising a single service – health, education or culture, villagers have a choice of places. They choose, of course as per geographic convenience, but in many cases the choice depends as per their behavioural attitude about a particular small town.

In India, share of small towns in total urban population is highest in the northern half of the country comprising the states of M.P., U.P., Orissa, Rajasthan, Assam and J&K. In these cases small towns constitute more than 60 per cent of total number of towns (Figure 10.2).

---

* Central place functions available generally in small towns of India include: (1) Restaurants, (2) Cinema Houses – may be temporary, (3) Banks, (4) Pan-shops, (5) Cloth-stores, (6) Gold and Silver-smiths's shops, (7) Hardware/Paints, etc shops, (8) Books and stationery shops, (9) Cycle – sale and repair, and on rent, (10) Ayurvedic, Unani and Medical Drugs, (11) Country-liquor shops, (12) Tractor and agri-implements – sale and repair, (13) Utensils shops, (14) Dispensaries – Government and Private, (15) Schools, College including primary and secondary, (16) Block-office, (17) Tehsil, (18) Lower Courts, (20) Agro-experiment Station of University.

Universality of the Phenomena

Small towns and their relationship with surrounding countryside, and also with a city are not related only to underdeveloped areas characterized by primary occupations. Their linkages form essential part of all sorts of countries, whether developed, developing or underdeveloped. In the USSR (formerly known), Baransky has pointed out, 'socialism leads to bridging the gap between the town and the countryside, but under capitalism, on the contrary, the gap is further intensified.[7] While, in the Soviet Union cities operate as strong points of the dictatorship of the proletariat in assisting the agricultural labouring population both economically and culturally, in capitalist countries cities operate as strong points of the political power of exploiting classes, oppress the agricultural labouring population, and increase their dependence. Howsoever, this cannot be denied that in both types of countries the common traits of small towns have very large significance. In USA, Nelson pointed out that rail-road centres were mostly small cities balancing the many urban centres of the country (small towns) that are strikingly low in their proportions of transportation.[8]

Small towns and roads are also closely associated and contribute to each other's development by virtue of their intrinsic qualities of functions. Initially each new town leads to the creation of roads leading into it and from it. And each new road contributes to the emergence of new population centres along the road, especially at key points such as intersections with other roads (Figure 10.4).

Cities, like the Corps of officers, too possess their hierarchy – they include country town, small town, full-fledged town and capital, regional or metropolitan centre. Within a major economic region, cities are subordinated to each other in a certain pattern. The coordination among them reflects their specific functions and range of activities. Each of them possesses

Figure 10.4
Theoretical Model Representing Towns and Rail-Road Association

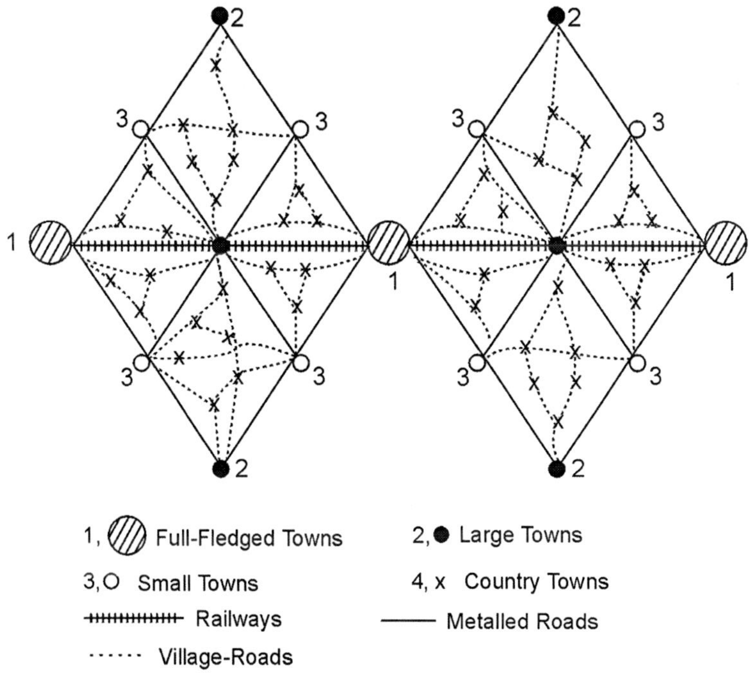

After Verma, L.N., 1976 in *Essays in Applied Geog.* (ed.), Misra, V.C., Sagar.

its own radius of influence and of attraction. This is particularly apparent in the USSR (formerly) where regional centres are economic, cultural, administrative as well as political ones.

To conclude the aforesaid, for urban geographers, the study of small towns is a focal point because it is associated with the knowledge of countryside entering into their sphere of influence. The study is also of significance because of role played by small towns in receiving the overgrown pressure in lakh-towns and million-cities. Small towns are instruments of stabilizing the balance of the rurban process by their being reagents in symbiotic relationship between the lowest and uppermost settlement system. In India, the problem is grave. Here, growth of towns, especially in remote areas, is yet to take sufficient time in its real sense. There has been poor filteration or rather penetration of urban values into the countryside. This has given impetus to exodus of rural skilled workers and job-seekers. It has resulted into transmission of unmatched tints into some of the cities to ultimately produce hybrid ecology. It would have been rather sound ecologically, had the Indian technocrats and planners too gone to keep harmony with nature and produced social and economic equilibrium. Unfortunately, in the lust of the urban-industrial model parallel to the West, Indian cities grew so haphazardly as to become parasitic on the surrounding countryside with widened gap between rural and urban areas.[9] It seems that reality behind the urban scene of India, as pointed out by Lambert, is in its 'hinge-like function' in which less urbanized areas are connected below it with larger centres above in 'multi-level hierarchies' of specialisms such as administration and politics, commerce, religion and education.[10] Million-cities of India have appeared to grow lopsidedly at the expense of small towns. Not only this, the point of worry is rather stagnation of many of the small towns. They have become sick and have been suffering from diseases, like lack of opportunities for growth, interplay of caste, class, social and economic bonds reflecting slow pace of mobility. Truly speaking, it is the rural countryside that seeps into the cities.[11] The end-product of the Indian urban scene is that cities have their feeble influence which is insufficient for meeting the demand of the consumers economically. Negligence towards the urban order of middle category and particularly of towns around the population of 20,000, is injuriously crucial and they need immediate attention of the urban planners of our country to bring them into a channel of sustainable development.

Notes

1. Raza, M., *A Survey of Research in Geography*, ICSSR, New Delhi, 1979.
2. Mukerjee, R.K., *Man and His Habitation*, Mumbai, 1968, p. 122.
3. Kambo, B., "Towns of Tomorrow", *Journal of Town Planning and Architecture*, New Delhi, 1978, p. 120.
4. Raza, M., op. cit., Foreword of the Report ICSSR, New Delhi, 1979.
5. Christaller, W., "*Die Zentralen Orte in Suddeutschland*", Jena, Germany, 1933, translated in English by Carlisle W. Baskin: *Central Places in Southern Germany*, Prentice Hall, 1966.
6. Ramchandran, R. and V.L.S. Prakasa Rao, "Mobility and Choice of Central Place", *Analytical Geography*, Vol. 1, No. 1, pp. 17-32.
7. Baransky, N., *Selected Works in Geography*, Progress Pub., Moscow 1981, p. 146.
8. Nelson, H.J., "A Service Classification of American Cities", *Eco. Geog.*, Vol. 31, 1955.
9. Bose, A., *India's Urbanization 1901-2001*, Tata McGraw Hill, 2nd Ed., p. 275.
10. Smailes, A.E., *The Indian City: A Descriptive Model*, Geographische Zeitschrift, Vol. 57, 1969, p. 182.
11. Turner, Roy (ed.), *India's Urban Future*, p. 59.

11

Central Place System

Nature of Distribution of Towns

Geographically speaking towns are unevenly distributed in an area. They are not only varying in their mutual distance, but they also vary in order of size and rank. Distribution of towns is governed by certain forces. Towns with specialized activities perform their task best at a point either centrally located with respect to accessible places or where a high degree of population is concentrated. This means that there are certain significant questions for probing into the distribution of towns. B.J.L. Berry has attracted attention towards certain innovative processes which reveal that distributional urban system of a country has its own organization model.[1]

Distributional patterns of towns theoretically reveal the following hypothetical cases:

1. Central place functions or general services are carried out by urban places for contiguous areas.
2. Special functions are carried out for non-local, non-contiguous areas.

3. Transport functions are carried out at break-of-bulk points along lines of communication.

Transport functions of a town are also linked with central place functions because these are media to meet demands of contiguous hinterland. General functions are characteristics of all towns, while special functions are only met by a few specialized functions to far and wide distant places located with enough of gap in between. This problem of two different sorts of networks for two different sets of services – general and special, is the main theme of the study of central place concept within urban geography. Nevertheless, the performance of central services is the character of all the three categories of cities stated above to some degree. The central function is the common denominator for a theory of location of urban centres.

Christaller's Model of Central Place

Christaller opined that there was regularity of spacing among urban centres concentrated on serving the areas around them. This was perhaps applicable to agricultural areas in southern Germany. Thus, the Central Place model of Christaller[2] is based on the premise that a certain amount of productive land supports an urban centre or central place. Hans Carol[3] defines the central place as the location either of a single central function, or the location of a group of central functions supplying the consumer goods or services for an area larger than itself.

Centrality

The concept of 'centrality' involves three dimensional process, viz., goods and services offered at the central place, the size of the complementary area for which the services are available, and also the number of people coming to the central place to avail goods and services. This means that goods and services of a place are available for the centre itself as well as for the surrounding area. Establishments of service institutions and goods offered exclusively for the people of the central place will not contribute to the centrality of a place, it is also the 'surplus' constituting the needs of the people coming from the complementary area.

Size of Central Place

Size of central places vary with the functions that a centre performs. The more complex are the functions, the larger the centre. Each central place of higher order performs all functions available in smaller central places, plus the additional more centralized functions as well. Thus, it is not the population but the complexity of functions which determines its rank as a central place.

Threshold Population and Range of the Goods

Berry and Garrison[4] consider the concepts of threshold and the range of goods are useful in the central place studies. Christaller did not use this term of 'threshold'. But it is significant in the sense that it determines the minimum number of consumers required to make an establishment profitable at the central place.

The range of goods or services is the maximum distance over which people will travel to purchase goods or derive a service offered at a central place. The range of goods depends upon (i) distance to the central place to obtain goods or service, (ii) distance in terms of time and money, (iii) number of customers decreases with the distance from the central place, and (iv) rate of decline for basic needs would be very steep, but for costly and infrequently needed items, the rate would be gradual.

Hierarchy of Central Place

The lowest level of the centre performs limited number of functions. A centre of the next higher order performs all the functions of the lower order centre plus a group of additional functions within its greater range. The new goods of higher-order central place have greater ranges and draw people from a considerably greater distance than the goods of the smaller centre do. The next higher order of centre will offer all the goods offered by the first two levels, but will be differentiated by a group of the newer goods than those offered by the next smaller centre. Thus, a sort of hierarchy of central places is evolved.

Shapes of Complementary Areas

On an entirely uniform plain having a purely agricultural economy, ideal complementary area for each central place should approximate a circle with radial traffic routes converging at the centre.[5] But circles do not use space efficiently and leave unserved space, and overlapping areas (Figure 11.1a). Christaller eliminated this difficulty by using a pattern of hexagons instead of circles. Hexagon is actually the most appropriate figure nearing circles that will use all the space without overlapping or leaving unserved space.

Figure 11.1a

Representation of Areas by Different Shapes

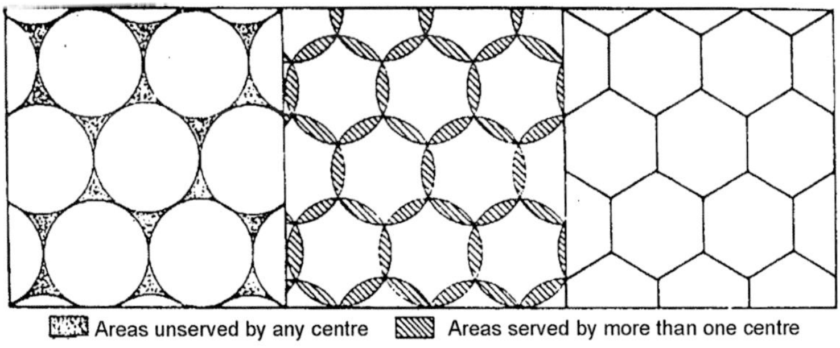

Christaller's System

Christaller developed his hexagonal theory to include various orders of central places and computed the population, their distances apart and their tributary areas. He envisaged three criteria known as (i) the marketing principle, (ii) the transportation principle, and (iii) the administrative principle (Figure 11.1b).

Figure 11.1b

Hexagonal Representation of Places

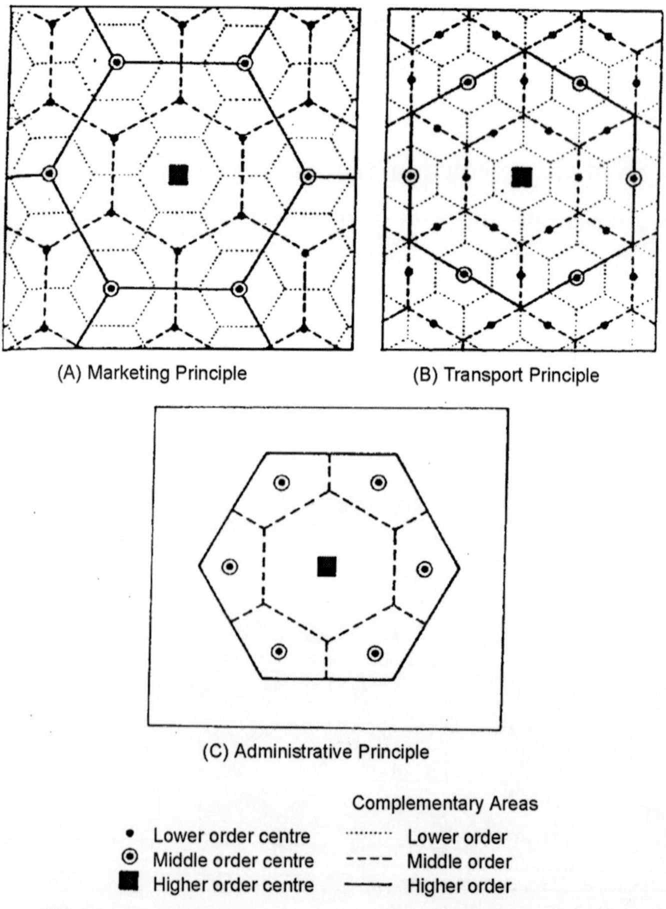

Marketing Principle

In Christaller's scheme, the market town is the smallest unit, having a population of 1,000 and lies at a distance of 4.5 miles from its nearest neighbours. It could be reached in an hour's walk approximately. For southern Germany, the tributary area of a market town was 17 square miles having a population of nearly 3,000.

The principle shows that there is strict ordering whereby each settlement serves its own hinterland and an area/population equivalent to the hinterlands of two other settlements in addition, hence it has been called 'the rule of three', expressed as k=3. The number of centres according to k-value hierarchy increases in geometrical progression as 1, 3, 9, 27, 81 and so on.

Seven Levels of Central Places

Christaller's theory has seven levels of central places performing the market-centre function in a hexagonal pattern. Their population, spacing interval and tributary areas are being tabulated below:

Table 11.1
Seven Levels of Central Places

	Grades	*Towns*		*Tributary Areas*	
		Population	*Distance apart (miles)*	*Population*	*Areas in sq. miles*
I	Market Town	1,000	4.5	3,000	17
II	Township Centre	2,000	7.5	11,000	51
III	Country Seat	4,000	13.0	35,000	154
IV	District City	10,000	22.5	100,000	463
V	Small State Capital	30,000	30.0	350,000	1,390
VI	Provincial Head City	100,000	67.5	1,000,000	4,170
VII	Regional Capital City	500,000	110.0	3,500,000	12,500

The distance between adjacent smaller centres amounts to the distance between those of the preceding grade times $\sqrt{3}$. For example $4.5 \times \sqrt{3}$ = approximately 7.5; $7.5 \times \sqrt{3}$ = approximately 13, etc. Christaller's system of central places is called 'nesting hierarchy' since each place performs the functions characteristic of its grade and all those of lower order centres as well. The nesting-hierarchy of central places is interwoven by route-hierarchy too.

Telephones as a Measure of Centrality

Christaller felt and decided that telephone was the best measure to link a central place with its tributary area. The number of telephones thus may be proved as best criterion to measure the centrality of a place. He proposed that its value of centrality would be measured by the formula T_Z-$E_Z(T_G/E_G)$, where T_Z represent number of telephones in the place; E_Z is the population of the place; T_G and E_G the number of telephones and population respectively in the surrounding region.

The criterion of telephone of determine centrality of a place has been questioned by many people on the ground that it may have been true of southern Germany when Christaller did his work; but for all times and all places it cannot be held valid.

Criticism of Christaller's Concept of Central Places

Ullman[6] points out that telephone may be of value for communication with out-of-town areas, but other measures might be better like an evaluation of actual central services performed over and above those for the town itself. Trade data and also the use of data on the number of automobiles entering a town may also be more significant and a better determinant than number of telephones.

The Christaller system is being criticized on the grounds that it is the least viable and can be disrupted by various local conditions. These include presence of important transportation routes, nature of terrain, soil-type and productivity, types of agriculture, cultivation and manuring including extent of technical advancement and administrative organization. Changing transportation and competitive railroads may change the shape of service areas. Christaller's hexagonal pattern of service area is based on assumptions rather than upon empirical evidence. He did not take into account the effect of large scale manufacturing and linear arrangement of centres along long-distance transport routes. It seems that his overall concept was designed as a deductive theory.

Nowhere in the world, the central-place system remains static. It is constantly changing with changing conditions. A common phenomenal change can be seen everywhere – that people go longer distances to the larger centres for availability of quality services that they formerly received in the local market towns. This is because of the development of good highways, and it has resulted considerably for changing smaller centres into more small, and the larger centres into more large.

General Significance and Applicability of Central Place Theory

The theory as propounded by Christaller, no doubt, is being criticized. But it is also true that almost all theories have both their attackers as well as defenders. It is true that industrial and technical changes have brought changes in world trade pattern, and the relationships between town and country have become obscured. But, it is also equally true that the changed large cities have not lost their role as service centres for their extensive tributary areas, thus reflecting to some measure a central-place pattern. Howsoever distorted in form, the central-place system of Christaller is applicable partially even to this day in countries of the developing world including India, China and areas where primary occupations predominate.

The theory, it is again emphasized, is normative in character. Therefore, it will be of no use to seek approximation in the real world. But, the impact of the theory is not absent. Let us examine the case of our country India, where administrative hierarchy of settlements exists. Its practical relevance and impact on daily life is obvious. Gram Panchayats which are rural in character provide legal, economic, administrative, educational and health services to the adjoining hamlets and smaller villages, are central places of the lowest order.[7] The administrative hierarchical system of India may differ but the spacing of tehsil and district level centres conforms to the theory. The overall difference may be due to wide gaps between the real and ideal world.

Table 11.2

Administrative Hierarchy of Settlements in India

Hierarchical Level	*Number of Settlements*	*Spacing (km)*	*Population Served (in lakhs)*	*Area Served (sq km)*
National Capital	1	—	6,840	32,80,543
State Capitals	25	428	311	1,49,116
District HQs.	412	100	17	7,962
Tehsil HQs.	2,500	40	2.8	1,250
Block HQs.	502	30	1.4	652
Gram Panchayats	2,00,000	5	0.04	20

Source: R. Ramchandran, *Urbanization and Urban Systems in India*, OUP, New Delhi, 1999, p. 219.

Table 11.2 shows that Christaller's concept differs from the system in India. Theoretically, the ratio between the higher and lower order settlements is expected to be 1:7. But in India it is 1:19 of districts to states. Moreover, the number and spacing between different hierarchical levels is far from the ideal. But as stated below demographic hierarchy in India reveals a different picture.

Demographic Hierarchical Order of Central Places

In India hierarchy of places as recognized in the census of population is popular. Ten categories, as shown in the Table 11.3,

Table 11.3

Demographic Hierarchy of Settlements in India (1981 Census)

Hierarchical Levels (based on Pop.)	*No. of Settlements*	*Pop. Served by each Settlement*	*Area Served by Each Settlement*	*Spacing between Settlements*	*Ratio of Spacing*
1. Metropolitan Cities (one million or more)	12	54,916,000	248,000	535	4.25
2. One-Lakh Cities (1 lakh to 1 million)	204	3,051,000	13,800	126	1.50
3. Intermediate Towns (50,000-99,999)	270	1,356,000	6,140	84	1.58
4. Medium Towns (20,000-49,999)	739	538,000	2,440	53	1.83
5. Towns (10,000-19,999)	2,881	160,000	727	29	1.71
6. Small Towns (5,000-9,999)	7,924	55,000	248	17	2.21
7. Large Villages (2,000-4,999)	46,729	11,215	51	7.7	1.60
8. Villages (1,000-1,999)	93,800	4,320	20	4.8	1.41
9. Small Villages (500-999)	1,34,213	2,298	10	3.4	1.42
10. Hamlets (less than 500)	2,67,493	1,189	5	2.4	—

Notes: 1. Population served by each settlement $= \dfrac{\text{Pop. of India (659 million)}}{\text{No. of settlements in each size-class}}$

2. Area served by each settlement (A) $= \dfrac{\text{Area of India}}{\text{No. of settlements of each size-class}}$

3. Spacing between Settlements (S) $= 1.075\sqrt{A}$

4. Ratio of Spacing

$$(R) = \frac{\text{Spacing of settlements in size-class}}{\text{Spacing of settlements in the immediate lower size-class}}$$

Source: Ramchandran, R., *Urbanization and Urban Systems in India*, 1999.

depict that there is significant relation between population size of a settlement and the centrality of a place – of course, approximately. It bears a close similarity to the theoretical principle of marketing; ratio of spacing of higher order centres to the immediate lower order centres varies from 1:41 to 1:83, which is approximately very near to the theoretical ratio of 1:7. But the computation reveals two cases of exceptions. The major one is related to million-cities which stand apart as primate cities. Another exception is in case of centres with population of 5,000 or more and the level below it. This is perhaps because of rural-urban divide in case of India. Conclusively this much can be inferred that demographically in India hierarchy of settlement system approximately exists at the lower levels of settlements. R.E. Murphy expressed the opinion about Christaller's scheme sufficiently in a balanced tone: "the scheme seems to have value in explaining the distribution of urban centres in certain localities, and with modifications it may eventually be much more widely applicable".[8]

August Lösch and Central Place System[9]

Lösch thesis, *Economics of Location*, first published in 1939, deals with the problem of the location of economic regions. He used the same hexagonal lattices for his theoretical landscape that were used by Christaller. He emphasized like Christaller, that raw materials were to be equally dispersed over a flat plain. But differences would emerge as postulated by Lösch "owing to the forces of concentration brought to play by the possibility of specialization and of the operation of economies of scale". The idea of a hierarchy of settlements in which some settlements provide specialized functions for others, the simple triangular lattice pattern has to be disturbed. Lösch thus developed a form of more sophisticated economic landscape by rearranging and superimposing the various hexagonal systems.

Figure 11.2
Lösch Representation

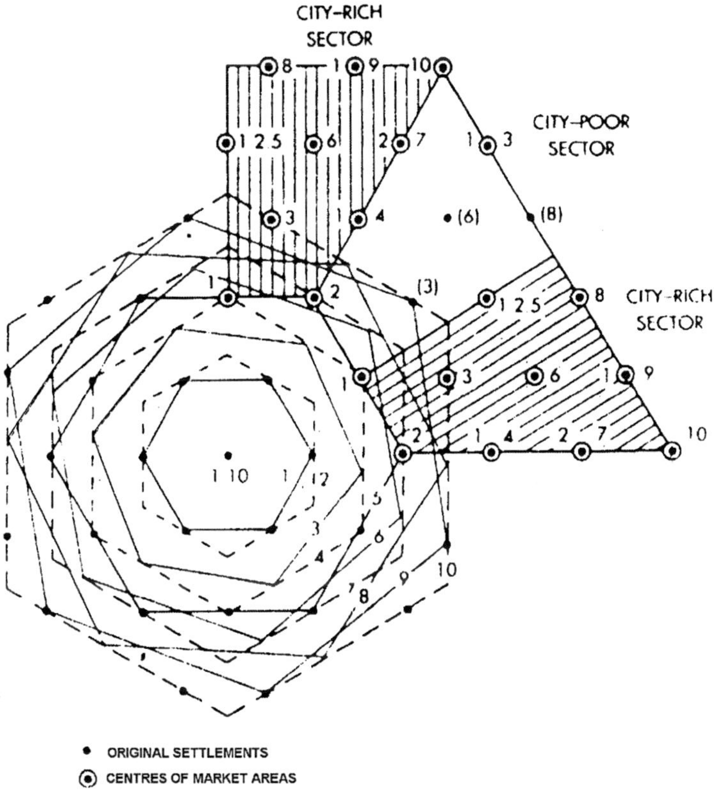

Figure 11.2 shows that central places performing specialist functions are double circles, the dependent places are open circles lying within the field of central place, and by closed circles if lying on the perimeter of each field.

Lösch proceeds and considered the ten smallest areas (Table 11.4 and Figure 11.2). The goods sold and services offered will have a different lower and upper-limit which could only be offered at a variety of different points. If all the meshes are made centring on one point and rotating the various nets about this point, six city-rich and six city-poor areas can be produced with a maximum degree of coincidence (Figure 11.2). The city-rich sectors have relatively many higher order central places, while other six sectors represent centres relatively of poor services.

Table 11.4

The Ten Smallest Possible Market Areas

Area No.	*No. of Settlements Completely Supplied*	*Distances Between Centres*	*Range*
1.	3	$a\sqrt{3}$	a
2.	4	$a\sqrt{4}$	a
3.	7	$a\sqrt{7}$	a
4.	9	$a\sqrt{9}$	$a\sqrt{3}$
5.	12	$a\sqrt{12}$	2a
6.	13	$a\sqrt{13}$	$a\sqrt{3}$
7.	16	$a\sqrt{16}$	2a
8.	19	$a\sqrt{19}$	2a
9.	21	$a\sqrt{21}$	$a\sqrt{7}$
10.	25	$a\sqrt{25}$	$a\sqrt{7}$

Source: After Lösch, *Economics of Location*, 1954.

k-Value of Lösch

Total number of settlements served by each central place is termed as its 'k-value'. Christaller's k-value is three of each central place. His hierarchy consists of a number of definite steps of tiers in which (i) all places in a particular tier are the same size and have the same function, and (ii) all higher-order places contain all the functions of the smaller central places.

But, in contrast, the Löschian hierarchy is far less rigid. It consists of a nearly continuous sequence of centres rather than distinct tiers, so that (i) settlements of the same size need not have the same function, and (ii) larger places need not necessarily have all the functions of the same smaller central places.

Difference between Christaller's and Lösch's Approaches

The major difference between the two approaches is that Lösch regarded the fixed-k assumption as a special limiting case and used all the various hexagonal solutions, both the nine and extensions on the same lines. By superimposing all the various sizes of hexagons on a single point, he rotated all the nets about that point to get six sectors with many and six sectors with few production sites. The rotation produces a strong pattern of variation, both between sectors and with distance from the metropolis, i.e., the demand decreases as the distance of the consumer increases from the point where the goods are offered.

Löschian system, when adjusted for concentration and resource irregularities, yields a pattern more in accord with reality than that of fixed system of Christaller. Vining[10] has attacked the fixed-k concept of Christaller on the grounds that it leads to a 'stepped' size distribution of cities, rather than the continuous distribution actually observed.

Notes

1. Berry, B.J.L., "Research Frontiers in Urban Geography", in Hauser and Schonore (eds.), *The Study of Urbanisation*, John Wily and Sons, N.Y., 1965, p. 403.
2. Christaller, W., *DieZentralen Orte in Sud-deutschland*, Jena, Germany, 1933.
   —, and Baskin, C.W., *A Critique and Translation of W. Christaller's Work*, University of Virginia, 1957.
3. Carol, H., "The Hierarchy of Central Functions within the City", *AAAG*, Vol. 50, 1960, p. 420.
4. Berry, B.J.L. and Garrison, W.L., "Functional Bases of the Central Place Hierarchy", *Eco. Geog.*, Vol. 34, p. 145.

5. Grotewold, A., "Von Thunen in Retrospect", *Eco. Geog.*, Vol. 35, 1959, pp. 346-355.
6. Ullman, "A Theory of Location for Cities", *American Journal of Sociology*, Vol. 46, 1941, p. 858.
7. Ramchandran, R., *Urbanisation and Urban Systems in India,* OUP, New Delhi, 1999, pp. 218-219.
8. Murphy, R.E., *American City: An Urban Geography*, McGraw Hill, N.Y., 1966, p. 81.
9. Lösch, A., *The Economics of Location*, Yale University Press, Newhaven, 1954.
10. Vining, R., "A Description of Certain Spatial Aspects of an Economic System", *Eco. Dev. and Cultural Change*, Vol. 3, 1955, pp. 147-95.

12

Rank-Size Rule

The study of distribution of urban places is of paramount importance in analyzing various urban concepts. Why is a town of specific cadre in terms of population situated there, and what is its relationship with the towns of preceding or succeeding cadres in the area? This question is related with economic as well as various other aspects of human life. Truly speaking, the problem of varying sizes of urban places is the reaction of their nuclei in terms of their functions and organization of the settlement pattern in the region.[1] One of the many conceptual problems in urban geography is to review correlations of city size distributions. Is there any system visible in the distribution of various sizes of urban centres? Do they reveal some kind of rank-size relationship? These problems occur even in a common man's mind and people remain eager to seek their appropriate answers.

Concept of Rank-Size Rule

It is an empirical concept and based on observation. When we look into the various sizes of urban places in an area, it is commonly observed that there are a few large cities, many medium sized and a host of small centres. This trend is universal and can be observed at the national or regional level. In other words, the number of settlements in any region is universally proportional to the size of the settlements.

If all the urban centres of a region are arranged in a descending order by population size, the system reveals a regular relationship between the first-rank city and other urban centres. The second ranked city will have half the size of the primate, the third ranked will have one-third, and the nth ranked will have 1/nth population of the first-rank city. This rank-size relationship may also be mathematically expressed as: $P = \frac{P_1}{(rn)}$, where P is the population of the nth ranked town, and P_1 is the population of the primate or largest city (first-rank) of the region, and (rn) is the rank of that town. Suppose, the primate or first-rank city in the region is having 100,000 population, the 4th rank town, as per rule, will have one-fourth of the population of the first-rank city, i.e., 25,000. This conceptual relationship may be graphically represented on three scales:

1. *Simple log graph*: This will represent a concave upward curve;
2. *Double log graph*: This represents a straight line; and
3. *Log-normal probability graph*: This also represents a straight line.

Development of the Concept

The empirical relationship among distribution of urban places according to their rank of population size was first presented by Falix Auerback in Germany.[2] In USA the same relationship was observed by Lotka.[3] But the concept was fully developed scientifically by Zipf.[4] Central place theory of Christaller had also discussed the size of urban places and their various grades in order to provide goods and services to the consumers of the surrounding complementary area.

The distribution of urban places by their size and rank plotted on a double log graph shows a S-shaped curvilinear trend, but in Western industrial countries it gives a straight line graph. The basic difference between Christaller and Zipf is about types of hierarchy generated by the two systems. Zipf's findings show a smooth relation, while Christaller postulated a stepped and ranked distribution of size classes. Another point which should be borne in mind about the Zipf's rule is that it measures size by population totals and not centrality of central places generated by general and special functions for surrounding areas.

According to Berry and Garrison[5] the two concepts (Central Place and Rank-Size Rule) are compatible even when applied to the same data because when all urban functions are massed together then it is perfectly possible to transform a ranked hierarchical array into a continuous rank-size relation.

Rank-size rule when examined empirically, it failed to convince its validity in the absence of favourable evidences. It is unable to analyze the relationship among urban places spatially. The rule of size and rank actually has no answer about varied functional structure of urban places, and also about their mutual locational pattern in an area. It is because of the incompleteness of the rule that Berry and Garrison have presented location theories of urban places as one of the several alternative schemes to the Zips's concept.[6] Beckmann[7] and Keynon[8] are some of the other thinkers who could analyze to some extent the relationship between functions and size of urban places of various hierarchical order.

Forces Governing Size

Zipf's concept about size and rank is related empirically with the two forces, viz., centripetal and centrifugal in the region. The balance between these two actually gives rise to a sort of regularity in terms of size and number of central places. The forces generating centrifugal from the centre towards outer areas are responsible for producing settlements of small size. The small-sized central places seek their locations around sporadically distributed raw materials. Thus, they are found to be governed by primary economic activities in the area. The dissemination of small-sized settlements is generally the rule where primary economic activities predominate. They are almost at a walking distance from the market town where their basic demands are met and where goods of their common necessities are available.

Contrary to the small-sized settlements, the forces known as 'centripetal' are responsible for developing specialized urban centres because of mobilization of secondary activities and unification of raw materials at the centres. Such centres, of course, because of the process of concentration are larger in size and located at a greater distance. Their location possesses magnetic attraction and is the focus of tertiary economic activities. These activities are essential for consumers who prefer to concentrate on a large settlement itself for utilizing services and goods industries of higher technical standard. Thus, forces of centripetal nature are responsible for the emergence of large sized urban centres. But it is not necessary that these centres create ranking order in terms of their size by population. It is because of this disequilibrium that the Zipf's rule is defunct and empirically unfit. It may be true that the population of cities decline with their lower rank, but not according to Zipf's rigid arithmetical relationship, i.e., the second largest city has one-half of the population of the first largest in a region, the third rank has one-third, and so on.

Studies in Rank-Size Rule

A number of scholars – foreign as well as of India, have examined and utilized the Zipf's rule in analyzing the distribution of urban places in their own universe.[9] Berry and Garrison, Beckmann, Browning and Gibbs, Clark and Evans, Duncan, Haggett and Chorley, King, Stewart, Bourne and

Sinclair, Davies and Lewis, Linsky, Wallerstein, Yantsky, etc., are some of the principal geographers outside India who have analyzed the principle of size and rank of urban places. Among Indians who have given thought about Zipf's analogy are Qazi Ahmad, D. Barai, K.K. Dixit, Mumtaz Khan, K. Lahiri, R.B. Mandal, H. Misra, A.B. Mukerjee, F.T. Moore, D.S. Negi, S.S. Narayanswamy, S.R. Patil, N.B.K. Reddy, P. Roy, O.P. Singh, R.N.P. Sinha, B.L. Sinha, L.N. Verma, H.S. Yadava, M.S. Yadava, B. Zutshi, R. Ramchandran, etc.

Rank-Size Case of India

On a national level in India, the R-S Rule of Zipf does not show positive relationship. Mumbai is the primate city of India and in 1991 it had a population of more than 99 lakh. By virtue of its population Mumbai is the first-rank biggest metropolis. But next lower population city of Delhi had much bigger size than one-half of Mumbai. Not only the second largest city but even the fifth ranking city in India shows much more concentration of people than one-fifth of Mumbai. If we examine in reverse order and estimate the population of the largest first-rank city given the population of the nth rank, then also the R-S case of India seems impractical. Bangalore in 1991 had more than 26.5 lakh population and its rank was seventh. This too confirms the same statement that Indian cities do not show positive relationship as was postulated theoretically by Zipf.

Rank-Size Relationship in States of India

Ramchandran observes that nearly 50 per cent States of India had primacy. In other words, at least 13 out of 25 States show that the population of the premier city is at least three times larger than that of the second city.[10] In these states the Zipf's Rule is ineffective. In Kerala, the three cities of Kochi, Calicut and Trivandrum have nearly the same population size. The same is the case in Madhya Pradesh where Indore, Jabalpur and

Bhopal are almost at the same demographic level. In Bihar and Orissa industrial cities have distorted the Rule of R-S relationship. Thus, it may not be true that the rule is applicable everywhere. Qazi Ahmad has pointed out that the R-S Rule holds good in the case of one-lakh cities in India for 1951 and 1961, when these are plotted on a double log graph against their ranks.[11]

In Rajasthan, Mumtaz Khan has come to the conclusion that excepting the smallest town, all other centres have more population than the expected according to this R-S Rule.[12] This is because of the fact that Jaipur which is the biggest city could not attain the true primate status even after two to three decades of India's Independence. Khan has also pointed out that in the State of Rajasthan, the expected population of urban centres is on the average 29.95 per cent above or below the actual size of the urban centres.

Conclusion

Zipf's R-S Rule is a theoretical concept and rarely would one expect to find an exact empirical fit. It attaches undue importance to the population size of the largest city in a region. It is practically not possible that other urban places of a region should have size descending in order of their nth rank. The population of urban centres, of course, decreases with their rank, but not in an arithmetically rigid manner, as postulated by Zipf's R-S Rule. Berry pointed that a theory or model as of rank and size of urban places has little meaning in the social services since it cannot portray "a direct representation of reality"; it can only be a means of understanding a reality which is highly complex.[13] Stewart too has remarked that "factual truth of the R-S Rule has shown that it applies only to large areas".[14] It embraces wide range of special functions of urban places which transform a ranked hierarchical array into a continuous relation. Truly speaking, the rank-size rule is essentially an economic one and explains the size of settlements in relation to economic activities.

Notes

1. Dickinson, R.E., "The Scope and Status of Urban Geography", in Mayer and Kohn (ed.), *Readings in Urban Geography*, Chicago, 1967, p. 10.
2. Auerback, Felix, "Das Geretz Der Bevol Kanings Kanztration", *Petermann's Geographische Mettalungen*, Vol. 59, Part 1, 1913, pp. 74-76.
3. Clarks, J., *Population Geography*, Pergamon Press, Oxford, 1966.
4. Zipf, G.K., *Human Behaviour and the Principle of Least Effort*, Cambridge, 1949.
   —, *National Unity and Disunity*, Bloomnighon, Illinios, Principia Press, 1941.
5. Berry, B.J.L. and Garrison, W.L., "Alternate Explanations of Urban Rank-Size Relationships", *AAAG*, Vol. 48, 1958, p. 83.
6. *Ibid.*
7. Beckmann, M.J. and McPherson, J.C., "City Size Distribution in a Central Place Hierarchy: An Alternative Approach", *Journal of Regional Science*, Vol. 10, 1970, pp. 25-33.
8. Keynon, J.B., "On the Relationship between Central Function and Size of Place", *AAAG*, Vol. 57, 1967.
9. Some of the Indian authors who have expressed their views on the Zipf's rule are:
   (a) Singh, B.L., "Rank-size Relationship in the Central Place system of Mithila Plain, North Bihar", *N.G.J. of India*, Vol. 31, 1985, pp. 129-46.
   (b) Reddy, N.B.K., "A Comparative Study of the Rank-size Relationship in the Krishna and Godavari Deltas and South Indian States", *N.G.J. of India*, Vol. 15, 1969, pp. 63-90.
10. Ramchandran, R., *Urbanization and Urban Systems in India*, OUP, New Delhi, 1999, p. 202.
11. Ahmad, Q., *Indian Cities: Characteristics and Correlates*, University of Chicago Press, 1965.
12. Khan, M., "Size of Urban Centres in Rajasthan", *Geog. Rev. of India*, Vol. 42, No.1, 1980, pp. 83-87.

13. Berry, B.J.L. and Pred, A., *Central Place Studies: A Bibliography of Theory and Application*, Pennsylvania Regional Science Research Institute, 1965.
14. Stewart, C.T., "The Size and Spacing of Cities', *Geog. Rev.*, Vol. 48, 1958, p. 222.

13

Urban Primacy and Hierarchical System

Concept of Urban Primacy

In a country, generally, many cities and towns carry out urban activities of various orders. Their size too varies and their institutions, service establishments, channels of social and cultural phenomena not only differ in number but also in their intensity to influence people. Out of the many centres designating urban places, one is the largest. It becomes naturally the dominant within the system of towns and cities of the country. Such a dominant city is known as the primate city. Its primacy empowers the urban milieu and the entire urban settlement system of a country revolves around the dominant centre.

The concept of primacy was originally introduced by Jefferson[1] in urban geography who observed in 1939 that the largest city was more than twice than the second ranked city. He also propounded the view that "the primate city was super-eminent not merely in size, but in national influence too". Its dominance as observed by Jefferson was all-round – in spheres of economic, cultural, social and political. This type of dominance of the overall nature by one city is associated with what is sometimes called 'The Great Tradition' or with a 'primary arthogenetic city'. It is actually a city with a regularly developed urban matrix. None has escaped of its influence and its common culture is also being shared by all levels of population.

The concept of primate city as presented by Mark Jefferson was based on the fact that the city is the largest by more than twice than the second ranked city. But, more recently, when the largest city is compared with other cities in the same country it is found that other cities are far larger than one would expect from the rank-size rule. Thus, the concept of primacy has tended to shift from the original definition of Jefferson.[2] Mehta also observed the change and stated that "the concept of primacy differs from the meaning given to it by more recent writers.[3] Jefferson's "hypotheses were stated in a loosely descriptive manner which precludes rigorous testing".[4] In India too the concept of primacy does not correspond with the Jefferson's idea and Mumbai, Delhi and Kolkata fall apart of the underlying spirit of primacy.

Berry[5] considered primacy – a feature of underdeveloped countries. Similarly, El-Shakhs[6] on the basis of the analysis related to 75 countries, has substantiated that primacy and development are closely related. Primacy seems to be at the low-ebb in the primary stages of urban development, in the intermediate stage its level reaches maximum while in the final stage of development the level of primacy again begins to show decline. Haggett is of the opinion that primacy is positively related with strong economic and political forces.[7]

Carol A. Smith has examined primacy against the empirical evidence in Guatemala. She substantiates three situations for urban primacy. The first is colonialism in which the colonial power usually established one dominant centre of control, leaving the rest of the territory in traditional and backward condition. India under the British Rule had Kolkata, and later on Delhi as primate city. The second is export dependency – i.e., primary products or raw-materials were for export via single primate port/city. The third situation has been developed by way of rural collapse and growth of industry in the largest city. This is one of the standard interpretations of urbanward migration and hence growth of the largest city and its elevation to primacy.[8] Smith argues that a process of shift in the city system organization as a part of the transition to capitalism and the transformation of class relationship are responsible for primacy. Free labour is released and encouraged to move to some cities, it is discouraged from entering others, especially provincial cities having their traditional relations intact. Where the attracted labour cannot be given job, a large informal sector is generated to create 'overlarge' or primate cities with their shanty-towns.

Rank-Size Rule and Primacy

According to Haggett, the countries with rank-size of urban system tend to be large, have a long history of urbanization and are economically and politically complex. The developed world generally represents normal rank-size distributions, and primacy does not seem to overshadow; whereas in countries where urbanization processes are smaller then average primate distributions appear. Chase-Dunn[9] attempts to calculate a Standardized Primary Index (SPI) which attempts to express the deviations of city size distribution from the log-normal (rank-size) rule. It is zero when the city size conforms to the R-S rule. When it is positive, the distribution is primate. In case of negative, the distribution is less hierarchical than would be predicted by the log-normal rule. It follows that a primate distribution marked underdevelopment and characterized Western countries at earlier times and the 'Third World' countries at the present. Walters[10] does not support such a simple relationship and expresses that it is the extent to which the system, primarily economic and political, has generated a system of cities at the highest level. The different organizations of city systems within regions or nations also reflect the growth or world capitalist order. There are variations due to economies within the countries. Urban primacy shows a shift due to transition to capitalism and the transformation of class relationships.

Rank-size rule is a changing concept in terms of temporal-spatial dimensions. Brutzkus[11] discussed the change in Tanzania's Dar-es-Salaam, and pointed out that the structural gap between the first ranking and the last ranking town has increased in 1978 in comparison with 1948 situations in terms of population concentration. This shows development in economy and transport linkages took place due to excessive pull of the above attributes in Dar-es-Salaam's environ in respect of other parts of Tanzania. The R-S curve too of urban centres for 1978 was 'S' shaped – a sign of primacy, and there were several steps identified. Harris[12] also suggested in case of the former Soviet Union "steps in R-S curve indicating separate sub-systems of cities or relatively independent regions with little functional integration".

Primacy at India Level

At present, in India, there is no primate city. India being a federal state, the situation does not warrant to give fillip to only one centre agglomerated voluminously leaving far behind other centres. The large areal extent of India, the colonial legacy of the past as well as the disintegration because of the rule of princely states have been some of the major causes disallowing urban primacy. In 1991, the population of Greater Mumbai was more than 12.5 million, and it was the leading metropolis. But, at the same time, Delhi which was the second in rank, had more than 8.4 million people. Thus there was no case of primacy. In 1981, Delhi was the national capital, but it has third rank after

Kolkata and Mumbai, their respective population being 5.7, 8.2 and 9.19 million. This was again not the case of primacy. Even in 2001, Mumbai had about 11.9 million against the second city of Delhi which was having the population of 10.5 million. Since then Delhi has been fastly growing and it is very likely that it will surpass Mumbai in the coming decade. The absence of primacy in India can be held both by political as well as geographical reasons. Geographically its extent in area did not favour centralization of infrastructure –economic, cultural and even social to bring about unitary growth at one-point. India was never a politically unified nation until 1947. Even after five decades of the independence, the country has not come out of crude regionalism and lot of confusion has been going on over sharing the essential resources of water, energy, forests, etc. This is primarily because India is not politically a unitary state. It is partially federal and partially unitary. Each federal state of India is seeking the development of its own prime city. This can be inferred that in India it is only the strong Central political power which would generate primacy. Some efforts have now been made to provide political as well as economic bases for Delhi to see it as a real primate capital of the Indian Union. But around Delhi there have developed a large number of low-index towns, and to some extent they are characterized for commerce and industries. This might be proving a constraint for Delhi's primacy vis-à-vis Mumbai. Delhi is yet to display its dominance. In India, political forces have been divided among various states because of the country's federal set-up. The tendency of normal rank-size distribution is visible at the State level.

Primacy at the State Level

India's vast size possesses quite a many diversities including diversity of language and culture. Reorganization of States (1956) in India is fundamentally language-based which subsequently fostered a regional bias. Each State in India is the representative of its own regional culture. This has ultimately developed a feeling of oneness at the regional level and there has been a tendency to boost a prime centre of culture. Each State in its headquarter could develop a primate city. In 1981, out of 25 states, more than 50 per cent (13 states) had primate cities. After two decades conditions have not changed and in the Census of 1991 and 2001, there were primate cities in one-third of the states of India. It can be said that on the level of entire India rank-size rule does not operate. Nearly all states in the Northern India show absence of primacy. While the larger states like West Bengal, Karnataka, Maharashtra, Tamilnadu, Andhra Pradesh and newly formed states of Jharkhand, Uttaranchal and Chhatisgarh show tendency for primacy.

Kolkata excluding Howrah shows unique example of urban agglomeration which is nearly twenty-five times larger than Asansol, the second largest city. But in 2001 census Howrah alone possessed more than ten lakh population, and it is only one-fourth of the size of Kolkata of forty-five lakh and even more people. Kolkata, Mumbai and Chennai show their primacy even today by the remanants of the colonial rule. The primacy of smaller states of the northeastern sector of India like Sikkim, Manipur, Tripura, Meghalaya and Mizoram is largely due to influx of migrants from various parts of India and Bangladesh. In Madhya Pradesh, Bhopal and in Rajasthan, Jaipur have been moving fast towards primacy, but Indore in M.P. and Jodhpur in Rajasthan have also been following neck-to-neck.

Applicability of the Concept Below State Level

Khan[13] has tested the applicability of the concept of primacy[*] in the districts of Rajasthan and he could identify five levels[14]:

---

* Although the use of the word 'primate city' for the urban centres of the level of district HQ. is inappropriate, yet it has been retained due to its popular usage for the largest urban centre of the region.

(a) Jaipur district shows *very high primacy* (33.903), and the primacy index as calculated is 33 times higher than the lowest order of the district of Jalore(1.010). This is because of the capital city's presence. The district of Jaipur is surrounded by the areas of low categories of the primacy index.

(b) Jodhpur district falls under *high primacy*. The city was formerly the capital of Marwar.

(c) Third category has areas of *medium primacy index*. It includes four isolated districts of Bikaner, Udaipur, Kota and Alwar occupying the four corners of Rajasthan. All the four cities have been the headquarters of the former princely states.

(d) Areas showing *low primacy index* include five districts of Ajmer, Tonk, Bhilwara, Pali and Banswara. Except, Banswara, this forms a belt and is surrounded by categories of very low, medium, high and very high.

Table 13.1

Districtwise Index of Primacy in Rajasthan

District	*Index*	*District*	*Index*
Ajmer	4.173	Jaisalmer	2.025
Alwar	9.134	Jalore	1.010
Banswara	6.569	Jhalawar	1.728
Barmer	1.979	Jhunjhunu	1.218
Bharatpur	2.372	Jodhpur	17.472
Bhilwara	6.344	Kota	8.530
Bikaner	10.497	Nagaur	1.181
Bundi	2.380	Pali	3.769
Chittorgarh	1.525	Sawaimadhopur	1.057
Churu	1.114	Sikar	2.016
Dungarpur	1.663	Sirohi	1.309
Ganganagar	2.059	Tonk	4.315
Jaipur	33.903	Udaipur	8.460

Source: Khem Chand Sharma, "Size and Spacing of Urban Centres in Rajasthan", M.A. Dissertation, 1981, University of Rajasthan, Jaipur.

(e) As many as fifteen districts of Rajasthan fall under the category of very *low primacy index.*

Conclusions

The above classification shows that:

(i) "the proportion of a nation's workforce engaged in agriculture will be positively associated with the degree of primacy of the leading city".[15]

(ii) "...a rapid rate of national population growth will be positively associated with high primacy of the leading city".[16]

(iii) There is no indication that primacy is associated with the level of urbanization.[17]

(iv) Population size and small areal extent show significant primacy.[18]

(v) "... population density of countries is not at all related to the degree to which primacy of urban structure is developed".[19]

The above conclusions are corollaries derived on the basis of the study conducted in case of Rajasthan by rank correlation-coefficient of primacy index[*] with the related variables[**], and the level of significance of the correlations was measured by 't' test.

Finally, this can be stated that in Rajasthan the law of primate city does not hold true, the value (1.93) being less than even half of the primate city. The State is tending towards the rank-size rule rather than primate city. It follows that after India's State reorganization, particularly in case of the various states of Rajasthan, the State as organized is moving steadily

---

* Index of primacy has been calculated by I=p1/p2, where I is the Index of Primcay, P_1 is the population of the First city and P_2 is the population of the Second-rank city.

** Variables considered: (1) Urbanization (by rank), (2) Total population (by rank), (3) Area (by rank), (4) Pop. Density (by rank), and (5) Agricultural Pop. (by rank).

towards the path of progress. However, as Walters comments, "attempts to demonstrate such a simple relationship have been at best inconclusive"[20]. It is also pertinent that the simple contrast of a primate as against a log normal pattern is too rigid. Primacy and log normal curve may vary from region to region under very unusual circumstances.

On the basis of the foregoing it is apparent that the urban system is the decisive factor whether it is primarily economic and political or having different organizations of city systems within regions or nations reflecting the growth of the world capitalist order - core, periphery or semi-periphery. It is because of the urban system that New York, London and Paris have primate position. But there are some countries also which have developed altogether a different system - Brazil, Italy, Australia and Spain are examples - that for one reason or another lack real primate cities. Hoselitz[21] postulated that a hierarchical structuring is indicative of advanced economic development. But others are having different views and advocated that such city system as envisaged by central place theory, if has any meaning other than as a purely static, contrasted situation was proposed in the dominance of the primate city. Calculations have proved that the hierarchy of ten largest cities of the capitalist world is always less hierarchical then the log-normal rule world predict thus, the idea of world system is mistaken, and a better position would be that to consider the globe having many separate urban systems to compare the sizes of the largest cities and primacy ought to be analyzed separately.[22] In this connection two issues are of relevance. The first is the extent to which that system, economic and political, has generated a world system of cities and overriding regional and national boundaries. The second issue is the way to which different organizations of city systems within regions or nations reflect the growth of world capitalist order within the core, periphery or semi-periphery.

Notes

1. Jefferson, M., "The Law of the Primate City", *Geog. Rev.*, Vol. 29, p. 227.
2. Shryock, H. S., et al., *The Methods and Materials of Demography*, New York, 1976, p. 101.
3. Mehta, S.K., "Some Demographic and Economic Correlates of Primate Cities: A Case for Re-evaluation", *Demography*, Vol. 7, 1964, Footnote 3, reprinted in Breese, G. (ed.), *The City in Newly Developing Countries*, Prentice Hall, 1969.
4. Linsky, A.S., "Some Generalizations Concerning Primate Cities", *AAAG*, Vol. 55, 1965, p. 506.
5. Berry, B.J.L., "City Size Distributions and Economic Development", *Economic Development and Cultural Change*, Vol. 9, 1961 pp. 573-587.
6. El-Shakhs, S., "Development, Primacy and Systems of Cities", *Journal of Developing Areas*, Vol. 7, 1972, pp. 11-36.
7. Haggett, P., *Geography: A Modern Synthesis*, Harper and Row, N.Y., 1979.
8. Smith, C. A., (a) *Theories and Measures of Urban Primacy: A Critique.*
   (b) "Class relations and urbanization in Guatemala: towards an alternative theory of urban primacy", in Timberlake, M. (ed.), *Urbanization in the World Economy*, Orlando, Flo: Academic Press, 1985, Chapters 6 and 7.
9. Chase-Dunn, C.K., "The System of World Cities", (800-1975), in Timberlake, M., Ibid., pp. 269-92, 1985, Quoted from Carter's *The Study of Urban Geography*, London, 1995, pp. 38-58.
10. Walters, P.B., "System of Cities and Urban Primacy: Problems of Definition and Measurement", in Timberlake, M., Ibid., Chapter 5., pp. 63-85, 1985.
11. Brutzkus, E., "Centralized versus De-centralized Pattern of Urbanization in Developing Countries", in *Soc. Geografie*, Vol. 64, pp. 11-23.
12. Harris, C.D., *Cities of the Soviet Union*, Chicago, 1970.
13. Khan, M., "The Law of the Primate City: Re-examined in Rajasthan", *The Geographer*, Vol. 26, pp. 35-42, 1979.
14. Class-interval prepared on the technique suggested by P. Toyne and P.T. Newby, *Techniques in Human Geography*, London, Macmillan, 1971, pp. 85-89.
15. Linsky, A.S., op. cit.

16. Ibid.
17. Mehta, S.K., op. cit., p. 305.
18. Ibid., p. 307.
19. Ibid., p. 306.
20. Walters, P.B., op. cit., p.73.
21 Hoselitz, B., "Generative and Parasitic Cities", *Economic Development and Cultural Change*, Vol. 3, p. 278, 1955.
22. Chase-Dunn, op. cit., p. 275.

14

Metropolises and Growth Poles

Metropolis under the present circumstances of population boom, forms an important part of the study of urban geography of a country. It forms a special category of urban agglomeration. It differs more from a 'capital' city, and also from 'conurbation'. But metropolis has qualities, magnet-like, to become in the real sense of the meaning, 'metro' which literally means 'very large'. Metropolis acts as a magnet and becomes dinosaur. The power of attraction in a metropolis is very strong, even stronger than a capital city. The best example is Paris. Its incomparable influence on the whole world would have been impossible had it remained the small capital of the Ile-de-France instead of having, even at the time of Louis XIV, a population of 500,000 in a country where no other towns reached a population of 100,000.

Concept of Metropolitan Area

For most of us, the word 'metropolis' suggests only the largest cities. But we are, in this way, facing with the same problem as with the definition of a town. Population alone cannot be a reliable and correct determinant of the status of a metropolis.

The criterion of function must be accompanied by one of size. It would be erroneous to think about terms like 'metropolitanism' and 'metropolitization', chiefly in connection with such places as New York, Chicago, and Los Angeles. Generally, the term 'metropolis' more commonly is used to indicate a place of large enough size serving as a regional capital. But this is not true, and there is by no means full accord on its such meaning. In USA, where it is supposed to be used widely, metropolise is being defined in the Bureau of the Census Publications.[1] This has been made clear in the census that data for an incorporated city alone generally do not convey the reality of the entire urban story. The phenomenon is much more related than the central incorporated city to an urban area or better expressed as metropolitan area.

At first, the 'metropolitan district' was used in 1910 in the Census of Population carrying a central city of 50,000 or more population and all adjacent minor civil divisions having a population density of 150 or more persons per square mile. By 1940, the concept of the metropolitan district had lost favour because the possibilities of correlating local data with district data were limited. Besides this, the metropolitan district did not truly represent social and economic integration with the central city. Therefore, a new areal unit, the standard metropolitan area, came into vogue in 1949. It was defined as made up of counties instead of minor civil divisions. It was succeeded by the 'standard metropolitan statistical area' (SMSA). It is defined below as it existed in 1970:

1. A contiguous county will be included in an SMSA if:
   (a) at least 75 per cent of the resident labour force in the county is in non-agricultural labour sector; and
   (b) at least 30 per cent of the employed workers living in the county work in the central county or counties of the area.
2. A contiguous county which dose not meet the foregoing requirements will be included in an SMSA if at least 75 per

cent of the resident labour force is non-agricultural and meets two of the following additional criteria of metropolitan character and one of the following criteria of integration:

(i) *Criteria of Metropolitan Character*

(a) At least 25 per cent of the population is urban.

(b) The county had an increase of at least 15 per cent in total population during the period covered by the most recent two censuses.

(c) The county has a population density of at least 50 persons per square mile.

(ii) *Criteria of Integration*

(a) A least 15 per cent of the employed workers living in the county work in the central county or counties of the area, or

(b) The number of people working in the county who live in the central county or counties of the area is equal to at least 15 per cent of the employed workers living in the county, or

(c) The sum of the number of workers commuting to and from the central county or counties is equal to at least 20 per cent of the employed workers living in the county.

As stated above it seems that metropolis is primarily a demographic concept. But this may be emphasized once again that metropolis is much more than an agglomeration. It possesses distinct character and functions which are not likely to be found either in agglomeration or in conurbation. In metropolitan cities each function has benefited from the conditions which brought about the other functions and has found reasons for developing there itself. There the power of attraction make them bigger and bigger, and consequently enormity of their size increases their power of attraction. This is happening in Mumbai which has grown tremendously during

1901-91 by 1000 times. In the real sense of the term, Mumbai's population is being exploded and estimated in 2001 more than 14 million and Delhi too had more than 10 million. Nonetheless, significant is the role of their multifarious functions. Mumbai is simultaneously an international port, one of the biggest commercial marts, an important industrial node of the country and a cosmopolitan centre. Delhi owes its position primarily to its political role as capital of the federated India, to commerce, industry, education and a place for tourists from all over the world.

After analyzing the conditions of this development, it may be observed that out of 300 cities with population over one million in the world (1991), more than 50 per cent are sea ports (including inland ports of Chicago and Detroit). In reality, ports possess immense potentials to concentrate functions, because, on the one hand, they are by definition commercial places, and on the other, they attract manufacturing industries by the materials of all sorts which they receive from various parts of the country. Even in the days of the ancient Mediterranean civilizations, and also, during the colonial times, the great commercial connections were then maritime links with the metropolis. The eastern and western sides of the Atlantic in Europe and America therefore, have great ports. Metropolitan cities acquire a sort of permanence and remain evergreen over time. Think of Athens and Rome, Paris and London, Tokyo and Shanghai, Delhi and Mumbai – they all possess rich historic legacy in their ever flourishing life-span. These gigantic towns have a strange power, a sort of predestination, defying time, and finding in every age and in every civilization a new reason to prosper.[2]

Cartographic Missing Link in SMSA

The size of a particular city depends on the way it is defined. In every country legal city is incorporated and its population is given generally in the census for its legal area. The corporate city, thus has a definite legal entity. In USA the Census Bureau also provides data for urbanized area, or better expressed, physical city and for SMSA or metropolitan community. It is rather erroneous and non-geographic to include whole counties which have substantial sections with entirely agricultural and sparsely settled forest or desert areas. In case of Ontario (California), for example, SMSA has devoured several small cities by its vast expanses of desert wasteland.

Metropolitan Sprawl

Another interesting point to make is about the phenomenon of sprawl in case of SMSA. It evokes a pattern of movement. Gradually, on the north-eastern sea-board of USA, the "super metropolitan character became a reality of this vast area". This has been termed by Gottmann by a special name of 'megalopolis'. It is actually the blend of metropolis and small town. Empirical observations have given him insight of the problem, and thus, appeared the classical essay of Gottmann, "Urban Sprawl and its Ramifications".[3] City growth thus is going to keep going on and on. Metropolitan sprawl in India has displayed its negative role as is visible in case of Delhi and Kanpur. Kolkata and Mumbai too are no exception. In these metropolitan areas terrible sprawling with their inadequate transportation facilities, polluted air and questionable water, ugly or monotonous suburban developments, numerous slums and blighted sectors infested with poverty and crimes have made the living a 'hell' in its real sense. Inspite of pathogenic conditions of metropolitan cities in various parts of the world, people have lust for them. These are centres of innovation, and with modern communication, our culture has become almost metro-oriented. Maximum opportunity in the metropolitan areas although produces immense constraints for smooth life, yet people have become addict in facing them, and they do not let the opportunity go unavailed. The larger the city, the greater the number and diversity of opportunity. Nearly hundred families from the cities of Rajasthan were interrogated about their children's prospective for future job placement. As many as 75 per cent replied and indicated the choice for Ahmedabad, Mumbai and Bangalore. Thus, cities everywhere will continue to grow and the urban sprawl will expand at an increasing rate. Increasing numbers of people will be oriented in their way of life to the largest cities and more cities will attain large size. In India at the time of Independence, Delhi's decadal growth (from 1941 to 1951) was 50 per cent and since 1951, the metropolitan Delhi has been increasing by leaps and bounds. Its population in 1961 was 2.35 million and in 1991 it grew to 8.42 million. In 2001, it rose to about 10 million. Delhi began to sprawl in all directions. Its metropolitan region is closely linked with the urban core of Ghaziabad in U.P., Faridabad and Gurgaon in Haryana and Narela urban communities of Delhi. Kolkata too has expanded enormously and in 1991 census, Greater Kolkata had a population of 10.9 million which rose to 12.5 million in 2001. In 1991 the density of population rose to 59,000 persons per sq. km from 10,085 persons in 1941. The rapid growth of Kolkata has been due to heavy influx of migrants, industrial labour and displaced persons from Bangladesh.

B.J.L. Berry has discussed factor-analysis to explain growth of metropolitan areas of the USA. The conclusions derived from Berry's exercise suggest that if the factors are uncorrelated then the economic base of urban centres tends to act independently of other urban structural features. Metropolises lose distinction in economic specialization and possess broader socio-economic dimensions. But the distinctive towns of specialized economic bases are small and unimportant.[4] Gugler has expressed that in developed countries growth of metropolises bringing urbanization has been largely due to technological progress transforming the occupational structure. But in underdeveloped countries it has been largely a product of demographic evolution. Third world metropolitan cities are over saturated "by an excess of labour with limited skills".[5] This, in turn has given impetus for under employment in most of the million-cities and those fully employed may be labelled as 'misemployed'.

Nature of Metropolis in India

In the first quarter of the 20th century Kolkata, Mumbai and Chennai were the premier urban centres. Their commercial supremacy along with railway transport had enough to support their status. These largest urban centres of the country had massive Roman style buildings used as administrative institutions reflecting alien culture. But the indigenous residential areas were haphazardly crowded. It was during the post-independence period that million-cities appeared. Since 1951, considerable urban growth has been witnessed around the million-cities. Around Delhi, the metropolitan area came into existence with the amalgamation of the standard urban areas of Ghaziabad, Faridabad and Gurgaon. But the phenomenon of this sort took place in the case of only a few of million-cities.

The Census recognizes the term 'metropolitan area' for places with a population of a million or more. India had 20 cities with a population of more than 1.5 million or more in 1991, whereas metropolises of one or more million people are 23 in number.* In 2001, Greater Mumbai and Delhi were

---

* 1. Greater Mumbai (12.57m), 2. Kolkata (10.91m), 3. Delhi (8.37m), 4. Chennai (5.36m), 5. Bangalore (4.08m), 6. Hyderabad (4.28m), 7. Ahmedabad (3.29m), 8. Kanpur (2.11m), 9. Pune (2.48m), 10. Nagpur (1.66m), 11. Lucknow (1.64m), 12. Jaipur (1.51m), 13. Surat (1.51m), 14. Kochi (1.13m), 15. Coimbatore (1.13m), 16. Vadodara (1.11m), 17. Indore (1.10m), 18. Patna (1.098m), 19. Madurai (1.093m), 20. Bhopal (1.06m), 21. Vishakhapatnam (1.05m), 22. Varanasi (1.02m) and 23. Ludhiana (1.01m).

having a little difference in their population and very likely in near future Delhi being the national capital may surpass Mumbai.

Spatial patterns of metropolitan areas have considerable significance in their growth and they deserve attention for urban geographers. The four principal metropolises account for the absence of million-cities in a number of states. Delhi has its shadow over Jammu & Kashmir, Punjab, Himachal Pradesh and Haryana. Kolkata has influenced the states of Bihar and Orissa. Kerala comes under the shadow of Chennai.

Some eight metropolises are located on the banks of the rivers for the reasons of supply of water for industrial establishments and also for providing water for irrigation to their surrounding areas. Their riverside location has been also important strategically and Delhi, Kolkata, Kanpur and Varanasi have been important during medieval and modern era turmoils in history. Mumbai, Chennai, Kolkata, Vishakhapatnam and Surat have been significant in their location on sea coast having their trade relations with the countries of the western hemisphere and also with China and south-east Asian islands from very ancient times. Most of the metropolitan areas are best equipped with rail-road transportation. The railways were aligned to connect these even before their existence. The railways followed the ancient trade routes and integrated various parts of the country through the metropolises. Mumbai, Ahmedabad, Kolkata, Chennai and Delhi through their rail networks have joined the country's east-west and north-south corridors, enhancing their economic and cultural ties which have been advantageous for the unity of federal states. The Mumbai-Kolkata axis has emerged as a major corridor on which are lying urban industrial cities of the national level.

Metropolises play their role in determining the 'urban system'. In India, the urban system primarily is rotated around four principal metro areas, of Mumbai, Delhi, Kolkata and Chennai. Some of the states' urban systems show single-nucleus independence. Rajasthan, Haryana, West Bengal, Kerala had one metro city each as per 1991 census. The impact of metro culture is being felt in these states administratively and economically around the nucleus only while the areas which are farther and even farthest from the metro city remain affected by much lesser degree. Nonetheless the significance of metro city cannot be totally ruled out because in these states, metro cities are less like capitals and possess close political links.

Urban agglomerations have also their close relationship with the metropolitan areas in India. Actually 'town group' forms an agglomeration, and in India since 1971, urban agglomeration came into vogue instead of 'town group'. The Kolkata metropolitan areas is the strongest having more than 120 urban units. Out of these nearly 25 possess population of more than a lakh. Other metro cities which have shown the trend of agglomerations are Delhi, Bangalore, Chennai and Ahmedabad. The larger the city, the greater attraction it possesses to agglomerate surrounding urban centres. But the phenomenon of agglomeration has given rise to spatial problems associated with slums, squatters including housing, water, electricity, transportation and pollution.

Metropolitan regions are based on the aforesaid characteristics in India. Primary region is governed by the principal metro cities of India. Kolkata, Mumbai and Chennai have been under the colonial rule. They have been playing significant role in the country's economic, social and cultural spheres since the beginning of the 19th century. They command their influence on several states and have their impact over areas far and wide covering most of the northern, southern and eastern India. North-western India has been under the sway of Delhi. The entire country of India politically is being integrated through Delhi. But Kolkata, Mumbai and Chennai were leading commercial and industrial metro port cities, and are still at the top of the country's urban scene. Thus, four major regions under the command of principal cities of metropolitan status

Figure 14.1
Map Showing Metropolitan Regions

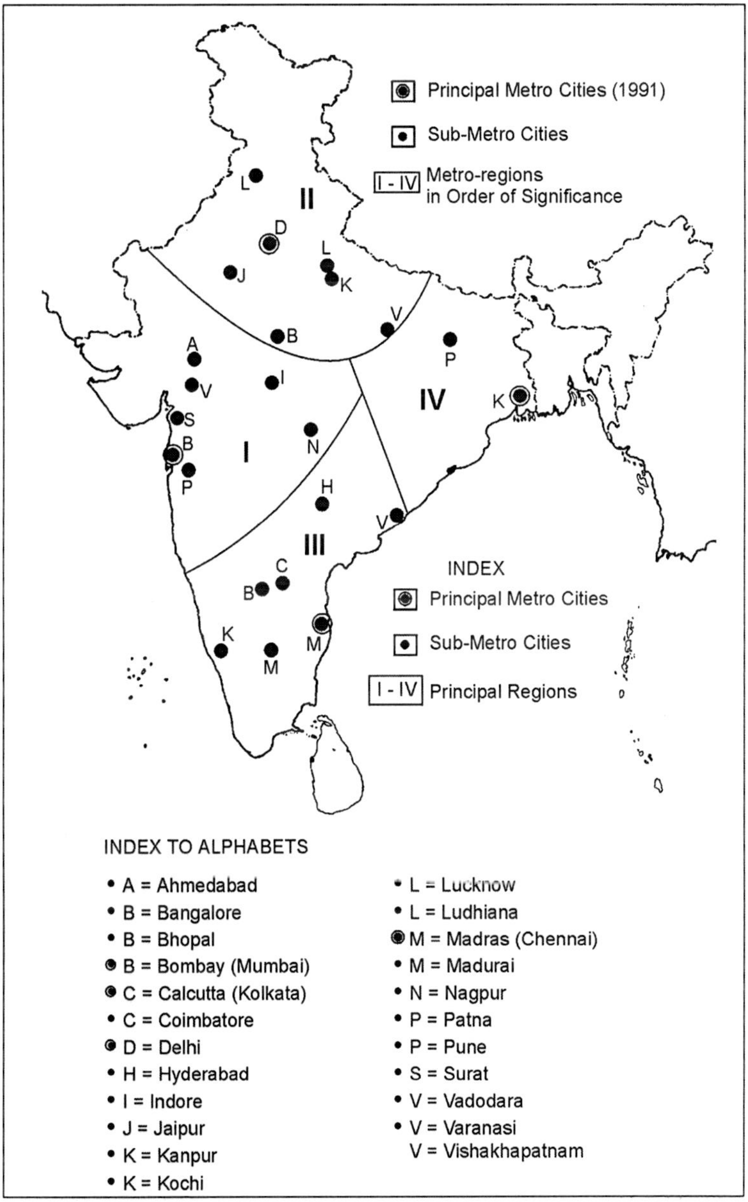

may be (a) Kolkata bound eastern section, (b) Mumbai bound the western section, (c) Chennai dominated the southern parts, and (d) Delhi region controlling the western Uttar Pradesh, Himachal Pradesh, Uttaranchal, Punjab, J&K, Haryana and the northern half of both Rajasthan and Madhya Pradesh (Figure 14.1).

Within the principal metropolitan region after tremendous economic growth and population increase during the last three decades sub-metropolitan areas have appeared. Recently with the development of economy there has been tremendous increase in the population of major cities and the number of metro cities rose from 12 in 1981 to 23 in 2001. The change in economy as well as in administrative status because of the state re-organization and also with exodus of people from rural areas there has been emergence of sub-metropolitan centres (Figure 14.1). Some eight centres had their place even in 1981, but eleven new centres attained the status of sub-metro cities under the command of principal four metropolitan areas (see Table 14.1 below).

Table 14.1
Showing Metropolitan Regions

Principal Regions		*Sub-Metro Regions*	
		(By 1981)	*(By 2001)*
I	Mumbai	Pune, Ahmedabad, Nagpur	Surat, Vadodara, Indore
II	Delhi	Kanpur, Jaipur, Lucknow	Ludhiana, Varanasi, Bhopal
III	Kolkata	-	Patna
IV	Chennai	Bangalore	Vishakhapatnam, Kochi, Coimbatore, Madurai, Hyderabad

Composition and Basic Structure of Metro Regions in India

The Delhi region has under its influences the states of J&K, Himachal Pradesh, Punjab, Haryana and northern parts of the states of Rajasthan and M.P. It has also under its sway the western parts of U.P. and the middle Ganga plains. The position of Delhi as the national capital has virtually its impact over whole of India.

The Mumbai region covers almost the entire western section lying between Rajasthan and Kerala. Besides the two states of Maharashtra and Gujarat, it includes Goa and the union territory of Daman and Diu. The southwestern part of M.P. and Indore also look towards Mumbai and are its clientele.

The Chennai metro region has its command over the states of Andhra Pradesh, Tamilnadu, Karnataka and Kerala. Besides these, the southwestern part of Orissa and south-eastern-most corner of M.P. also fall under its limits.

The Kolkata region encompasses the north-eastern states of India including Assam, Meghalaya, Nagaland, Arunachal Pradesh, Tripura, Manipur and Mizoram. Bihar, Orissa and Sikkim are also under the influence of Kolkata region.

This may be understood that the regional limits of the four principal metropolitan areas are only broad generalization and must not be taken for granted objectively.

Ramachandran has taken into account some of the basic attributes of the four metro regions.[6] He considers that Kolkata (formerly Calcutta) is the oldest and most important in India. But recently the Kolkata metropolitan region has shown decline in its economic prosperity. Mumbai, according to him possesses number of distinct cultural regions besides its own Konkan, Gujarat, Pune and Nagpur are its sub-regions and represent the distinctive culture of Saurashtra, Maharashtra and Vidarbha respectively. Delhi has its sway over far and wide areas like Kanpur and Lucknow in U.P., Jaipur in Rajasthan and Bhopal in M.P. The Chennai region has important metropolises of Bangalore, Coimbatore, Hyderabad, Kochi and Vishakhapatnam – all them being economically and culturally significant sub-metro regions of the southern India.

Future Prospects

The quality of life in the metropolitan cities of India has deteriorated steadily over several decades with their ill and haphazard extension, unplanned construction pitted against aging infrastructure and decaying civic institutions. On the contrary urban areas in the neighbourhood of India like Singapore, Hong Kong and Shanghai have recently developed skyscrapers and gleaming shopping malls. In these metropolises, commercial areas have been rejuvenated completely. India has a glorious ancient past and possesses invaluable architectural heritage which can be reshaped, rejuvenated and given the new-look befitting for modern metropolis. Now, there is an opportunity for Indian metropolises to relieve them of overcrowding and dilapidated structures.[7] S. Sanyal of Singapore proposes some steps to regenerate the metropolitan scene. One device is to 'pedestrianize' whole areas and utilize in the best way the traffic-free spaces to give place for institutions of all sorts to meet the 'mod-way' of life but not overlooking our soil-rooted cultural values. Another step for action is to continue using the buildings for their original purpose but steadily update the usage. Sanyal stressed over the point that this is not just applicable to the four metropolitan cities but a myriad of smaller towns across India – not just in case of forts and palaces of the pre-princely states. The main thing is to create a framework to provide incentive for the process of urban restoration.

Growth Centres

Need and Meaning

In India, people of all status and of all areas are not equally benefited by spatial opportunities. This is because of the fact that economic opportunities along with distribution of resources are generally restricted to large cities and towns.

Although India is a country of villages but paradoxically villages have been most neglected as far as facilities for life are concerned and rural areas are devoid of opportunities for development. Plans and programmes and their implementations are generally oriented towards only a few privileged sectors of communities, and areas which actually are in need for assistance remain neglected. There is need for ameliorating the condition of the downtrodden in backward areas where scheduled tribes and scheduled castes as well as people living below poverty line form a considerable size of the population of villages and even small towns. These settlements have least accessibility with the areas where opportunities may be available and do not possess linkages either with towns or large villages where the required services may be utilized within their means based on cost-benefit principal. These circumstances draw our attention to rethink about spatial distribution of centres and the nature and degree of amenities and services available there. There is also a need for their re-alignment and linking them to the areas where need is imminent.

Growth Centres Defined

Within a region or some particular areas on a continuum basis such centres are located or aligned which could provide opportunities for development to all sections of people of the areas associated. These centres are known as centres for development or 'growth centres'. Growth centre has its own area of influence or hinterland. The size of hinterland is based on the degree of specialization of a growth centre. The nuclei or central settlements within a region which provide essential services and opportunities for growth around their respective areas in a successive manner are 'growth centres'. There is hierarchy among the settlements in a region for their functional process, and dependent villages are linked by service villages, and service villages are associated with growth centres. They all form a network around the regional nucleus.[8]

Figure 14.2
Czechoslovakia Settlement

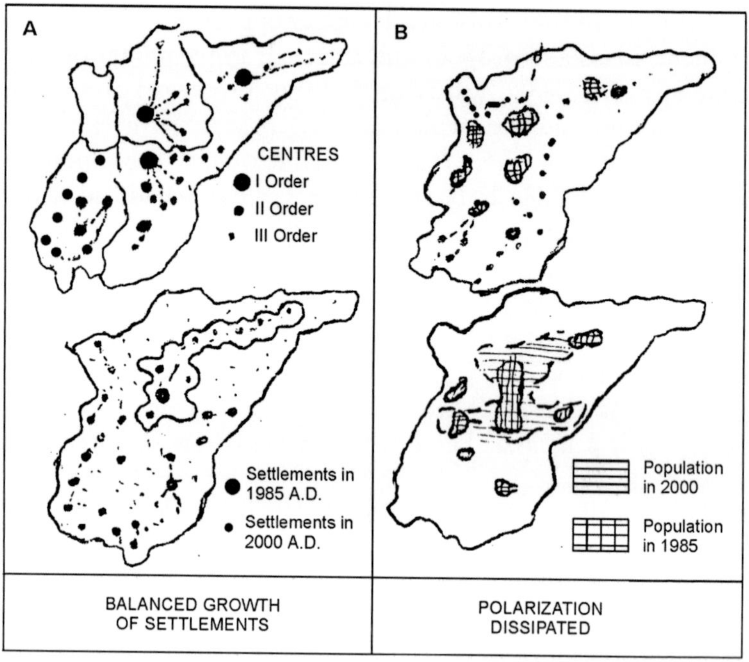

Each growth centre is equipped with its own special infrastructure. This is related to key service institutions providing amenities and services like health, education, administration, community life, transport, communication and marketing. Amenities including water and electricity, irrigation, agricultural implements and seeds, manures and labour also become part of resources available at growth centres. Growth centres to a sufficient extent provide a bridge between a small village and a large town or even a metropolis.

Application of the Concept of Growth Centres

An alternative settlement structure can be suggested for the maximum growth of an area by means of realignment of centres of growth in view of the prospective population increase and new opportunities of growth. A case of Czechoslovakia[9] presented by Imrich Jankovich reveals the role of growth pole and counter-magnet in the alternative settlement structure of the country (Figure 14.2).

The map (Figure 14.2) shows in its pattern (A) projects of the overall and balanced growth, and in its (B) part, polarization is dissipated by counter-magnets. The counter-magnets

Figure 14.3
Balanced Growth and Polarization of Towns

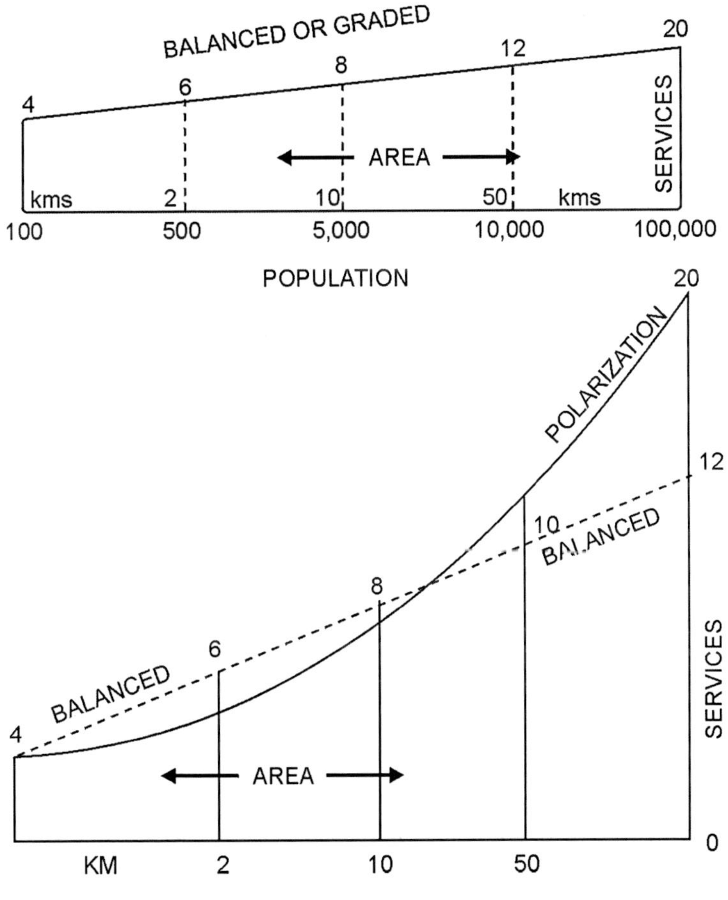

are growth centres realigned to meet the requirements in the various parts of the region. Their functions vary as per meeting the prospective development of the areas in question (Figure 14.3).

The alternative suggested in (A) part of the Figure 14.2 is based on the Christaller's central-place system. It shows the static relationship to achieve the balanced growth in the region. But the alternative in (B) part has different objective than (A), and it is based on the ever growing prospects of the development. The prospective development can be achieved by realignment and changing the status and number of settlements.

In India, settlement realignment[10] was proposed by M. Alam for the urban system of Andhra Pradesh in 1974. He suggested the diversified development against the centralized urban agglomeration. Alam suggested that metropolises may be dissipated for realignment by regional modes which may be proved counter-magnets. In other words, for sustainable growth their decentralized realignment is a necessity. This may be useful for dispersal of economic activities and equitable distribution of potential resources among the principal towns of the region. In Figure 14.4 (A) and (B) centralized and decentralized patterns of growth are shown of the Rayalaseema (Andhra Pradesh).

In India, four principal metropolitan areas had more than 26 million population in 1991 and 20 cities, each one having 1.5 million or more population. Such a polarization had been considered uncontrollable by Bharadwaj. He was of the opinion to decongest some large cities by providing for the overspilling population in satellite and new towns specially constructed for the purpose.[11] This would be beneficial ecologically also. Small towns in form of growth centres would ease the problem because they might make environment of emerging metropolises worthy of living comfortably. Under present circumstances of growing metropolises it is the need of hour to establish counter-magnets against giant urban centres to

Figure 14.4
Rayalaseema

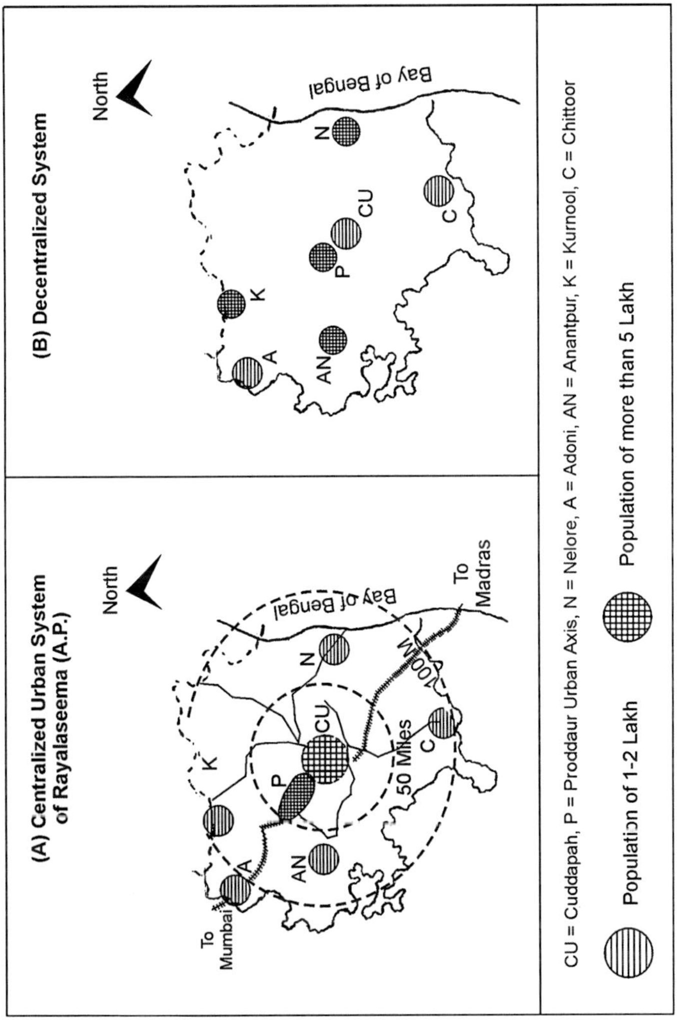

control them without further delay, otherwise their deterioration would make urban life a 'hell' in the real sense of the term. "One can't directly interfere with urban growth. But what we can do is to feed inputs into other parts of the system so as to create counter-magnets and a balanced urban structure".[12]

Notes

1. U.S. Bureau of the Census. Census of Population, 1970.
2. Beaujeu-Garnier, J. and Chabot, G., *Urban Geography*, Longmans, 1967, p. 203.
3. Gottmann, J. and Harper, R.A. (eds.), *Metropolis on the Move*, John Wiley and Sons, N.Y., 1967.
4. Berry, B.J.L., "Latent Structure of the American Urban System", in Berry, B.J.L. (ed.), *City Classification Hand Book*, John Wiley, N.Y., 1972, pp. 11-60.
5. Gugler, J. (ed.), *The Urbanization of the Third World*, Oxford University Press, 1988.
6. Ramchandran, R., *Urbanization and Urban System in India*, OUP, New Delhi, 1999, pp. 284-286.
7. Sanyal, Sanjeev, "Hope in the Cities", *Times of India*, New Delhi, January 12, 2004.
8. Sen, L.K., et al., *Planning Rural Growth Centres for Integrated Area Development,* National Institute of Community Development, Hyderabad, 1971.
9. Jankovich, I., "Alternative Settlement, Structures: Central Czecholovakia", *Ekistics*, Vol. 34, December 1975, Athens, pp. 408-409.
10. Alam, S. Manzoor, "A Note on the Realignment, of the Urban System of Andhra Pradesh", in Misra, V.C. (ed.), *Essays in Applied Geography*, University of Sagar, 1976, pp. 177-185.
11. Bharadwaj, R.K., *Urban Development in India*, National, Delhi, 1974, p. 44.
12. Correa, C. M., "Patterns of Urban Growth", *Ekistics*, Vol. 34, 1975, p. 434.

15

Urban Problems

Water: Problem of Immediate Concern

Everywhere cities have grown both in size and considerable population; especially large cities like metropolises have grown by leaps and bounds. In the countries of the Third World rate of increase per annum is more than 3.5 per cent. World's urban population has gone up from 300 million to more than 4 billion during the last four decades. The tremendous increase of cities has given rise to number of problems like the lack of essential amenities of life. Acute among the various problems, water problem in cities recently has become very serious. As many as two billion people do not have ready access to clean water. Nearly three billion people have no sanitation facilities. Six thousand children die every week due to consumption of contaminated water. Fresh potable water is going to be so scarce over the coming decades that it is being predicted that the next world war would not be over territory or politics, but water!

Water is one of the major problems of urbanization. No town can exist without it. Both its quality and quantity are important and it has no substitute. Water is necessary both for human consumption and for industrial use. People in Los Angeles (California) have to go very far for its supply, and in India too some of the cities meet their water supplies from the sources which are as far as 100 miles. Lake City of Udaipur depends on its supply of water from sources situated nearly 50 kilometres ahead of the main city. In some areas there has been inter-state struggles for water. In USA the struggle between New Jersey and New York for the use of the Delaware river went up to the Supreme Court.[1] In India too Andhra Pradesh, Tamilnadu and Karnataka have been fighting over the use of Krishna river water. Narmada Dam is also an issue on differences among Gujarat, Madhya Pradesh and Maharashtra and the project of Sardar Sarovar struggle is under the Supreme Court for seeking the settlement over the issue of utilization of water. In Great Britain, Liverpool had lot of opposition in Wales over construction of reservoirs.

Our Requirements

The requirements of water vary tremendously. A normal figure in India's metropolitan cities estimates between 150-200 litres per person per day. The industrial use of water is also not the same everywhere and it varies according to the industrial base of a city. According to a survey report published in *India Today* (9 June, 2003) while 12 major cities each require 14,000 million litres of water a day, they get only 10,000 mlt. Mumbai is facing everyday a shortfall of 4,000 mlt. This has made life of the people there almost like hell.

Nearly 90 per cent of the water required for irrigation is met from groundwater resources and the rest of 7 per cent and 3 per cent the country spends for industrial and domestic purposes, respectively.

Repercussions

Rapid pace of urbanization in India has led to drying up of traditional water sources like tanks and lakes. In Bangalore, for example, out of 262 tanks, about 181 have dried up. In South Delhi, tube wells are now dug routinely at a depth of over 200 metres and everyday the level is going down. Groundwater levels of over country have plunged in more than 300 districts. The Ministry of Water Resources estimates that the demand of water in top 35 cities including metros of our country is expected to double to 12,906 million cubic metres (mcm) as the population in these cities shoots up from 107 million today to 202 million in 2021, while water availability stays at the 2001 level.[2] It seems that after a period of 20 years, eleven river basins of our country including the Ganges will be facing huge deficit, threatening 900 million lives. Tourist city of Jaipur in Rajasthan in the coming five years' period will be consuming water just the double amount what is consumed today. The sources are going from bad to worse and, the consequences would be drastic.

Apathy Towards the Capital City

In the metropolis Delhi which is the capital also, water has become a serious problem. In fact, in and around the capital the onslaught on the existing water bodies is continuing and the mandatory rule for water harvesting is not yet implemented. Major sources of drinking water are dying due to urbanization, illegal encroachment and also pollution. According to the Delhi Development Authority (DDA), there were 102 water bodies in the capital. But now it is maintaining only 22. Eighty of the water bodies were lost because of the carelessness of authorities. The area of Bhalswa lake near Jehangirpuri was 44 hectares which is now spread only in 22 hectares. The localities in South Delhi have been facing acute water shortage. But contrary to the grievances of the people, huge 'malls' and other commercial complexes are coming up in Vasant Kunj which would make the problem of shortage of water go out of control. Massive construction work will only be adversely affecting the green belt and water harvesting areas. The water table in the area is going down and would be continuing to go further below the present level because of the cutting of the trees all around illegally. Water conservation laws are either being flouted or not implemented even though the directives of the Supreme Court were there to implement strictly.[3] New building have been coming up without having water harvesting plant and also without recycling process. Serious efforts have also not been done to preserve the green belt around Badkal lake near Faridabad which is a tourist spot. The World Bank granted a loan of 300 million dollars for afforestation to keep the water-bodies intact and also to maintain the underground water level around the lake area.[4] It is disheartening and to the dismay of the people that the sanctioned amount has not been used.

Impact of Poor Water Quality

The World Bank and WHO have estimated that in India 21 per cent of all communicable diseases are related with poor quality of water.[5] The specific diseases are diarrhoea, trachoma, intestinal worms, hepatitis and the 'tropical cluster' of diseases. It is estimated that every year 1.5 million children under 5 years, die in India of water-related diseases. The following Table 15.1, makes it clear that enough of burden, about 30.5 million of DALYs (Disability Adjusted Life Years), has to be born in India because of water-related diseases.

Table 15.1

Disability Adjusted Life Years

	Diseases	*Persons Affected (in DALYs millions*)*
1.	Diarrhoea	28.01
2.	Intestinal worms	2.09
3.	Trachoma	0.11
4.	Hepatitis	0.31
	Total	30.51

Source: World Dev. Report, 1995.
* DALY is a quantitative measure that integrates premature deaths and temporary disability due to diseases.

Imagine, every year in our country 30.51 million of life years are lost because of poor water quality, sanitation and hygiene.

The Major Sources of Water Pollution[6]

These are primarily (1) domestic waste water, (2) industrial waste water, and (3) agricultural run-off. In India, domestic and human waste water is most problematic. It is affecting our cities because of inadequate, and at places, even absence of waste water treatment facilities. In 1988, class I cities generated 12,146 MLD (million litres per day) of waste water. The figures have increased by 25 per cent in 2001, and at present nearly 18,000 MLD of waste water is being generated by cities of first order. Mumbai (more than 2,000 MLD) and Delhi (1,800 MLD) jointly generated more waste water than all class II cities put together. Out of the all class II towns' waste water only 2.5 per cent has the facility of treatment plants. Class I towns too do not have more than 25 per cent facilities for treatment of waste water. From the above, it is clear that water bodies in India are under great stress.

Urban Transport

Movement of people and goods within city limits and also from one city to another has recently become a serious problem in the wake of rapid urbanization. Growth of metropolitan cities in India from 5 in 1951 to 23 in 1991 has increased the share of urban population in the total population from 19 to about 33 per cent. This does not only mean that more people have started living in cities, but more people and more goods have started making trips to and fro in urban areas, and often to longer distances.

What is the Impact?

There has been tremendous vehicular growth on urban roads. Motor vehicles are also instruments of economic growth of cities. Increasing dependence on cars of people in cities is apparent. The impact of increasing pressure on roads and costs of increasing dependence on cars include expensive road building and maintenance, frequent road blockades and traffic jams, and streets' congestion, increased consumption of energy, unbearable noise and air pollution, road accidents, mental tensions, etc.

Pattern of Urban Transport

Urbanization and vehicular growth are closely linked. In the developing countries there has been tremendous growth of two and three wheelers with the increasing of city size. In Figure 15.1, it is shown for two decades (1980 and 1990). It shows that the number of vehicles in a city is likely to grow along S-shaped logistic pattern[7] as city size increases. The trend is more pronounced in the 1990s than in the 1980s. Data in case of Delhi has been excluded because vehicles in Delhi rose many a times higher than other cities, and hence is considered an outlier. The trend also shows that as city size increases, the number of vehicles tends to grow slowly until the city reaches a

Figure 15.1

Logistic Pattern of Growth of Vehicles (1980s and 1990s)

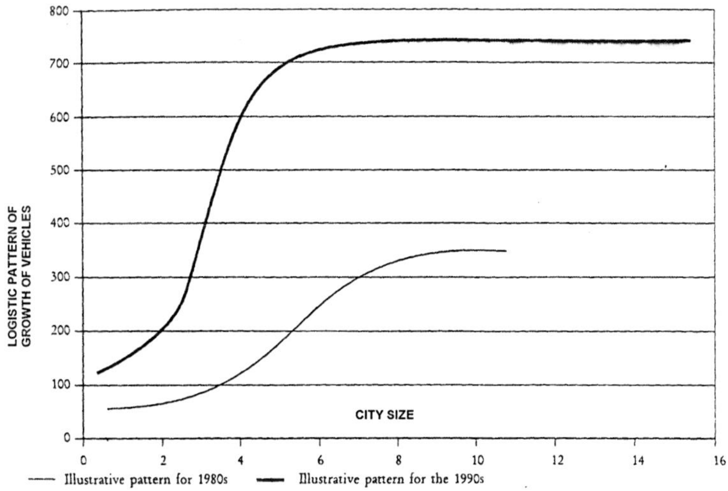

Source: R. Ramanathan, India Dev. Report-1997.

certain critical size. This takes place when demands of vehicles and economic activities become in consonance with each other. The logistic pattern of growth of vehicles in urban India can be altered under conditions such as encouraging walking and cycling. Some of the cities have provided all the facilities for change of travel mode and have encouraged its population for using cycles. In Lucknow, cycling and walking accounted for nearly 55 per cent of the total trips in 1994.[8]

Growth of Public and Private Transport

Personal vehicles in cities of India are on the rise than the public transport. In the major four metropolitan cities nearly 85 per cent (two wheelers 60 and cars 25) of the total number, forms personalized vehicles. Number of public transport buses constitutes 30 per cent of the total buses (1991-92). But it has been remaining static or even decreasing in Mumbai and Kolkata against the use of personalized vehicles and taxis including auto-rickshaws. In Delhi also personalized vehicles and auto-rickshaws show a rise of nearly 25 per cent during the last two decades. Statistics of the US metropolitan areas also shows that in the largest metropolises, the private car has become a dominant mode of travel. The following figures in Table 15.2 are for a selected few US and Britain metropolitan areas.[9]

Table 15.2

Per cent of Journeys by Different Modes

City	*Private Transport*	*Public Transport*	*Walk*	*Other*
New York	47	44	8	1
Baltimore	83	12	5	1
Greater London	44	17	37	1
Manchester	38	17	44	1
(All Urban Areas in Great Britain)	44	13	40	22

Source: Whitelegg, 1985.

The table indicates that private car has become dominant as the prime mode of travel. In Britain a greater number than the US prefer walking to reach the place of work.

Smaller cities everywhere have limited public transport facilities, especially in India. Udaipur which is one of the premier cities for tourists has no facility of public bus transport system as yet.

Problem of Trip Generation

Intra-urban travel varies temporally everywhere. It is found that there is heavy concentration of movement into clear peak periods.[10] The morning time remains very congested and busy, being related largely to commuting journeys to work and to school. This is again repeated in the late afternoon with

Figure 15.2
Temporal Characteristics of Intra-Urban Travel

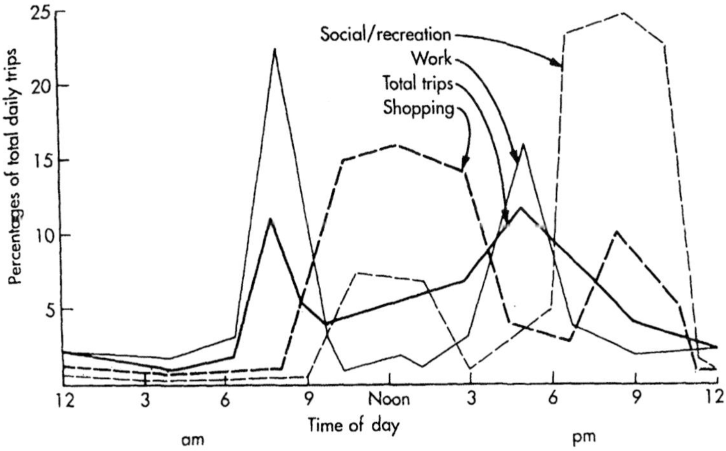

Source: G. Barber 1986: Aggregate characteristics of urban travel, in S. Hanson (ed.), *The Geography of Urban Transportation*, New York, The Guilford Press. p. 77.

returning home. This adds to the problem of all metropolises and has several implications like road congestion, reduction in speed, increase in accidents, energy consumption and also emission of pollutants.

Urban Roads

The share of urban roads to total roads in India has declined from 8 per cent to just about 6 per cent in 1996. The number of users of urban roads has been increasing and there has evolved a situation of inadequacy in the supply and demand. Lately, the government at the centre is trying to meet the demand. The state governments have been directed to acquire land and shift utilities coming in the way for building roads under various phases of the National Highways Development Project. Some of the states like Tamil Nadu, Maharashtra, West Bengal and Karnataka have been lagging behind, in so far as, land acquisition is concerned. Rajasthan, Bihar, U.P. and Orissa have shown good results. Gujarat is barely 1 per cent short of the acquisition-target. There have been success in the completion of the Golden Quadrilateral and North-South, East-West Corridors as achievements in the highway building. But still much is left for reducing the pressure which was created because of disproportionate growth of personalized vehicles in Indian cities. More than 20 projects have been going on, and some of them have completed for manufacturing cars. At present annual sale of all vehicles is estimated around 5 million which was around one million in 1990. The growing number of vehicles will add to existing congestion, unless sufficient road networks are made available. In comparison to 1980s, the situation in 1990s became more worse in the three metropolitan cities, where passenger car unit (PCU) per 1,000 population increased three times. Whereas per capita road length decreased during the same decade. In 2005, the situation has become worst because of the increase of vehicles more than four times, and per capita road length decreased because of urban explosion in the metropolitan areas.

Delhi Transport System

Majority of Delhi's middle-order population uses bus-service to reach its various areas which are far-flung from the Central Bus Terminus. The city-bus system is circular to join the city in different directions as shown in Figure 15.2A.

The Central Bus Terminus is located near the Rashtrapati Bhawan joining the various significant areas by circular route service.

The city, is also served all around by 'ring-railway. It connects Delhi Junction in the northwest to Azadpur and

Figure 15.2A
Mudrika Bus Service

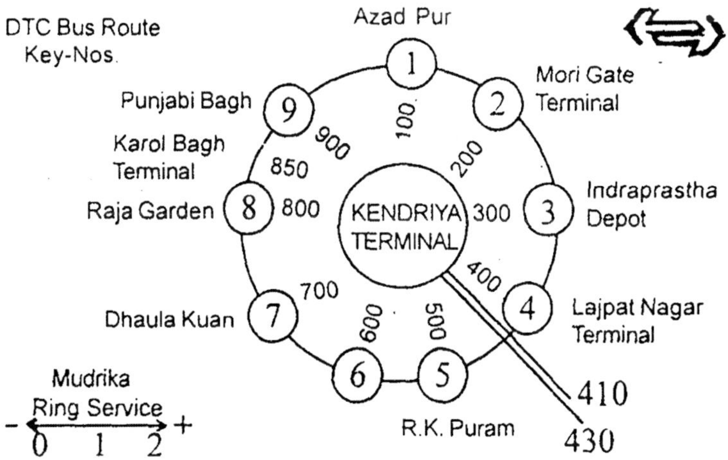

further to Panipat. In the west of Rohtak through Dayabasti and Shakoorbasti. In the southwest the railway joins Delhi Cant. The southern sector of Sardar Patel Marg, Safdarjung, Sarojini Nagar, Lodi Colony, Lajpat Nagar are connected to finally complete the Ring in the east by joining Nizamuddin, Tilak Marg, Minto Bridge and Sadar Bazar. The route to Shahdara is also connected to join Vivek Vihar and Sahibabad in the east (Figure 15.2B).

Connaught Place (CP) which is the central and busiest area of Delhi is estimated to be used by as many as 12 lakh passengers (2003). The figure will climb up to 50 lakh by 2021. The CP has now been converted into the most congested place, because of unwieldy traffic without a proper control. There is now a move to rationalize traffic flow of CP. It is proposed that motorists should only be allowed to enter the Inner Circle only from Janpath and exit from Baba Kharag Singh Marg.

Figure 15.2B
Delhi Ring Railway and Other Services

New Delhi Municipal Council has made several proposals to meet the surge in traffic. Among them key points are: (a) Increase pedestrian space and provide walk-ways; (b) all intersections of the middle circle to be provided with coloured zebra crossings to ensure slower vehicular movement; (c) middle circle be enforced by raised walk-ways on either sides; (d) create more subways across places like Panchkuian Road, Minto Road, Bhagat Singh Marg, Barakhamba Road, to ensure conflict-free pedestrian crossings; (e) reduce number of buses in congested places; (f) multi-level parking be added on Kasturba Gandhi Marg and Baba Kharag Singh Marg; (g) during peak hours, a bus should run every two minutes and in non-peak

Figure 15.3
Showing Rite's Plans in CP

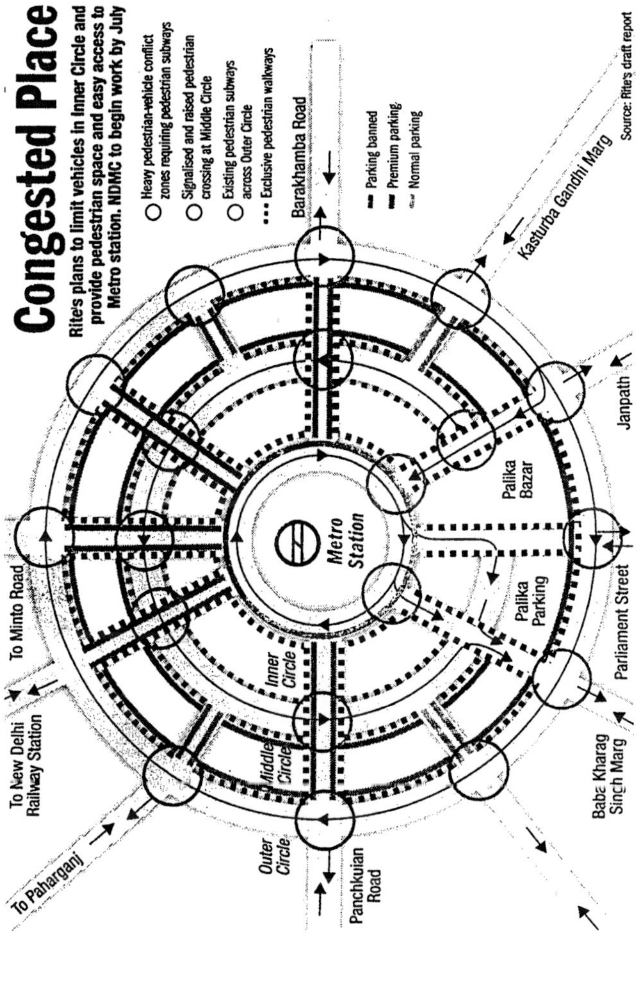

hours the same should have a five minutes frequency; and (h) discourage surface parking and ban it in the Inner Circle (see Figure 15.3).

There is an urgent need for planning the CBD areas of the metropolises in India on the similar lines or as conditions warrant in their own cases. But planning the transport of CBD is essential to rationalize the busiest areas.

Residential Areas in City and Problem of Housing

Use of urban land in cities is very significant and it is related with the problem of housing. The problem of housing has become acute because of the tremendous increase of urban population and unplanned growth of the city. Industrial growth and rush of immigrants are also responsible for making the problem critical. Construction cost and land values have gone too high to be within the means of medium-class population to think about owning a house. Above all, the game of brokers and middlemen in acquiring a land and to construct house on it has become a nasty process.

In the American metropolitan cities, land under residences varies in areas from 30 to 50 per cent of the total development area of the city.[11] The use of land for residences in Detriot is 46.5 in Pittsburg 51.3, in Philadelphia 52.3, in Chicago 32.2 and in New York is 39.8 per cent of the development area. In India average area under the residential use of a city is found 40 per cent of the developed area.[*]

Generally the following categories of residential areas are visible in the cities of our country. These form:

1. Dense and fully built-up central zone,
2. Moderately dense built-up area of middle zone,
3. Partly built-up outer residential zone,

---

* *Development area* of a city is equal to the total area of an administrative city minus the areas under water bodies and recant land.

4. Suburban and satellites areas, and
5. Police line, cantonment, railway colony, etc.

The 'central area' of a city is occupied by old and traditional residences. It has houses of business population and is a mixed area having shops and business units on the ground floor of a two-storied building. It forms the hub of both residences and markets. In Kolkata, the density of the central zone is more than 2,000 persons per acre. Out of the total residences, nearly 70 per cent are rented buildings. Only 10 per cent families have three-room houses, and 40 per cent families live in one-room space. Only 10 per cent houses have the facility of independent toilet.[12] The central residential area of Udaipur in Rajasthan has about 900 acres of land[13] where mixed land use is the characteristic like other towns of India. The area up to 1955 has been within the historic city walls all around with its four principal gates in the four directions.

The 'middle zone' occupies areas between the central and outer zones. It has residential houses along lines of principal routes on both sides. It has houses both of people of middle- and low-income groups. The density varies between 100-150 houses per acre. The middle zone has been occupied recently by new buildings for residences. At places 'residential complexes' have also come up occupied by families on rent. These families include service-class and large number of immigrant's families. The middle zone near the centre of city is occupied at places by people below the poverty line and are labourers. Gradually their site is being developed into 'slums' and is generally an unauthorized occupation of land.

The 'outer residential zone' is an area resembling 'urban' landscape and found scattered on the urban fringe. The dwellings include semi-built-up units and some of them are 'kachha' and without water, light, roads and drainage facilities. The sporadically occupied residences have density of less than 100 units per acre. The area is generally near the industrial units of a city and is characterized by deplorable living conditions.

Neighbourhoods, Suburbs and Satellites

Beyond the fringe of an administrative city there appear residential sectors, It is a general feature of most large modern cities. It is partly the result of the increasing population with the attraction of migrants due to their dynamic economies. People also have now started to live in areas of lower densities and there is also now a tendency for smaller and independent family units. In Britain, Hampstead Garden suburb is an ideal example. It was designed to attract a variety of social classes in houses of different sizes. It was provided with social amenities, making it more than a mere dormitory.[14] In India, the design and style of suburbs make difference by being inadequately equipped by life amenities. Hiran-magri suburbs in Udaipur even after two decades of their origin, do not possess adequate facilities.

Figure 15.4
Neighbourhood

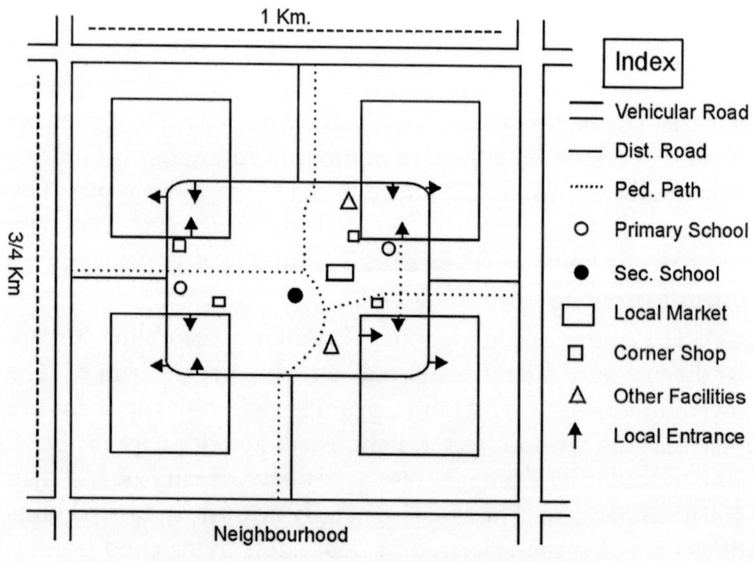

Neighbourhood is also a modern concept and its built-up area is being designed to relieve the overgrowing pressure on metropolises' residential centre (see Figure 15.4). Ruth Glass' work on Middlesborough defined it as a self-sufficient world where residents carried on almost all their legitimate pursuits. Clarence Perry considered neighbourhood as an embodiment of actual development of all its residents for play, school, shopping, community life, etc. In India, Noida near Delhi was planned for the same objectives but the residential area of Noida is being disintegrated and has become heterogeneous in landuse. Residential facilities for all age-groups have become almost nil and safety of movement from one place to another including commuting between residences and work places too is uncertain.

Urban Satellites

Expansion of cities gives rise to residential satellites depending on the main city. They are like Sputniks. Soviet geographer[15] defines it by indicating three characteristics: (a) workers of satellite-town have to come to work in the central town because it is the central town which guarantees a certain number of services, (b) the satellite town reciprocally provides facilities for holidaying and relaxation, and (c) there is found easy and frequent transport and communication between the two. Around Delhi, there are urban centres performing the services of satellites, e.g., Ghaziabad, Bahadurgarh, Gurgaon, Sonepat, and Faridabad. Similarly, Kolkata encompasses number of urban centres of the surrounding area. They are closely linked and have become centres for service activity. Some of these satellites may be counted as Kalyani, Barrackpur, Jadavpur, Bansdrori. Purba Putiary, Gobindapur and Sutanuti also form the status of satellites. Tollygunge and several peripheral towns are closely linked with the city. Kanchanpura, Nabapally, Halisahar, Ishapure are towns other than satellites of the conurbation.

Satellites differ from suburbs in that they are separated from the central city by many miles. They have little daily commuting but their economic activities are closely geared to those of the central city. Suburbs are primarily joined with the central city for commuting to or from the city. Growth of automobiles and commuter rail lines in metropolises have stimulated suburbanization. Kolkata encompasses a number of urban centres which are satellites on the Hooghly side. They are distinctly attached economically with the Kolkata conurbation.

Nature of the Problem

Bartholomew after surveying found that the residential units in USA fall into three main categories[16]: (a) single family, (b) two family, and (c) multiple family dwellings. More than 80 per cent families live in single family tenements. It seems that the American culture is largely single family oriented, and people prefer rather independent social life. But with the increase of population in metropolitan areas of the USA, the proportion of single family dwellings go on decreasing. In India, single family housing units in cities (average of the four main metropolises) is about 70 per cent.[17] In Kolkata, it has reached nearly 80 per cent. Only 20 per cent of Kolkata-population has the facility of a complete living unit. Kenneth B. Keating, formerly the ambassador in India, observed that "the most important problems of Calcutta in India that we face are of living environment".[18] People in lakhs have no proper place for living and they have to squatter on footpaths in the night.

Shortage of Residential Units

Shortage of residences in India is one of the serious problems. The population is growing rapidly and every year the shortage is fast increasing because the houses are not built in the same proportion. In 1991, the census indicated the shortage of houses to about 40 million.

Although there have been efforts by the government to solve the housing problem, but it is going on continuously to become serious day by day because of the vicious circle of housing-markets. The process involving the demand and supply may be tabulated as:

Table 15.3

Demand-Supply Marketing

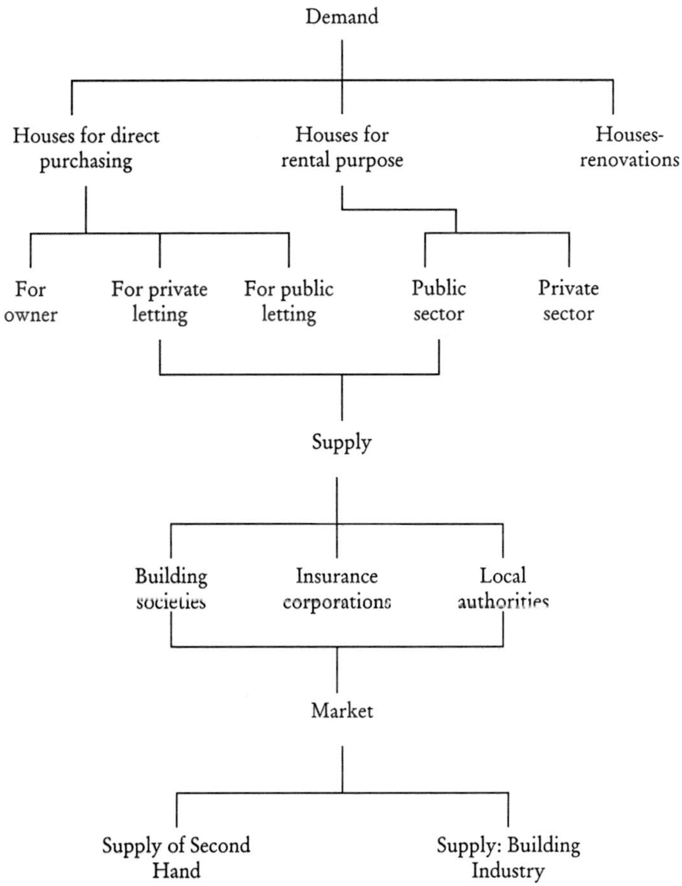

Market involving the process of demand and supply is overwhelmingly occupied by middlemen and brokers who manage for the purchasers either land for construction of new houses or for making a purchase of old houses. The process is too intricate and difficult that a common man hardly gets out of it any suitable solution. They remain largely unserved.

Efforts by Government Sector

The government including local bodies like improvement trust in urban areas have made some efforts to solve the housing problem. Some of the schemes include:

Subsidization

A scheme for industrial labourers was initiated in 1952 to provide loan to the extent of 65 per cent for purchase of houses which were provided by the cooperative societies.

L.I.G. Scheme

It was initiated in 1954 under which a loan upto 80 per cent was granted for constructing houses. It was open only to families having an income of less than Rs. 6,000. Later on, under this scheme the Urban Improvement Trust provided constructed small houses to be leased to owners on fairly convenient instalments.

M.I.G. and H.I.G. Schemes

Under these schemes loans were sanctioned by various banks and also by the Life Insurance Corporation of India to be utilized either by the people who have insurance policies or property of sufficient value. The loan can be returned with interest within 20 years' time in instalments or when the life policies become matured for payment.

Land Allotment Scheme

The government could acquire land for development and the same could be allotted to people in open bid.

Recently in metropolitan areas and also in many of the lakh-towns because of the increasing problem, high occupancy rate, skyrocketing rents and land values, people are forced to live in housing apartments. These apartments vary from flats in residential complexes, duplexes in posh-colonies to 'chawls', 'cheries', 'bustees', 'ahatas', having subhuman living conditions. 'Kalras' in Kanpur, Lucknow, Agra, Delhi, Meerut, etc., have no facilities for water-tap, toilets and sanitation. Kolkata is a pre-mature metropolis[19] where all the garbage and refuse are dumped everywhere; only 12.3 per cent families have water taps and 55.8 per cent families share the facilities with others, while 32.9 per cent are devoid of these basic amenities of life. In India, problem of the residential facility has gone out of control because of middlemen and builders whose sole aim is to exploit the needy masses. The government has no control over their dealings and rackets in the metropolitan areas. The price of houses for sale is not determined by what they cost to build, but what buyers can afford. And what buyers can afford depends on the levels of wages, credit, subsidies, etc. But if wages rise, house prices also rise. If government subsidies increase, house prices also rise. If credit gets cheaper, and easier, house prices too rise. As soon as decent housing comes theoretically within the reach of the common workers, house prices rise and it becomes out of reach again.[20]

Problem of Squatters and Slums

Metropolitan areas almost everywhere and especially in the 'cities of the Third World' are occupied by squatters near the city centre (see Figure 15.5). B.J.L. Berry[21] while discussing the problems of pseudo-urbanization of Africa, pointed out that squattering was one of the many ills that invaded development.

Figure 15.5

Conceptual Location of Squatter Settlement

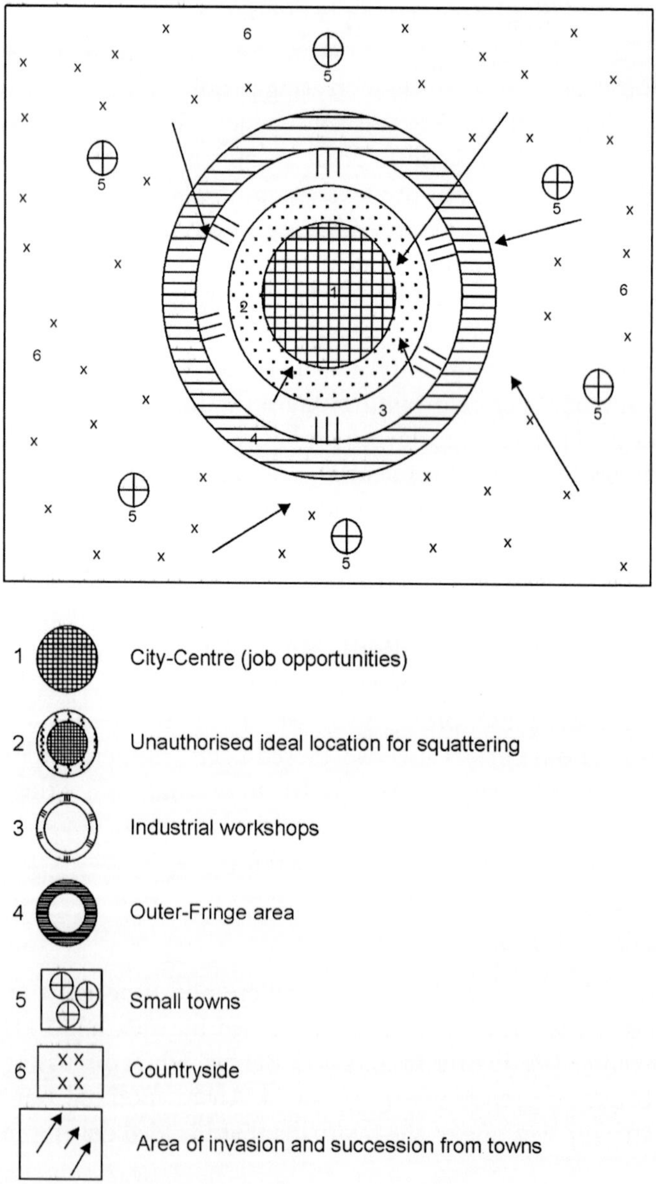

Unwieldy growth of the colonial capitals and squattering of floods of immigrants have in reality altogether changed their environment into nasty landscape totally undesirable for human living. Their subhuman living has made life fungus-ridden. From Cairo to Manila the middle urban areas near the city centre have been infested overwhelmingly by the unauthorized occupation of land for 'Jhuggi-jhonparis', which are piles of tinsheds, rugs and waste materials. These are areas illegally occupied by spontaneous or squatter settlements.[22]

The term 'squatter settlement' or 'squatter housing' is defined as any housing which contravenes existing legislation on the occupation of land of the construction of dwellings. The illegal nature of such housing strongly affects all aspects of life in the squatter community from the physical environment through types of economic activity to relations with the urban authorities.[23]

Criticizing the policy and programmes of the million-cities, Misra pointed out that in India, these serve only a few well-to-do immigrants...the poor are left to fend for themselves. As a result squatter slums tend to multiply in big cities.[24]

Dickinson defines the concept of slum as "extreme condition of blight in which the housing is unfit as to constitute a menace to the health and the morale of the community".

Table 15.4

Growth of Jhuggi-Jhonparis in Delhi (1951-1991)

Year	*No. of Squatter Households (Jhuggis)*
1951	12,749
1961	42,814
1971	115,961
1991	275,900

Source: Town and Country Planning, Delhi.

Table 15.4 above indicates that nearly 20 per cent of the population alone was living in 'jhuggis' in Delhi. In Kolkata, nearly one-fourth of the total population used to live in 'bustees' nearly four decades ago.

Now, the following Table 15.5 makes the position clear of the squatters and slums in various states of India (1981).[25] This shows that in India nearly one-fourth of the total urban population is living a subhuman life in slums and squatters.

Table 15.5

Showing Per cent Urban Population Living in Slums

States/Union Territories	*Percentage of Squatters and Slums*		
	Urban areas of Population between 1 Lakh-10 Lakh	*More than Million +1,000,000*	*Total*
India	21.50	35.50	23.00
States:			
Bihar	37.48	37.51	37.50
Maharashtra	32.49	37.50	32.62
West Bengal	27.48	37.49	31.53
Andhra Pradesh	32.50	22.51	30.47
Punjab	27.48	37.49	31.58
Gujarat	17.82	22.50	18.84
Tamilnadu	15.00	32.50	18.75
Orissa	19.95	X	18.49
Assam	-	-	17.46
Haryana	22.49	X	15.98
Uttar Pradesh	17.49	40.63	15.76
Madhya Pradesh	12.50	X	15.15
Karnataka	12.49	10.43	14.43
Rajasthan	14.95	27.50	14.06
Kerala	9.98	X	8.81
Union Territories:			
Delhi	-	17.50	47.50
Chandigarh	12.47	X	12.47

Source: Planning Commission, N. Delhi 1981.

In Mumbai, after independence, nearly 85 squatter settlements were present which rose to 206 in 1969. At present more than 10 lakh people have been living in 'chawls' where nearly 10 per cent have no more than 15 sq. ft. of living space. Metropolitan Mumbai has nearly 2,000 squatters and slum areas and about 40 lakh population is without legal-land and proper services and live in slums and on pavements.

Some Redevelopment Schemes

J.F.C. Turner favours the proposals for redevelopments of slum-dwellers and squatter settlements. In his opinion, "inspite of many severe drawbacks slum-dwellers and squatters are forward moving vehicles initiating social and economic change".[26] They should be granted first of all 'legal rights' or 'pattas' to claim themselves as landowners. The ownership-right would make them active participants in the developmental schemes.

Eyre[27] while studying 'shanty-towns' of Jamaica had four-point proposal for the renovation:

(a) Squatters remain under tension, fear and insecure about their future, and they should be relieved of this situation by granting ownership rights.

(b) When squatters begin their new changed life, they face a transitional stage.

(c) Under the third-stage squatters when they come out as victorious, begin to feel secure by becoming owners.

(d) The last stage is very significant when squatters are merged into the main channel of the city. Actually, this is the stage of social-revolution in the real sense of the term.

Mangin[28] has also expressed the feelings for the amelioration of the conditions of Lima squatters in Peru:

> Given any recognition and encouragement by the government such as the paving of the street or even the collection of taxes

> from them, the people respond with a burst of activity in improvement of their homes. There is a compensating trend... the two largest 'barriadas' now have elected mayors and town councils.

In India, urban renewal schemes were being planned during the decade of sixty on the initiative of the then Land and Building Secretary of Delhi. He vehemently expressed:[29]

> ...if we plan according to our needs and situation and be not led away by what is being done in the affluent societies, if we exploit our resources to the maximum and distribute them on more equitable and rational basis... if we show greater courage to deal with the vested interests and impart a clearer sense of direction and purpose to our administration, and if we reorient our national economic policies to correct the fundamental imbalances in our society and "kill the microbes which produce the disease", the twin challenge of massive urbanization and poverty (indirectly problem of squatters) could be successfully met.

In India social and cultural integration is more urgent a step rather than investing funds and resources sporadically to uproot blindfoldedly the areas occupied by slums and squatters simply to gain political motives.

Notes

1. Garner, B.J., and Chabot, G., *Urban Geography*, Longmans, London, 1967, pp. 131-132.
2. *Employment News*, 1-7 November, 2003, New Delhi.
3. *Times of India*, New Delhi, 19 July, 2005.
4. Annual Report (1994-95): Ministry of Environment and Forests, Govt. of India, New Delhi.
5. World Bank: Investing in Health, *The World Development Report*, OUP, New York, 1993.

6. Central Water Commission: Water and Related Statistics, Statistical Directorate, New Delhi, 1993.
7. Ramanathan, R., "Transport: A Critical Infrastructure", in *India Development Report, 1997*, OUP, New Delhi.
8. "Improvement of Urban Public Transport in Developing Countries", Habitat - UN Centre for Human Settlements, 1994, Nairobi.
9. Whitelegg, J., *Urban Transport*, Macmillan, 1985.
10. Barber, G., "Aggregate Characteristics of Urban Travel", in Hanson S. (ed.), *The Geography of Urban Transportation*, New York, 1986, Chap. 4.
11. Abrams, Charles, "The Use of Land in Cities", *Cities - Scientific American*, 1973, p. 228.
12. Bharadwaj, R.K., *Urban Development in India*, National, Delhi, 1974, p. 92.
13. Udaipur Master Plan, 1992, State Planning Dept., Udaipur, 1999.
14. Johnson, J.H., *Urban Geography*, Pergamon, 1967, p. 34.
15. Davidovitch, V.C., *Soviet Geography: Review and Translation*, Moscow, 1962.
16. Bartholomew, H., *Land Uses in American Cities*, Harvard U.P., Cambridge, 1955.
17. Bharadwaj, R.K., op. cit., p. 72.
18. *American Reporter*, Vol. 19, 1969.
19. Bose, N.K., "A Premature Metropolis", *Cities Scientific American*, pp. 251-262.
20. Ambrose, P. and Colenutt, *The Property Machine*, OUP, 1975.
21. Berry, B.J.L., *Urbanization and Counter-Urbanization*, Vol. II, Sage, London, 1976, p. 259.
22. Turner, J.F.C., "The Squatter Settlement", *Ekistics*, Vol. 23, 1967.
23. Drakakis-Smith, D.W., 'Shelter': Overview, Australian Nat. Univ., Canberra, Dept. of Human Geography, Pub. No. 2, 1978.
24. Misra, R.P., (ed.), *Million-Cities in India*, Vikas, Delhi, 1978, pp. 346-66.
25. Data Source: Housing and Urban Development, Planning Commission, New Delhi, 1981.
26. Turner, J.F.C., op. cit., p. 78.

27. Eyre, L.J., "The Shanty Towns of Montego Bay", *Geog. Review.*, Vol. 62, Jamaica, pp. 394-418.
28. Mangin, W., "Squatter Settlements", in *Cities – Scientific American*, California, 1954, pp. 235-40.
29. Jagmohan, "The Souvenir", Town and Country Planning Seminar, Delhi, 1968, p. 51.

16

Central Business District

Central Area of a City

City is a complex agglomeration of multiple activities – economic, social, cultural, etc. Its 'central area' is its distinct section which is identified as the centre of marketing, business and financial activities as well as dense built-up sector where lines of transportation converge from various parts and nearly from all direction. It is therefore known as the hub of a city. In other words, city centre is a specialized area and a "distinctive region with a complex web of associated and interwoven land uses".[1]

The central area of a city is known by various names such as City Centre, Central Business District (CBD), Premier Shopping Centre, etc. Its nomenclature is associated by varying order of city size. In Great Britain, city's 'downtown' is also the city centre and a principal area for marketing and business. Besides being the core of commerce, the central city serves as retail district flanked by stores, shops, office buildings, banks, clubs, hotels, theatres, museums, and organizational headquarters.

Johnson is of the opinion that there is hardly any distinction between the city centre and CBD. Here residential and industrial uses of land have merged spontaneously with the specialized uses of CBD... "and a distinction between the central area of a city and CBD is easier to make in theory than in practice".[2] If non-central business uses such as places of worship and educational institutions which are also commonly located in the city centre are excluded, the delimitation of a compact CBD will be almost impossible.

Characteristics of CBD

Accessibility is one of the most significant attributes of CBD. It possesses the quality of being accessible from almost all residential areas lying all around in the far-flung middle and outer zones of a city. The city centre itself is a jumble of neatly placed multi-storeyed buildings on both sides of a principal broadway. The multi-storeyed buildings are generally occupied by commerce and business offices. In CBD area, competition for land has become too acute to cope with, and it is for this reason that buildings show vertical expansion rather than horizontal. The buildings are rarely used for residential purposes because of intensity and density of business uses. However, in the cities of the developing areas, the central business area is also occupied sporadically by residences, and in some cases upper storeys are used for residences. In Delhi, Mumbai and Kolkata more than 25 per cent upper-storeys of the multi-storeyed buildings are used for residential purpose. But the case of the Western world is different. In London, not more than 5,000 population was estimated in 1961. Besides this, although manufacturing does not form an attribute of CBD, yet newspaper and book publication are found centrally located in many cities. This is perhaps because of the facility of their sale and circulation including convenience of transport and communication.

Business dominated central area of a city should not be misunderstood as 'homogenous' in its aspect of urban land uses.

It is characterized by internal specialization of mixed-uses regarding retailing. There one may find readymade dresses, utensils, general merchandise, footwears, electronic goods, medical stores, tailoring and outfit, confectionary, watches, restaurants and fashionable ladies wear, ornaments, etc. The competition for the central location has increased with diversification of shopping and with specialization.[3] Diamond[4] has identified three specialized areas at the CBD of Glasgow. These are offices, wholesaling and retailing.

Recently, there has been a danger that the central function of the city might break down completely because they are becoming painfully inaccessible. Traffic breakdown has become a common phenomenon, especially in the metropolises of the Third World countries. "...cities have much to offer us when the quality of life within them is high and much to trouble us when it is not".[5]

Practical viability of CBD is not even 50 per cent possible for it to function. Even the developed countries' CBD areas are not perfectly meeting their objectives, and are engrossed with incorrigible problems. Actually, there is little coordination between the theory and practice on the concept of CBD. Nevertheless mixed motives of the CBD have not been able to minimize its overwhelming attraction.[6] With the sprawling of cities and coming up of the residential sectors in different parts far and wide, the metropolises like Delhi, Kanpur, Hyderabad-Secunderabad in India are disintegrated into subsidiary retail business areas. The significance of the primary CBD has been minimized because people do not prefer to reach the downtown under traffic-tension and uneasy movement out of their own residential sector. The outlying business district fulfils nearly all needs – social, cultural and economic – of the residents who are living about ten to twenty miles off the main city centre.

Hierarchical Order of CBD

Now in cities at various places, facilities are available meeting the requirements of central business type. B.J.L. Berry has identified an hierarchical order among various business areas. The demand can be met at the various levels but of varying degree of threshold. Only the very essential goods are made available at the lowest order or at nearest point for consumers. This is the lowest level where only essential goods stores are located and are within easy reach. At this most convenient point, frequency of consumers is very high. But with the increasing level of hierarchical order, the level or degree of threshold changes and more special nature of goods centres are found with lesser degree of consumers' frequency[7](Figure 16.1).

Edge of CBD

Degree of specialized nature of consumers' goods goes on decreasing as one moves away from the CBD towards its edge. The land values too show a gradual decline. The areas are occupied towards the edge by parks, public institutions, etc. Dickinson[8] has termed the area of edge of CBD as a 'zone of deterioration', whereas it was called 'blighted zone' by Firey[9]. The edge of CBD in many million-cities are infested by unauthorized occupation of land where mixed land uses have developed. Urban centres in this stage grow on the expense of the surrounding countryside, destroying the surrounding landscape on which it ultimately depends. It is also known as area of neglect and somewhere as zone of discard.

Shape of CBD

Generally CBD resembles with 'Quardrate Cross' in shape[10] (Figure 16.2). It is not necessary that CBD occupies the geographic centre of a city. It may be away from it where specialization of land uses develop to make the point of space a

Figure 16.1
Hierarchical Order of CBD

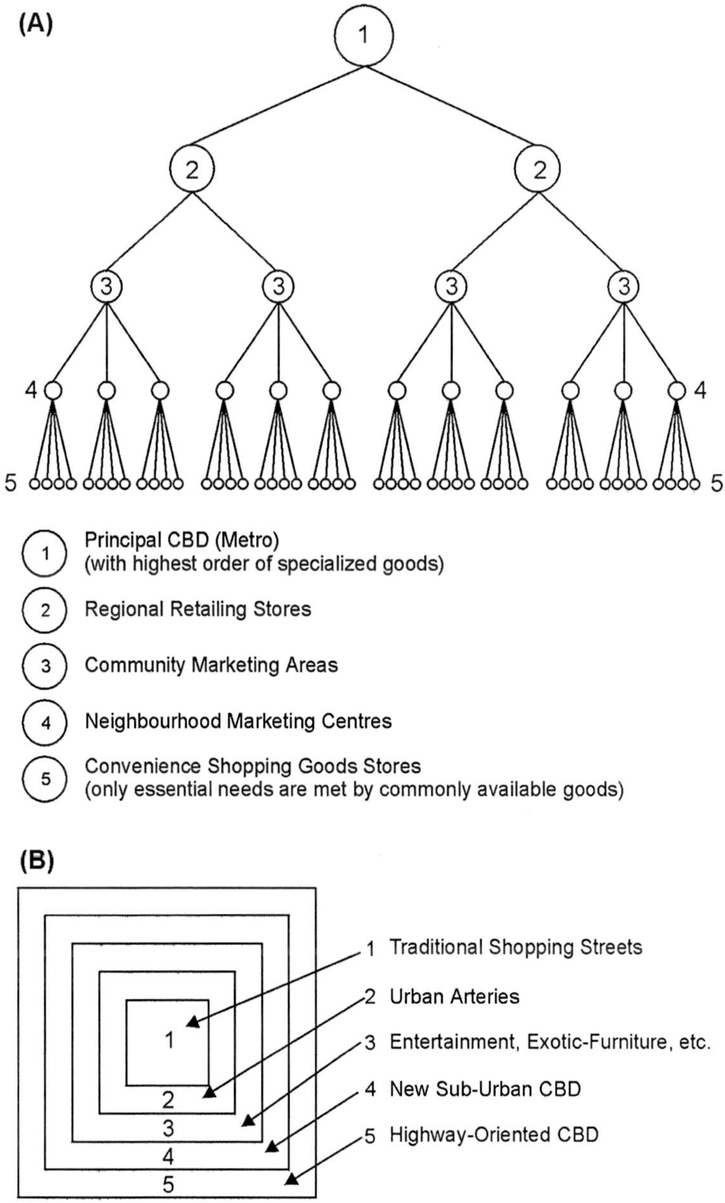

Figure 16.2
Shape of CBD

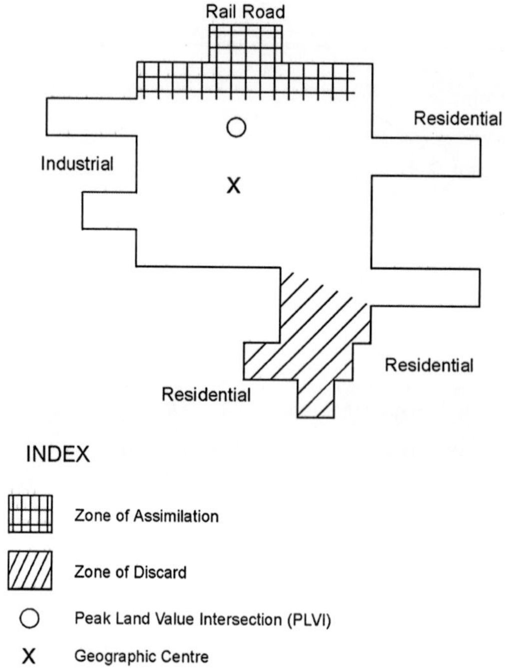

business-area of central order catering all sorts of people for all sorts of goods from all parts of a city.

The shape of CBD depends upon nature of a city, its population, areal extent and above all, land uses. It has also its relations with the social and cultural institutions.

The shape and size of the CBD do not evenly spread on all directions. Near its edge, zone of neglect or discard may distort its regular shape. Similarly, zone of assimilation also affects the shape by residences over its edge occupied by business community. On a map, the shape is seen two-dimensional as a quadrate cross, but in reality it is three-dimensional, and best visualized as a pyramid – like figure with an irregularly shaped base, and a height varying in proportion to total central business floor area.[11]

Land Uses in CBD

Two groups of land uses are on average visible: (a) service-financial-office uses, and (b) retail business uses. Wholesale business activity and residential units as well as factories do not form part of it. Besides these some of the institutions like administrative municipal council, other public institutions, parks, churches, place of worship, etc., also do not form its part. The following list of the various uses may indicate various CB and non-CB uses:

Groups of CB Uses	*Non-CB Uses*
1. Profit earning retail and services	1. Permanent residential units
2. Financial institutions	2. Govt. offices, educational institutions, parks, etc.
3. Retail marketing stores	3. Place of worship, university campus, college-buildings and play-ground
4. Shops and services for repairing job	4. Industries-Manufacturing, etc. (Exception: Newspaper and Printing Books, etc.)
5. Banks, L.I.C., legal-offices, restaurants, hotels, clubs, etc.	5. Vacant plots and buildings
	6. Wholesale units
	7. Commercial storages
	8. Railways

Delimitation of CBD

It is a difficult job to delimit CBD accurately because land uses in the central part of a city also vary from cities to cities. There is lot of difference in the central areas of the developed and developing countries. Whatever methods are used by the western authors hardly suit universal urban environment.

There is not yet any standard method of its delimitation. However, some of the methods have been given here which may reflect on the nature of fieldwork involved in its delimitation.

(1) W. William – Olsson Technique: This method takes into account a 'shop rent index' which is the total of shop rents of a building divided by the length of its frontage. But because of the difficulties involving in the collection of such data, it is impracticable. In India nobody discloses the correct value of rents.

(2) Sund and Isachsen used total turnover or trade instead of total shop rents. But, again, this is rather more unreliable to obtain and in the developing countries this type of data obtained from the Municipal Council (Department of Marketing) are totally fake.

Therefore, it is very difficult to prepare a map out of the aforesaid data and the picture which is thus obtained is mostly diffused.

(3) Proudfoot used to locate intra-city business areas by block-frontage-volume of sales for each side of a block of all stores whose addresses indicate that they front on that side. But Proudfoot method too involves weaknesses being unconcerned about the activities of offices and banks.

(4) Other possible efforts include the data of building heights, population distribution, traffic and pedestrian flows, valuation data and land uses. Some minimum building height may be taken as a cut-off point to mark higher heights on a lot basis as the boundary of the CBD area. If the resulting boundary obtained is irregular, the same may be smoothened out by basing the map on blocks rather on lots. Population of dwelling units, pedestrian flows, traffic volume may, similarly help in delimiting the area in question.

An appropriate criterion may be selected after close empirical studies of the central city. Of course, it varies from

Figure 16.3
CBHI and CBII of Worcester

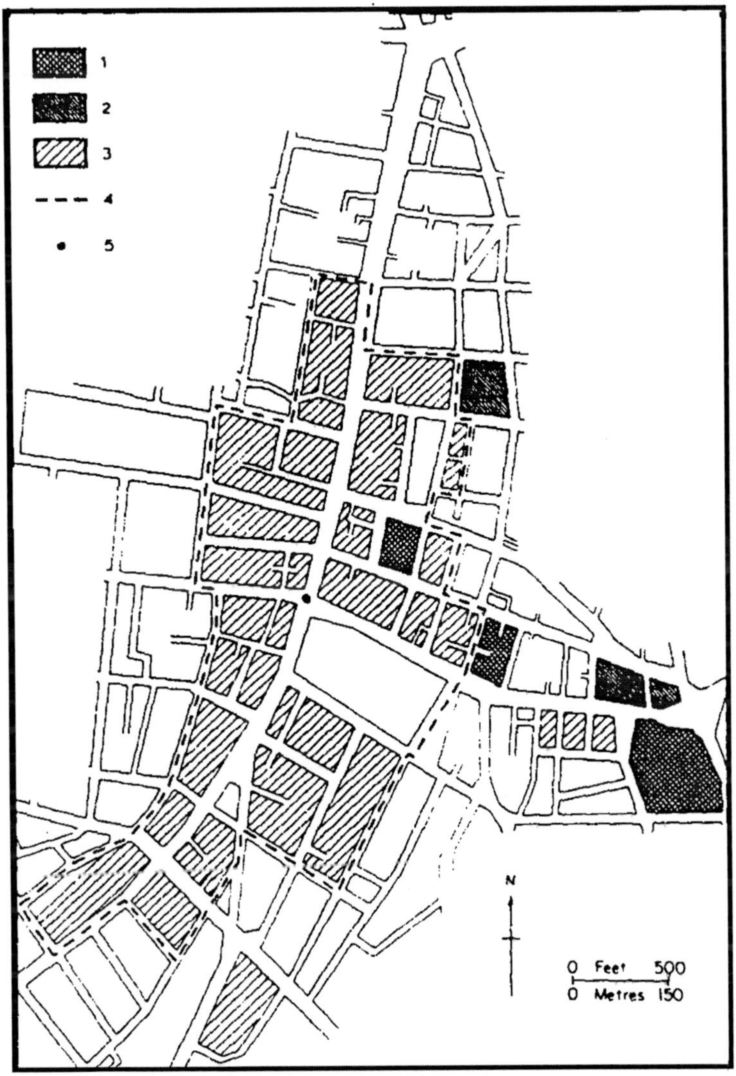

The definition of the Central Business District (CBD): Worcester, Mass. (after R. Murphy and J.E. Vance, 1954a). 1:Central business height index (CBHI) of 1 or more; 2: Central business intensity index (CBII) of 50 or more; 3: CBHI of 1 or more and CBII of 50 or more; 4: CBD boundary 5: Peak land value intersection.

city to city, to their size, to economies, to culture and to various activities which are centripetal to the area.

The simplest method is plotting of the landuse for delimitation of the CBD. Wherever there is a break in CB-use and non-CB use on a map, a point can be plotted for each street. But this must be carefully decided that, "how much of a break must there be in order to locate a point?" This problem is being solved by an application of Central Business Index Method (see Figure 16.3).

The delimitation may be done as:

(a) A block must have a Central Business Height Index (CBHI) of 1 or more, and
(b) A Central Business Intensity Index (CBII) of 50 per cent or more,

where CBHI stands for C space ÷ ground floor area and

CBII for $\dfrac{\text{C Space}}{\text{Total Space}} \times 100$

A profile for each story of the block is prepared. Its horizontal scale is equal to a base map of a city. This method is not suitable for small cities where only a few blocks could meet the CBHI and CBII measures. In India, the method may only be applicable in case of main four metropolises. CB area in other cities can be identified by plotting CB uses on maps.

Some Problems Faced by CBD

Nearly all CBD areas are overwhelmingly becoming crowdy during peak hours and near the Peak Land Value Intersection (PLVI) point traffic movement becomes a serious problem. This must be channelized by planning arterial roads and indicating places for disallowing traffic movement. Parking spaces should be provided on all sides at least one-to-two furlongs off the PLVI. In the absence of parking facility there is always insecurity and danger for pedestrians. Kolkata has the largest volume of pedestrian traffic and the problem in the

CBD area is being enhanced by encroachments by vendors. Calcutta Urban Development Project (CUDP) constructed underground parking plazas in the CBD. Usurpation of road-frontage and unauthorized occupation of footpaths should be strictly prohibited. The edge of CBD is notoriously occupied by slums and blight areas. In Delhi, old CBD including Sadar Bazar and Chandni Chowk is inflected by slums and blights.

Commonly in India, an average size of city does not have a distinct CBD resembling the cities of USA and Western Europe. One may identify a compact CBD in the metropolises of Kolkata (Chowringhee), Mumbai (Kalba Devi-Tank Rd.), Bangalore (M.G. Road), Delhi (Old Chandni Chowk), New Delhi (Connaught Place), etc.

Identification of CBD area in India is not possible through the Murphy-Vance Index Method. There may not be a single compact area. But in our cities, being multiple nuclei in structure, there may be small central areas developed on and around different nuclei. Their delimitation may be possible by plotting on map central-business uses of land. Unplanned cities of India possess CB areas of distorted shape and may not be like 'quadrate cross'. Another distinction which makes CB areas of India different in nature from their western counterpart is their residential use. Most of the central areas in India are occupied by semi-residential buildings and possess high density of population which is an uncommon feature in the Western Central areas.

CB areas of Indian cities are considerably flanked by haphazard retail marketing stores, narrow and tortuous roads, traffic congestion, in sanitary conditions, absence of footpaths and parking space, and above all, slums and squatters. These possess an unhealthy look and movement within the central business areas of our country is rather unpleasant and rather a difficult job.

Notes

1. Murphy, R.E., *The Central Business District*, Longmans, London, 1972.
2. Johnson, J.H., *Urban Geography*, Pergamon, London, 1967, p. 107.
3. Jones, Emrys, *Towns and Cites*, OUP, London, 1966, p. 62.
4. Diamond, D.R., "The Central Business District of Glasgow", in Norberg, K. (ed.), *Proc. of the I.G.U. Symposium*, Lund, 1960.
5. Sampson, W.A., "Is There Help for Our Ailing Cities", *Northwestern Alumini News*, January 1982.
6. Jones, Emrys, op. cit., p. 110.
7. Berry, B.J.L., *Geographic Perspective on Urban Systems*, Prentice Hall, New Jersey, N.Y., 1970, p. 456.
8. Dickinson, R.E., *City Region and Regionalism*, London, 1947, p. 90.
9. Firey, W., "Ecological Consideration in Planning Urban Fringe", *American Sociological Review*, Vol. 11, 1946.
10. Murphy, R.E., *The American City: An Urban Geography*, McGraw Hill, 1974, Second Edition, p. 363.
11. Murphy, R.E. and Vance, J.E., Jr., "A Comparative Study of Nine CBDs", *Eco. Geog.*, Vol. 30, 1954, pp. 301-336.

17

Rural-Urban Fringe

Concept and Meaning

Urban fringe of the modern city is a significant area because it signifies both urban as well as rural characteristics. This should not be treated as two distinct zones as the city merges perceptibly into rural countryside by way of mixed land uses. In most of the western cities there is no break in its continuity which is strengthened by the journey to work. People using automobiles make their daily trips to perform their jobs, from the rear end of a city to its central area where their offices and economic institutions are generally located. In India also, the same job has been performed by other-side population, i.e., by village people who travel daily to earn their bread and come to neighbouring towns. But greatest is the role of land uses which bind together town and village everywhere and "there is the absence of clear break".[1] Thus, urban fringe is a marginal area both of town as well as countryside. It can be better identified in terms of land uses or modifications of land uses than in any other way.[2] Rural-Urban fringe (R-U fringe) is a transitional zone and could be recognized recently on social grounds by the presence of rural and urban groups. But modern means of communications as well as means of movement of people and goods, are making the social attitudes between the two groups of rural and urban practically much diffused. In various parts of western Europe and North America, urban impact on social life has been felt well away from the immediate surrounding of cities. Therefore, it is no longer worthwhile to recognize a rural-urban fringe. Herington[3] defines R-U fringe more or less in the same context as "an area with distinctive characteristics which is still partly rural and where many of the residents live in the country but are not socially and economically of it".

The city does not grow outwards in well-defined patterns. It sprawls haphazardly, making rapid advances at one point, and hardly moving at all at another. This results into incoherent landscape which is the characteristics of the fringe.

Another characteristic and an unique quality is a wide mix of land uses ranging from a variety of commercial developments, including out-of-town shopping centres, to the city services and industries which are conveniently located at the margins.

Fringe areas of the USA were like an 'institutional desert'[4] because of the uncontrolled location there of unpleasant and noxious establishments such as slaughter houses, junkyards, and wholesale oil storage, and of utilities such as sewage plants and cemeteries. But in the present context the various land uses, older and newer, are intermingled in a random fashion.

To sum up the concept, it forms the outer suburban zone or, R-U fringe lying beyond the city administrative limits. It is a wide rural area into which residential development is intruding and new industrial sites and other urban uses are in the process of development along its main lines of communication, often clustered around existing villages and small towns.

Distinction Between the Inner and the Outer R-U Fringe

The distinction between the inner and the outer R-U fringe lies in the fact that the inner fringe is almost continuously occupied by all urban uses, while the outer one still contains much farm and woodland with sporadically distributed compact build-up areas and a considerable scattering of urban residences and other uses in rural surroundings.

Complex Pattern of Transition in R-U Fringe

R-U fringe generally produces three distinct aspects[5] as its constituent parts; (Figure 17.1) – physical, social and economic:

(1) Fringe as a distinctive physical area or region of the city,

(2) Fringe area where urbanization impinges on rurality to produce conflict between ways of life, and

(3) The impact of urban expansion on agricultural land.

Physical aspect is represented by an inner zone. The area is in an advanced stage of transition 'from rural to urban uses'.

Another aspect is of social change in attitudes of the people of the outer fringe. Although primarily attitudes were rural, now with the impingement of urbanization, city influences have begun to infiltrate and social transformation takes place.

Beyond the above stated two aspects, the third one constitutes economic transformation in the area forming 'an urban shadow'. It is here that agricultural land is being transformed with the impact of urban expansion. One may observe there a sporadic and scattered representation of the city in some non-farm residences.

Characteristics of R-U Fringe

Walter Firey[6] has also discussed some of the characteristics of R-U fringe while describing the Flinct city, Michigan, USA. These include:

Figure 17.1

Hypothetical Model Showing City-Countryside Infringement

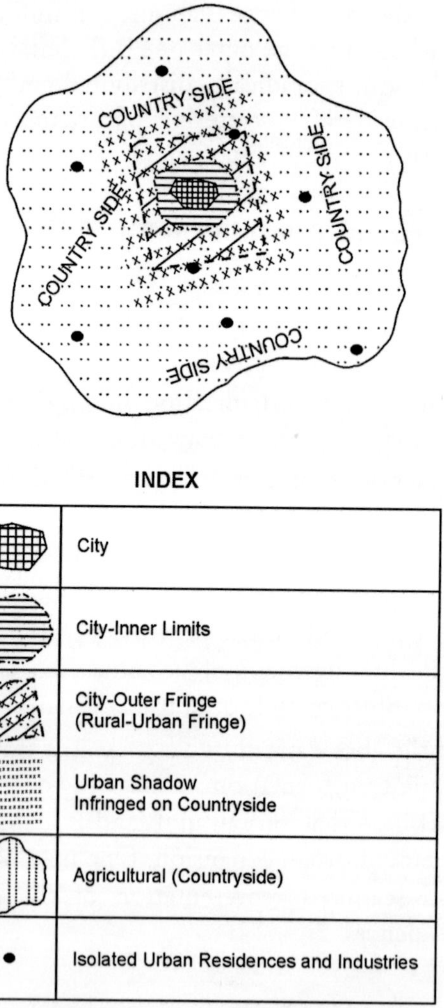

R-U Fringe : Rural-urban landuses bind R-U Fringe and there is not clear break in between. R-U Fringe is the sub-uban zone where urban and non-urban landuses are mixed. The process of infringement goes on as development along the main lines of communication.

(a) There is a vast usurpation of agricultural land by residential tracts of the suburbs including commercial, educational uses, etc.
(b) Industries have sporadically cropped up.
(c) People of the fringe area are overburdened because of the heavy taxes incurred to manage urban amenities.
(d) Land values have gone too high due to new constructions to be borne by medium-class population.
(e) One could observe a social shift in the attitudes of people.

In India, Sudesh Nangia[7] studied Delhi Metropolitan region (1976), and highlighted some of the chief characteristics

Figure 17.2
R-U Fringe of Delhi

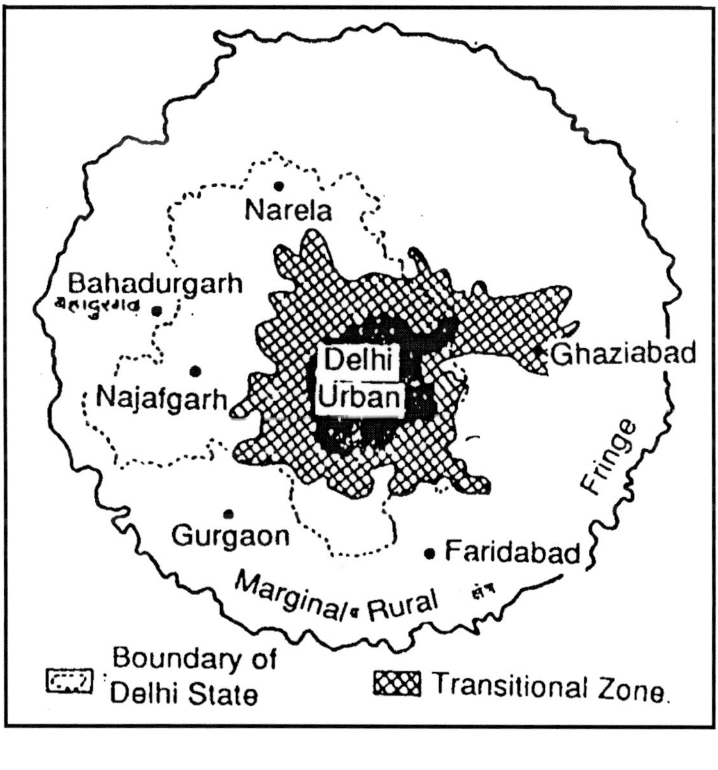

of the R-U fringe around the metropolis. She pointed out that the fringe area extended over 212 sq km and encompassed 177 villages within its fold. The zone is not concentric but polygonal in shape (Figure 17.2). Its structural units include slums and squatter-settlements, built-up dwellings without any proper plan, mixed land uses, areas of agricultural production usurped by lot of industrial units, dispersed location of settlements suffering from urban facilities, and also it commands sewerage treatment plant and recreation centres as well.

R.L. Singh studied R-U fringe of Varanasi[8] and called it an extension of the city itself, actual and potential. According to him, "the R-U fringe is an area where most of the rural land is forced into urban uses prematurely". U. Singh studied urban fringe of 'KAVAL' towns[9] and concluded that their fringe areas coalesced together inheriting all the evils of large conurbations such as horrible slums, appalling house and traffic congestion and long daily trip to work.

Pahl[10] attempted to summarize the characteristics of the fringe as segregation, selective immigration, commuting and collapse of geographical and social hierarchies.

The British Countryside Commission organized a conference on the urban fringe which revolved around five topics.[11] This is clear from the report that the major issues of urban fringe includes:

(a) Changing agricultural milieu of R-U fringe,
(b) Competition and development pressures,
(c) Prospects of recreation in the urban fringe,
(d) Landuse relationships and conflicts, and
(e) Interaction between policies in the urban fringe.

Delimitation of the R-U Fringe

An ideal method of the delimitation of R-U fringe actually depends upon intensive fieldwork from village-to-village around a limit of nearly 10 to 15 kms from the central city

Figure 17.3

Structure of R-U Fringe

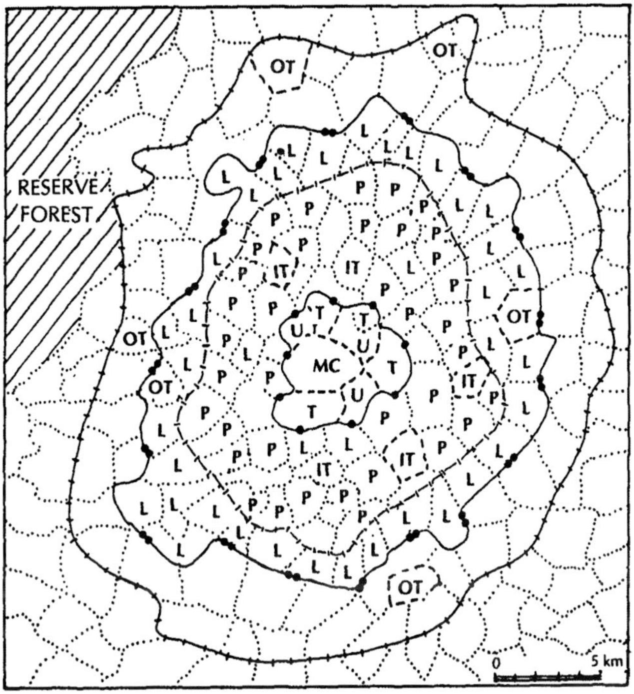

MC Main city (municipal corporation)
T Municipal and census towns contiguous to the city
U Villages substantially urbanized
IT Municipal and Census towns away from the city—inner ring towns
P Villages with urban land-uses—partially urbanized
L Villages having no urban land-uses but having other linkages with the city
OT Municipal and Census towns outside the rural-urban fringe—outer ring towns
⁘ Rural villages with no urban land-uses and no linkage with the city
...... Revenue village boundary
--- Municipal town boundary
Geographical city boundary—
—•— Inner boundary of the rural-urban fringe
—••— Outer boundary of the rural-urban fringe
—ı—ı Inner boundary of the green belt
—+— Outer boundary of the green belt

Source: After, Ramchandran, 1999.

limits. But the scholars have not yet been able to delimit the fringe of a city based on actual studies from village-to-village, especially in India. Whatever work is being done in this respect it is based either on a sample survey of the villages or it is wholly based on the secondary data of the censuses.

Some of the metropolitan cities have been studied and none of these studies in India is based on actual field survey for delimitation of the R-U fringe.[12] Delhi, Bangalore, Varanasi, Hyderabad, Kolkata are notable studies but these suffer from an inadequate and ambiguous conceptual framework for the delimitation of the fringe zone, being overwhelmingly based on the census of India.

Practically, the delimitation of the R-U fringe is a matter of thorough understanding about its structural composition. It is composed of several attributes like city municipal limits, contiguous small urbanised towns, urbanised villages around the city, and also villages associated with the city by virtue of their other functions. Figure 17.3 reveals the structure of the R-U fringe by pathetically in its spatial perspective. On the above basis as indicated in the figure the fringe area of a city may fall into the following three main categories:

(i) Generally around the central-city limits for about two kilometres, an innermost ring of the fringe may develop. It contains small towns and urbanized villages. In case of metropolitan area, for example, the Greater Mumbai, the fringe may begin within the city limits.
(ii) The next level of the fringe area extends further for a distance of five kilometres or more around the previous one. It forms the middle zone of the fringe and includes non-municipal towns and urbanized villages.
(iii) The third category forming the outer zone includes the villages having little or no urban land uses. Nonetheless, they are linked with the city by their allied functions.

The above categories are imperceptibly merged into each other and cannot be easily identified without closely examining their land uses in the concerned area. It is once again reiterated that for a proper demarcation of the inner and outer boundaries of the R-U fringe, a field survey of all the villages is a necessity.

The Delhi and Bangalore studies in the R-U fringe used the following variables to determine the outer boundary: (a) density of population - 400 km^2 or more, (b) population growth in the preceding decade - 40 per cent or more, (c) females per thousand males - 800 or less, (d) proportion of workers to non-agricultural activities - 50 per cent or more, and (e) the out limit of city bus services or local train services.[13]

Conclusion

On the basis of the discussion as stated above this can be concluded that the inner zone of R-U fringe is in the advanced stage of transition from rural to urban uses. The outer zone shows that gradual change is in the process and city influences have begun to appear. Beyond the outer zone is a diffused area where dispersal of some non-farm residences appear.

At the city margins everywhere, the fringes contain a wide mix of land uses ranging from a variety of commercial developments to the city services and industries. Some of the cities of the Western world have their fringes turned into 'unpleasant environment'[14] by noxious industrial units, junkyards, wholesale oil storage, sewage plants, and even cemeteries. Out-of-town shopping centres also form a part of the western cities' fringes.

In India, urban fringe has become almost jumbled by coalescing of settlements inheriting all the evils of conurbations such as slums full of 'jhuggi-jhonparis', drainageless unpaved narrow lanes and traffic congestion not far off the city centre.

Figure 17.4
R-U Fringe in the Developing Countries

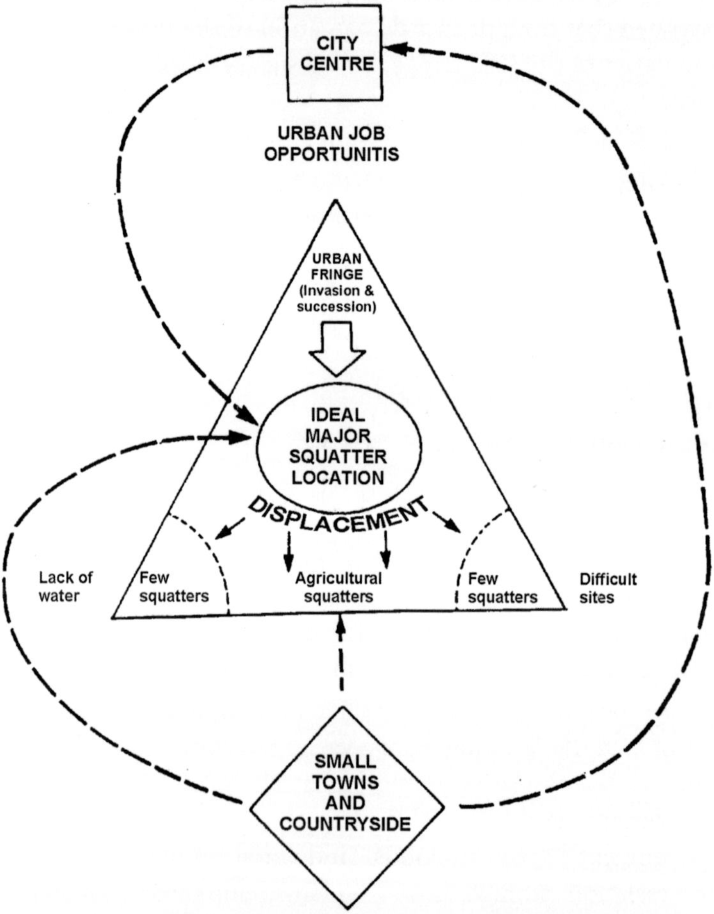

Fringes have usurped the land which was formerly under the agricultural production – 'baris' and orchards. In brief, R-U fringe areas in India offer the greatest challenges to the urban planner.

Notes

1. Johnson, J.H., *Urban Geography*, Pergamon, London, 1967, p.142.
2. Wehrwein, G.S., "The Rural-Urban Fringe", in Mayen, H.M., and Kohn, C.F., (eds.), *Readings in Urban Geography*, University of Chicago Press, Chicago, 1959, pp. 533-543.
3. Herington, J., *The Outer City*, Harper and Row, London, 1984.
4. Wehrwein, G.S., "Rural-Urban Fringe", *Eco. Geog.*, Vol. 18, 1942, pp. 217-228.
5. Bryant, C.R., Russwurm, L.H. and McLellan, A.G., *The City's Countryside, Land and Its Management in the Rural-Urban Fringe*, Longman, London, 1982.
6. Firey, W., *Land Use in Central Boston*, Cambridge, Harvard University Press, 1947.
7. Nangia, S., *Delhi Metropolitan Region: A Study in Settlement Geography*, K.B. Pub., New Delhi, 1976.
8. Singh, R.L., "The R-U Fringe Studies", *The Geographer*, Vol. 14, A. M. University, 1967, pp. 9-21.
9. Singh, Ujagir, "Urban Fringes of KAVAL Towns: A Study in Their Delimitation and Landuse Changes", in *Applied Geography*, R.L. Singh (ed.), NGSI, Varanasi, 1968, pp. 41-48.
10. Pahl, R.E., Urbs in Rure, "The Metropolitan Fringe in Hertfordshire", London School of Economics, London, Geogl. Papers 2, 1965.
11. Carter, H., *The Study of Urban Geography*, Arnold, 1995 – IV Ed., pp. 307-308.
12. Studies about the R-U Fringe have been conducted by R.L. Singh, M.M.P. Sinha, Debnath Mukerjee, Sudesh Nangia, V.L.S. Prakasa Rao, R. Ramachandran, Maya Ganguly, K.N. Gopi, G.S. Kulkarni, Manzoor Alam, etc. This may not be treated as a complete list.
13. Ramachandran, R., *Urbanization and Urban Systems in India*, Oxford, Delhi, 1999.
14. Carter, H., op. cit., p. 304.

18

City Regions in India

Meaning of City Region

City regions are the products of relationship among various orders of cities and their surrounding areas. A city has its 'dependents' which are linked with it by virtue of their dwellers' requirements fulfilled by the city's various service-institutions. Dependent centres of a city are generally smaller in size and they do not possess those specialized services which are only available at the neighbouring city of higher order than the dependent centres. In this way there are two types of relationship, and these two types produce two different nature of regions around a city:

(i) City region comprising towns of lower order of services, and institutions, and

(ii) City region and surrounding countryside.

No city is independent. An independent city cannot exist. A city may be administrative, industrial, agricultural, cultural or of any type; it must have its connections with the outside world. Similarly, areas outside a city are also not independent. They too somehow have to give and take and are not independent. The fact is that there exists mutual relationship between a settlement and area surrounding it. Sometimes, the relationship is concomitantly not restricted locally or regionally but it has its far and wide spheres of influence.

Distance and Nature of Transport Link

Intensity and frequency of city and its region also depend on linkages in terms of distance and the available nature of transport and communication. The more the distance between a city and its dependent town the lesser will be the interaction. And, similarly, the frequency of reaching to a city of people and commodities is also affected with the inter-distance. With the increment in distance the movement of consumers for utilizing services goes on decreasing from daily to weekly, and also from weekly to monthly or becomes irregular. If the service centres and consumers of the countryside are associated with quick or auto-transport the law of distance decay, operates negatively. Consumers visit frequently centres of special services using automobiles. Departmental stores also distribute commodities to the distant areas by means of automobiles. Perishable products like milk and vegetables reach as quickly as possible from far and wide areas by special trains, and by auto-vehicles. The relations of a city with its surrounding region are a matter of available means of transport to a large extent. Even small towns and urban centres have their regional functions fulfilled by their means and modes of linkages with the countryside, they being the main channels of "collecting the agricultural produce from the entire region, distributing and directing and coordinating the sale of imports and manufactured goods".[1] The extent of an urban regional influence depends as far as communications permit ease of movement. As a matter of fact it is the development of a transport network around an urban centre which makes the unison strengthened between the town and countryside.

Nature of Influence of Town

Before entering into some special cases of Indian towns and their regions, it is worthwhile to make clear the related concepts of city region. Urban influence is of varying nature. It may have its influence on agriculture, on industry, on administration and also on certain services like medical, cultural including educational, recreational, etc.

Town and Agriculture

Much has already been discussed about town's influence over surrounding countryside. Everywhere and in every age towns people have owned rural properties. In India, 'zamindari' system has been in vogue for a long time. Formerly, in princely states of India there were landowners owning rural properties and used to live in the state capital town. In modern times also rich people have lands and properties in the villages of their forefathers, but they themselves live in the neighbouring town. People possess farm-houses in the mid of their agricultural farms to look after and supervise their farm operations and visit intermittently. It has become almost a status symbol of a few well-to-do urbanites to have properties and land in nearby villages. It is not an exaggeration, therefore, to state that "the country is very often the property of the town".[2]

Town also depends on agricultural production. Dickinson while describing agricultural regions of Europe identified roughly concentric zones of various crops in relation to the town. There would be floriculture, market-gardening, rearing of dairy-cattle for milk, etc., and then cultivation of sugarbeet and cereals.[3]

Often some of the industries located in a town such as based on wool, sugarcane and sugarbeet for wine, wood products, mats, baskets, 'bidi' (in India), flax (in Europe) for linen industry, products for dyeing obtained from plants, mulberry for silk industry and so many other products are rural based. A town actually acts as a market for the rural products based on local raw materials. Thus, a town, through middlemen, offers required supplies and the facilities for products meant for export. In this way a town exerts a very real control over the surrounding country.

Town is a Shopping Centre for Country People

Villagers come to town to do their shopping. They purchase goods of their choice. Large cities have goods collected from different parts of the world.

Importance of extent of market lies in a region not by its large or small size. But it is the sale which determines the significance. The evaluation of sales to the inhabitants of the town, and also to those outside the time, determines the strength of the area of influence.

Among towns there is found an hierarchy for performing central administrative functions within its regional limit. Christaller in his classic treatise[4] while discussing the central places in southern Germany pointed out hierarchy ascending in order as market town, township, country town, district city, state capital, provincial capital and regional capital. The structure of the hierarchy varies from country to country. The town however serves as the regional centre is equally significant of all administration, business, legal affairs, medical and educational services. People from the countryside rely on their regional capital.

Nature of Spheres of Influence* of City

Each city generally forms the core of a larger area, and dominates the area by virtue of several service areas within it. The dominant area is actually the city's spheres of influence.

---

* The term 'spheres of influence' of a city is used by the American geographers. It indicates several areas of dominance around a city.

The area of dominance of 'spheres of influence'[5] consists a number of single feature nodal regions within it.

City's area of dominance tends to wane gradually with the distance outwards from the city core. Finally, the dominance disappears at a point where the influence of some competing urban centre reaches.

Areas of City Dominance and City Region

A city tends to exert a dominant influence over a small area in its immediate neighbourhood by virtue of the provision of specialized services. It must be borne in mind that there are several areas of dominance because a city possesses more than one service to provide around it. In case of India, majority of cities have no clear specialization in any one economic activity, but in reality they have diversification of several economic functions and services. This has resulted into several areas of dominance around a city. Each of the areas of dominance has its own hierarchical level. The largest of these areas of dominance forms the limit of influence of the city known as 'city region', while the smaller ones are known as areas of dominance (see Figure 18.1).

Recently, this has been noted that clusters of urban settlements have grown around large metropolises such as around Delhi in India. It also results into formation of what is called sometimes as 'city region' because it is made up of several areas of dominance by towns and country-towns falling within the ambit of a major city or metropolis.

Mckenzie aptly described the concept long back:

> The metropolitan (or city) region thus considered is primarily a functional entity. Geographically it extends as far as the city exerts a dominant influence... The metropolitan region represents a constellation of centres, by the interrelations of which are characterized by dominance and subordination. Every region is organized around a central city or focal point of

Figure 18.1
Areas of Influence and Zones of Competition and Overlap

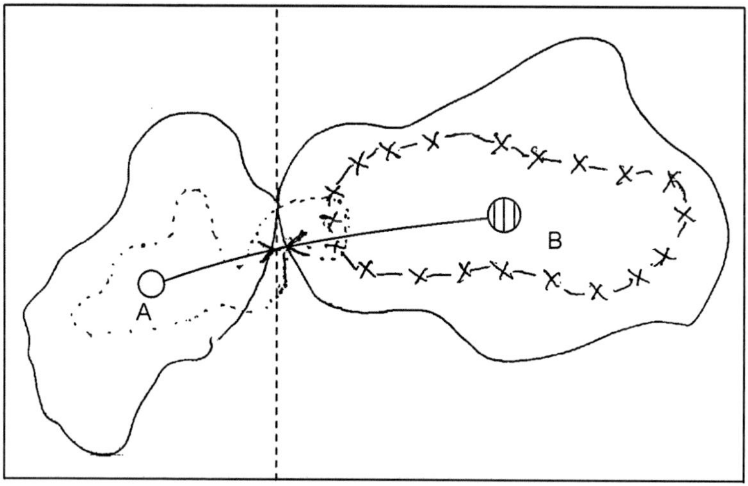

INDEX

A ○ Town

B ⦶ City

→ Distance from City A
← Distance from City B

¦ Zone of Competition between A & B

Area of Influence of X-Service of the Town A

Area of Influence of X-Service of the Town B

Overlapping Influence

dominance in which are located the institutions and services that cater to the region as a whole and integrate it with other regions.[6]

The concepts of city influence and city dominance give rise to an hierarchical order within a region. Areas of city influence are contiguous areas around a city. There are various institutions present in a city for different services such as medical, educational, marketing, cultural, etc. Each of these has its own area from where people commute to the city to obtain goods or services. The areas of their influence may cover varying sizes

Figure 18.2

Hierarchy within Scania, South Sweden

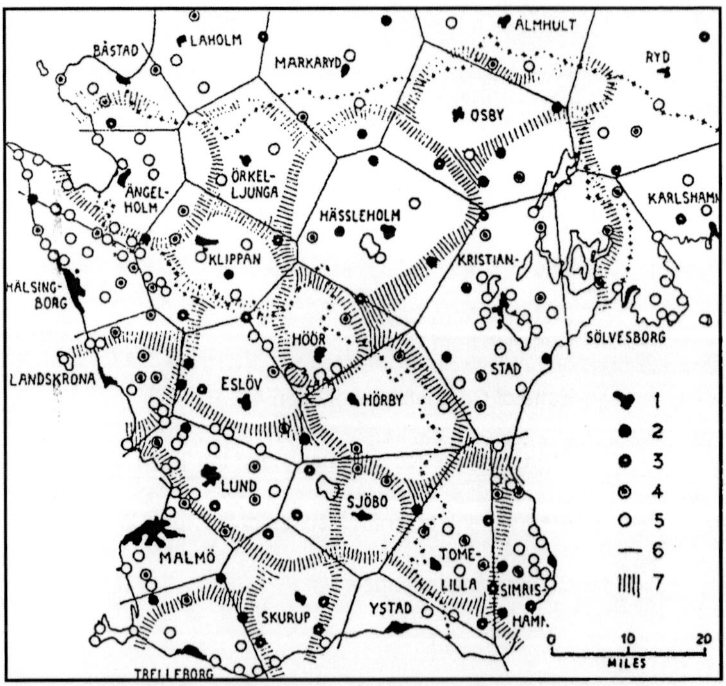

1. Regional Centre; 2. Townlet Centre; 3. Township Centre; 4. Market Centre; 5. Special Urban Settlement.; 6. Boundary of Theoretical Hinterland; 7. Actual Hinterland (defined by bus traffic)

Source: After Godlund, 1951.

and shapes. They may overlap also. The influence of neighbouring cities may generate a zone of competition. The zone of competition separates the areas of dominance of the two competing cities. And, the dominant areas is formed not by areas of one or two services, but it is formed with respect to all services of a city (Figure 18.1). In the diagram only one particular x-service area of the two towns are shown.

Regional Hierarchy

Hierarchy of towns within a region is based on the services and institutions offered by them, and not on the basis of occupational data as given in the census. The hierarchy reveals two principles: (i) services are arranged in ascending order from the hamlet to metropolis, and (ii) the spacing of such centres follows certain regularities, and the systems of distribution differ from one area to another according to circumstances of historical development in the area. The hierarchy resembles Christaller's theory of central place. Figure 18.2 shows urban settlements in the Scania region of South Sweden[7] discussed by Godlund. In ascending order the hierarchy within the region displays location of urban settlements (special), market centre, township centre, townlet centre and finally regional centre. The hierarchy represents centralization of retail services. The centres are graded by index of centralization. The index equals the number of persons engaged in retail trade and service as percentage of the total population in the settlement. The regional centres are fully-fledged towns having 19 selected branches in trade and services (with Index over 6.5), while the lowest in the hierarchy are special urban settlements with Index 3.5 to 4.4.

Existence of hierarchy of urban centres creates sets of areas of influence and areas of dominance, one within the other. Therefore, the city region may be defined as the area of dominance of a city corresponding to its hierarchical level (Figure 18.3). In this way each city may have more than one

Figure 18.3
City Region
(simplified three level hierarchy of a city region)

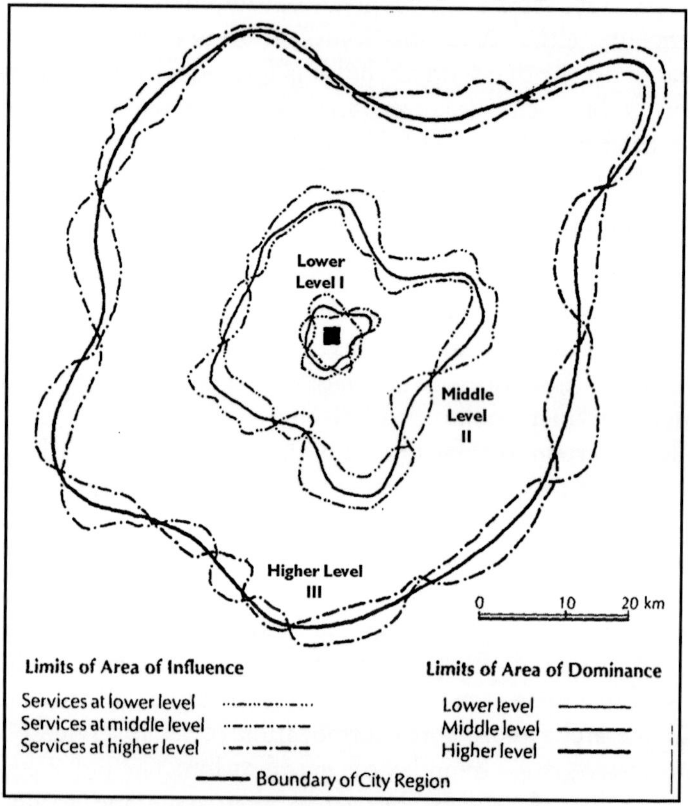

Source: After R. Ramchandran, 1999.

area of dominance – lower, middle and higher. Similarly, areas of small towns' influence are restricted to only a few in number, while larger towns have more service-areas, and finally the city performs all of the services rendered by the centres of lower-order hierarchy in the region. On the hierarchical level, areas of influence should be delimited based on the city's functional specialization. These may be agricultural, educational, medical, recreational, marketing, etc.

Urban settlements everywhere have grown to form clusters around a large city. Often these are constituted by country-towns and villages and are attracted to fall within the ambit of a major city by virtue of mutually associated functions. Thus, a 'city region' is formed around a city and metropolis. The city region is linked socially and economically to its urban centre. Various names have been assigned by geographers to the region around a city. Germans have adopted the term 'hinterland', while the British geographers preferred 'urban field'. In America, it is known as 'sphere of influence'. Other expressions like 'zone of influence', 'tributary area' or 'catchment area' have also been used, but they are not flawless and have some difficulties to bring the meaning of a region explicit. Actually the city region is an area influenced by an urban centre two dimensionally. Town acts both as centripetally as well as centrifugally. Goods and services flow both into and out of a city, and thus the region of city is economically interdependent. It is neither a sphere of influence, nor does it necessarily form a continuous zone. A city cannot sustain by itself but it is linked by its surrounding countryside interdependently. For this very purpose an appropriate word 'umland' was used for the first time by Andre Allix[8], a French geographer in 1914. The word umland, according to him meant the areas immediately around an interior city, more particularly a centre for holding 'fairs'. Whittlesey defined the word umland for an immediately tributary area extending fifty or sixty kilometres on all sides of a city. However the word was substituted by many geographers for urban hinterland, sphere of influence, catchment area, urban field, city region, etc.

In India, R.L. Singh used the word 'umland' in 1955. For the usage Singh was obliged to Prof. Stamp. According to him it is the area in which the region and the city are interrelated economically as well as culturally and politically. Stamp stresses that the definition and delimitation of an umland becomes actually a matter of definite practical importance in commerce and industry.[9] In practice a large manufacturer whose products are in wide demand must decide for himself his centres for distribution and the umland which each must serve. Conversely, if he is using local raw materials he must decide his centres and the umland from which each draws. This means that the concept of umland or region around a city has its significance in economic affairs.

Many scholars worked on the delimitation of umland in India after 1955. Manzoor Alam worked on Hyderabad-Secunderabad to identify various orders of urban influence according to their extent and intensity. Around the metropolis he could determine 'areas of dominance' and 'areas of association', V.L.S. Prakasa Rao also identified three grades of influence around towns of Mysore state – areas of least influence, greater influence and intermediate area. But his method was mostly theoretical and he assumed that the area of influence of a town is circular, the radius being calculated statistically.[10] Among the various methods used in India, Singh's study of Varanasi[11] was popular and was adopted by most of the geographers in India by revising a little as per local conditions.* Some of these criteria used, do not constitute central place functions. Moreover, the studies by and large focussed on large cities (population with several lakhs). There is also an excessive dependence on secondary data rather than first-hand collection of information by actual field enquiry.

City Regions in India

City region is not very different in concept than the area of urban dominance. The primary difference is that the areas of dominance of a city may be many, but city region is only one. M. Alam pointed out three levels of areas of dominance as:

---

* Most studies followed a set pattern, the model being Singh's study of Varanasi. Most students do not go beyond the six criteria – (a) Vegetable supply, (b) milk supply, (c) supply of grain, (d) bus service, (e) newspaper circulation, and (f) administrative area boundaries.

(a) areas of metropolitan dominance which is immediately around a metropolis. It is of the lower order; (b) areas of metropolitan prominence which play their role in assigning a significant position to the metropolis, being a complex of specialized services; and (c) areas of metropolitan association which is a higher area than the former two with respect to dominance. It is the net hierarchical level of the city and known as city region.[12]

The delimitation of city region must involve three concepts simultaneously, viz., dominance, cluster of services

Figure 18.4
Proximal Method

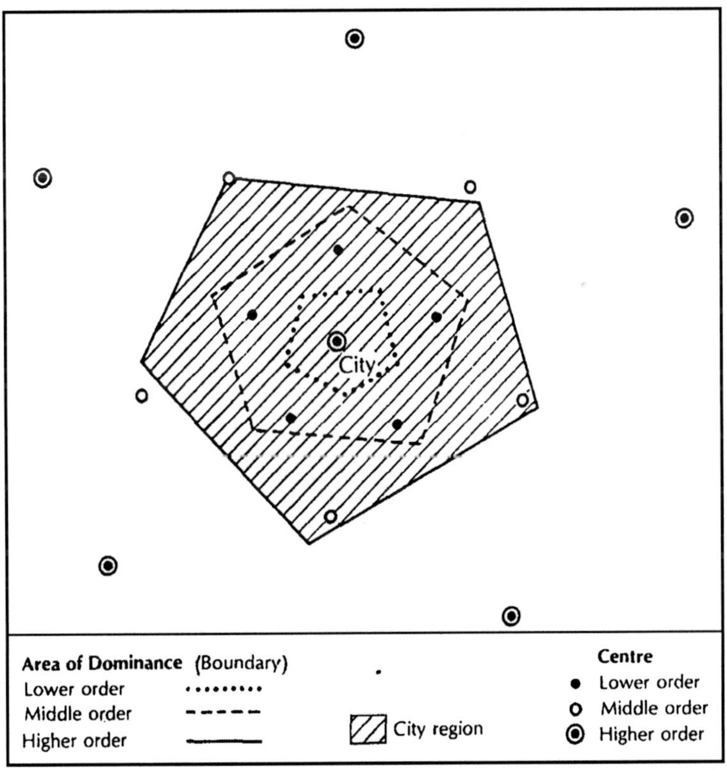

and hierarchical level of the city including levels below it. It must be clear in mind that city region cannot be an area of dominance delimited on the basis of a single criterion. City region is a multifactor based area of dominance. It is not an isolated area, but continuously remains under competing effects of centres surrounding it. Therefore, it should also take into account of the influence of competing centres too. Ramchandran[13] suggested 'proximal method'* for its delimitation. This is not an easy job and cannot be done in case of India which is a vast country, without the aid of computer. Moreover, it is not an empirical method and being theoretical cannot bring forth reality.

Dutta[14] divided India into broad urban regions which cannot be treated as city regions. The zones as suggested by Dutta are based on secondary data and are only generalizations indicating density of urbanization.

India is a vast country. The four premier metropolitan cities have been governing her urban status. Delhi, Mumbai, Kolkata and Chennai have their profound impact on city regions of what-so-order they are determined. They are situated in the four distinct parts of the country and have around them areas of urbanity covering the entire country. But, recently, a significant change has also taken place with regard to cities, besides the four old and recognized metropolises. Some new cities of million-cadre have been growing rapidly to challenge the urban life in India. They are fairly distributed in various states of our country except in Jammu & Kashmir and eastern states lying near the borderlands. They too have their significant role to play in the delimitation of city regions in India. Similarly, number of lakh-cities has been increasing in every state. They too affect city regions.

---

* Proximal method is a geometrical device which can be derived by joining surrounding centres of equal level. Perpendicular bisectors may be drawn to a given city from the midpoints of lines joining all its neighbouring centres of higher ranks in all directions (see Figure 18.4).

Figure 18.5
City Regions in India

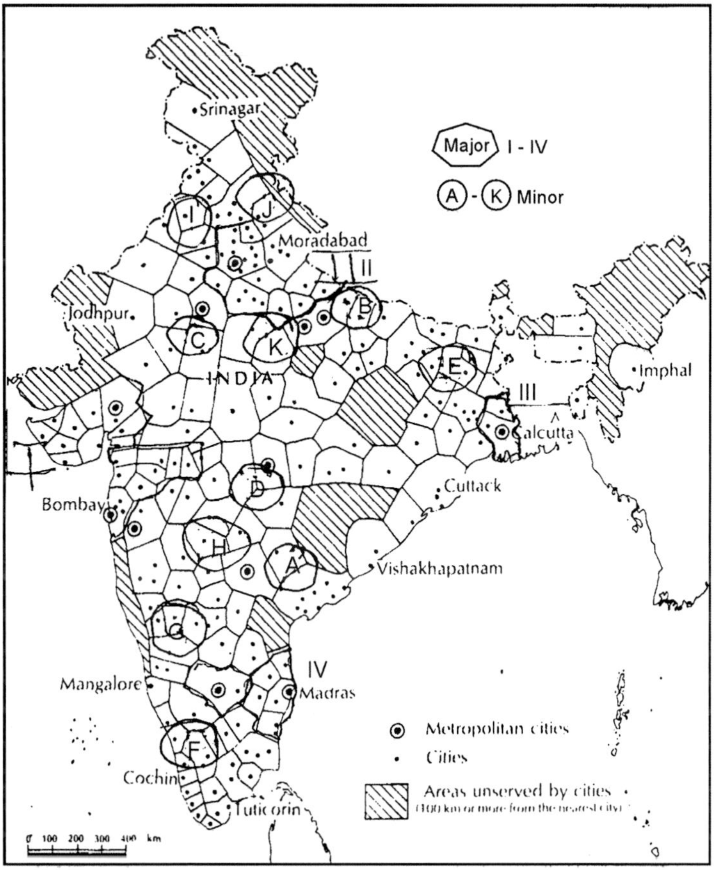

Two grades of city regions may be identified by merging roughly drawn areas of clusters around million- and lakh-cities (see Figure 18.5). Major city regions may be: (1) Maharashtra – Gujarat sector, (2) Delhi nucleus, (3) Kolkata-Howrah node, and (4) Chennai-Bangalore sector.

The minor level city regions may be around (1) Hyderabad-Vishakhapatnam, (2) Kanpur-Lucknow, (3) Jaipur,

(4) Nagpur, (5) Patna, (6) Kochi-Madurai sector, (7) Coimbatore, (8) Vijayawada, (9) Ambala-Amritsar-Jullunder, (10) Chandigarh, and (11) Agra.

It must be followed here that city regions are not as entities independent of other centres of various levels around them.

Notes

1. Mukerjee, R.K., *Man and His Habitation*, Mumbai, 1968, p. 132.
2. Beaujew-Garnier, J. and Chabot, G., *Urban Geography*, Longmans, 1967, p. 395.
3. Dickinson, R. and Jonasson, O., "Agricultural Regions of Europe", *Eco. Geog.*, 1925, pp. 284-6.
4. Christaller, W., *Central Places in Southern Germany*, Prentice Hall, N.J., 1966.
5. Murphy, R.E., *The American City: An Urban Geography*, McGraw Hill, N.Y., 1974, 2nd Ed., pp. 61-81.
6. Mckenzie, R.D., "The Metropolitan Community", 1933, p. 70, quoted from Dickinson, R.E., *City and Region*, London, 1964, 4th Imp., 1967, p. 12.
7. Godlund, S., "Bus Services, Hinterland and the Location of Urban Settlements in Sweden: Scania", *Lund Studies in Geography*, Series B, No. 3, 1951.
8. Allix, A., "*The Geography of Fairs*", G.R., Vol. 12, 1922, p. 532.
9. Stamp, L.D., *Applied Geography*, Pelican Books, 1960, pp. 167-168.
10. Prakasa Rao, V.L.S., *Towns of Mysore State*, Asia Pub. House, Statistical Publishing Society, Kolkata, 1964, pp. 30-32, Fig. 9.
11. Singh, R.L., *Banaras: A Study in Urban Geography*, Nand Kishore & Bros., Banaras, 1955.
12. Alam, S.M., *Hyderabad-Secunderabad (Twin Cities): A Study in Urban Geography*, Allied Pub., Mumbai, 1965.
13. Ramachandran, R., *Urbanization and Urban Systems in India*, OUP, New Delhi, 1999, pp. 287-290.
14. Kusum, L. Datta, "Urban Zones of India", *The National Geographical Journal of India*, 1967, pp. 97-100.

19

Urban Planning and Democratization

For geographers, concept of urban planning has a different meaning, other than what is generally being understood by common people. Generally, planning of a city and its practical application is not an activity falling within the scope of any one academic discipline. It involves practical knowledge of history, geography, architecture, geology and geomorphology, hydrology, engineering, demography, economics, public administration, futurology, etc. etc. The concept of planning about town and countryside is in its real sense and meaning 'an interdisciplinary activity'.

Geographer within the scope of his or her knowledge can identify spatial problems on the surface of the earth and can also evaluate their locational fitness in terms of time, place and distributional patterns, but their solutions and making them fit for the common good lie in the hands of a team of workers and academicians of various disciplines. Nonetheless important is the role of a geographer who actually prepares a base on which planning activity begins to take shape.

Meaning and Definitions

The main object of the city planning is to enable every inhabitant to enjoy full health of mind and body from the place. City is a land where people live, where they do and perform work, where they learn, where they play and pray. The planning of a place of that importance must be superb in all respects. Patrick Abercrombie[1] declared long back the mottos of urban planning as 'health, beauty and convenience'. These encompass total well-being of people and it is the process of democratization of our living-standard.

Dudley Stamp[2] stressed on the underlying objective of city planning as the 'welfare of the citizens'. City is for citizens and it takes care of their all-round development. It is the city space which actually provides its dwellers a suitable stage to act conveniently, to move to a place of work with ease and to reach safely and return after earning their daily bread. City provides its people joys of community living, opportunities for academic pursuits, entertainment and cultural affairs, and for growth – physically, socially and economically. Planning for a city therefore "is the projection of teamwork into a city form which serves as a common objective, a form in which urban development may proceed with order..."[3]. According to Gallion, city-planning is an activity of the highest order since it controls the destiny of city people, both of the present and future,

Patrick Geddes, a sociologist, insists through planning upon 'the reorganization of place, work and folk'.[4]

Its role as a democratic activity is wide enough. Its real and practical approach lies in following the situation and economy, also needs of the areas, people's participation – coordinated in all sections – private and public. It takes into account increasing responsibility for the welfare of citizens, municipal income, poor amount of taxes, land values and valuation of houses.

Town planning is an act involving science, art and policy matters simultaneously to fulfil the social and economic needs of the society. It takes into consideration the urban layout arrangement, setting the conditions of land utilization, transport management and construction of buildings in a systematic, healthy and efficient manner.

To sum up, town planning is a technique to seek ordered land use, adequate sites for buildings, commercial establishments and channels for transport and communication network. The major objectives which are inherent in planning and remain in the mind of a planner include practicability, economic growth, convenience, beauty and safety. This is done by a section of people from the local government who draw up and implement schemes of plan and programmes. Urban plan, therefore, is geared to control and protect urban environment, and other related measures to ensure that there is smooth life, security and convenience within the area.

Planning activity seeks an objective in future time by way of ability to predict. Prediction must be based on tested theory.

What is Master Plan?

Master plan is a long-term plan, may be for several decades. It is therefore a comprehensive one. People's participation is an essential element in its outline. It seeks a balance among different elements of a city likely to grow up in future. It also maintains cohesion within the regional and national planes. Le Corbusier[5] for the 'city of tomorrow' pointed out some principal ingredients such as rectilinear pattern, skyscrapers for business and tenements for housing. He also stressed on buildings surrounded by vast open spaces, a well organized city centre, uniformity in detail with variety of general layout. He favoured grid-iron street-system to separate different types of traffic for easy and speedy circulation. His future city preferably is built on level site, and he proposed the whole area to be surrounded by a protected zone.

Zoning

The concept of zoning is an essential part of the Master Plan. It means establishing regulations as to what may and may not be done with the land hereafter. Zoning regulations should be strictly enforced to prevent overcrowding and also to check unhealthy land uses in the areas where they illegally occupy the ones fixed for a particular use. Several small and big administrative offices and financial units of mini-type business have come up within the residential areas. Shops of variety and sale-windows, beauty-parlours, general merchants' establishments recently have started intruding the lower parts of the residential quarters which disturb the privacy, place and security of the residential areas of a city. In India this has become a common nuisance, and many of the residential units are now occupied by the coaching centres and nursery schools in the lower storey of residential buildings. Kota in Rajasthan at present has largely been infested by the menace of educational coaching centres and by hostels of immigrant-students. The city has become an example of the violently occupied illegal zone. It has become a headache both for administrators and also for residents of the city.

Zoning plan decides the minimum requirements of space for present and future use of land in various aspects of city life such as residential, commercial, industrial, transportational, recreational and open spatial areas.

Maps for Planning

Generally two types of maps are used:

(a) Published maps are part of zoning ordinance. These maps show land uses as prescribed rather than existing.

(b) Unpublished maps are detailed maps available in the urban planning offices.

These maps are on quite a large scale and show actual land uses. They are generally prepared on a scale of at least 1 inch to

50 feet. But the maps for central area of a city are on a scale representing 400-600 ft to an inch because of the extreme density of buildings under various uses.

In USA maps for American cities are also prepared by private companies. Sanborn Map Atlas is an example. In this Atlas, the cities of less than 50,000 population are covered.[6] They are plotted on uniformly sized sheets at a scale of 1 inch to 50 ft./1 inch to 100 ft. The maps are revised through periodic surveys by the Sanborn map company.

Bartholomew's[7] map are constructed to indicate land uses by alphabetical index. They show various types of residences and property under commercial, industrial, recreational and railroad uses.

Urban Renewal[8]

Redevelopment Agency of a city undertakes urban renewal programmes. Three different levels of urban renewal are recognized: (a) Conservation, the first of the three levels, is a more permanent measure. It is a type of renewal treatment aimed at restoring the economic and social values of deteriorating areas. Some structures are classified as standard, some as conservable requiring certain improvements, and, some as requiring demolition; (b) Rehabilitation, is the second level of urban renewal; and (c) The third and most drastic level is "Clearance and redevelopment". Structures with cleared utilities are installed and others are sold or leased to redevelopments who build new structures on these sites according to an urban renewal plan prepared by the local public agency. Blights are also arrested in the areas where they have cropped up through urban renewal programme.

Conclusion

Land is a primary resource both occupied by towns and by villages. But it is extremely limited and it requires control.

Control and its maximum adequate use is essential for welfare of the community. Best use of land is possible through planning and its management for future. Day-to-day problems can also be solved through extensive long-term plan. No problem can be handled unilaterally.

Physical planning of land is like a game of chess. It needs shifting, re-allocation, redevelopment and even surgery. Its planning is a matter of its best use for the community living. It depends upon the trend of growth, both human as well as economic. It is necessary for the future development. This involves decisive efforts and planned policies. It is fulfilled by a master-plan which is a complete and foolproof structure. It is a written document containing plans and policies. It shows land use plan for coming decades reinforced with maps indicating spatial transformation land uses according to set policies. Master plan of a city actually is an encyclopaedia to be used by future generation to give a convenient, healthy and beautiful shape to the city.

Gandhinagar

It is one of the most recently planned Indian cities. It is lying fifteen miles north of Ahmedabad on the right bank of Sabarmati river and is a new capital of Gujarat State. Its planning is based on the pattern of Le Corbusiar's Chandigarh. The main objective behind its establishment was to relieve the overcrowding and polarization of the old city. Its total area of 21 sq miles is divided into 30 sectors, each one of 1×3/4 km rectangle. It is flanked by light manufacturing industries besides residential areas and public institutions. Gandhinagar is being planned in a manner to keep it off from all types of pollution. It has for miles together rows of trees on both sides of the main road which provide 'beauty, health and convenience' to the residents. An area between sectors 7 to 9 and the river bank is being developed as 'recreational ground', where a lake is providing it a scenic sight (Figure 19.1).

Figure 19.1
Gandhinagar Plan

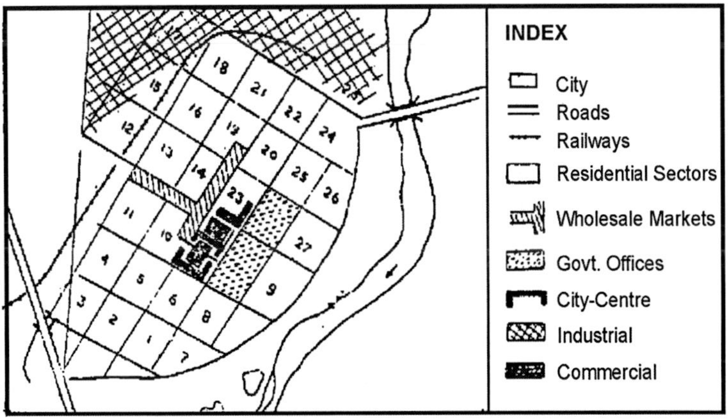

Each of the sectors of Gandhinagar is independent where school, local shopping centre, hospital, etc., provide basic amenities to consumers of all levels. Highways and roads are joined by sub-ways to keep the residential houses safe from vehicular traffic. School-children and tiny-tots have play field near their residences and they are within their walking distances. They need not to cross vehicular-roads for making use of their schools, playfield and a shop.

Jaipur

Jaipur is another ideal example of city planning. It is one of the most early modern cities in India which is based on the principals of planning. Even after five decades of independence of our country and its booming population and built-up areas, the city has been able to preserve its original glamour. It was planned by Sawai Jai Singh in 1727, on some of the geometrical principles and mathematical measurements. Its plan was prepared by Vidyadhar according to the science of architecture. It is for this reason that roads are viable even today to control the transport and human movement which have increased in volume and number more than four-fold. Its main roads may be compared with roads of New Delhi and New York and in no sense should be considered inferior to any of the world's cities.

Jaipur was planned only for two-three lakh population, but its population is now increased nearly ten times. It is surprising that even today the city is functioning smoothly, whereas Delhi, Mumbai and Kolkata are grieving distressly due to the lack of housing facility and means of transportation and communication. British architect, Sir Huge Caisson used to count Jaipur in the three most beautiful cities, i.e., Peking, Jaipur and Venice. Certain buildings of Jaipur are unique in the history of architecture and have none to compare. Ishwar Singh, son of Jaisingh who ruled for nearly seven years got a victory-pillar built which was used to be known for the city's 'sky-line'. His successor Madho Singh got built a garden-palace on the bank of Jaisagar lake flanked by beautiful fountains. Pratap Singh's 'Hawa Mahal' has its no parallel in the history of architecture.

A dam along Amanishah 'nallah' is meeting the problem of water even today. Jaipur's rectilinear plan is divided into nine blocks. Its main roads are 110 ft. in width cutting each other rectilinearly. The old town is surrounded by a city wall having eight gates for entrance. In the neighbourhood, a fort is perched on hills.

With the wave of immigrants coming in the city after the partition in 1947, a second phase of planning began. For resettlement of the people, Adarsh Nagar and Raja Park came into being. The service-class population had their own residential areas in the centres like Bapu Nagar, Bajaj Nagar and Gandhi Nagar.

Pink-coloured buildings have given the city a unique landscape and nomenclature known all over the world as 'Pink City'. Unauthorized occupation of land, incursions and usurption were strictly checked to maintain uniformity. The city has now sprawled considerably out of city walls. A sad state of affair of the planned city is the role of middlemen which has begun recently and unauthorized occupation of land on the outskirts is taking place. There has now started an ugly competition for land in Jaipur, and consequently laws for establishing industries, commercial units, residences have been flouted with little check of the administration. Recent developments have given rise to numerous problems of civic amenities, and the planned city of status is groaning for healthy civic life.

Notes

1. Abercrombie, P., *Greater London Plan-1944*, London, HMSO, 1945.
2. Stamp, L.D., "Land Reclamation in Relation to New Towns", *The City Planning*, No. 9, 1941, pp. 14-15.
3. Gallion, A.B. and Eisner, S., *The Urban Pattern*, 2nd. ed., New York, 1963.
4. Geddes, P., *Cities in Evolution*, London, 1949, Assoc. for Planning, Reprint of 1915.
5. Le Corbusior, *Concerning Town Planning*, Trans. by C. Entwistle, Architectural Press, London, 1947.
6. Applebaum, W., "A Technique for Constructing a Population and Urban Land Use Map", *Economic Geography*, Vol. 28, 1952, p. 24.
7. Bartholomew, H., *Landuses in American Cities*, Harvard, 1956.
8. *Standard Land Use Coding Manual*, Urban Renewal Adm. and Bur. of Pub. Roads, Washington, D.C., 1965.

Index